GEZİ

GEZİ

The Making of a New Political Community in Turkey

Kaan Ağartan

EDINBURGH
University Press

Edinburgh University Press is one of the leading university presses in the UK. We publish academic books and journals in our selected subject areas across the humanities and social sciences, combining cutting-edge scholarship with high editorial and production values to produce academic works of lasting importance. For more information visit our website: edinburghuniversitypress.com

Edinburgh University Press Ltd
13 Infirmary Street
Edinburgh EH1 1LT

First published in hardback by Edinburgh University Press 2024

Typeset in 11/15 EB Garamond by
IDSUK (DataConnection) Ltd

A CIP record for this book is available from the British Library

ISBN 978 1 3995 2590 9 (hardback)
ISBN 978 1 3995 2591 6 (paperback)
ISBN 978 1 3995 2592 3 (webready PDF)
ISBN 978 1 3995 2593 0 (epub)

CONTENTS

ABBREVIATIONS

AKM	Atatürk Cultural Centre (Atatürk Kültür Merkezi)
AKP	Justice and Development Party (Adalet ve Kalkınma Partisi)
HDP	Peoples' Democratic Party (Halkların Demokratik Partisi)
PKK	Kurdistan Workers' Party (Partiya Karkerên Kurdistanê)
SMO	Social Movement Organisation
TBB	Turkish Bar Association (Türkiye Barolar Birliği)
TEKEL	Turkish Tobacco and Alcoholic Beverages Company (Tütün, Tütün Mamulleri, Tuz ve Alkol İşletmeleri Genel Müdürlüğü)
TKP	Turkish Communist Party (Türkiye Komünist Partisi)
TMMOB	Union of Chambers of Turkish Engineers and Architects (Türk Mühendis ve Mimar Odaları Birliği)
TOKI	Mass Housing Agency (Toplu Konut İdaresi)
TTB	Turkish Medical Association (Türk Tabipler Birliği)
WSF	World Social Forum
WTO	World Trade Organization

ACKNOWLEDGEMENTS

I became indebted to several individuals and institutions for their support and encouragement in the long process of writing this book.

The Center for Excellence in Learning, Teaching, Scholarship and Service (CELTSS) at Framingham State University generously provided research, travel and course release grants at various stages of the project. Thanks to the centre's support, I was able to present some of the ideas that were later developed in the book at a number of events including: the American Sociological Association's 2014 Annual Meeting in San Francisco, the Sociology of Development Conference in Providence in 2015, the Council of European Studies' (CES) 2016 Annual Meeting in Philadelphia, the Mid-term Conference of the International Sociological Association's Research Committee RC 48 in Catania in 2017 and the International Sociological Association's Virtual Forum in Porto Alegre in 2021.

A visiting fellowship by the International Affairs Program at Northeastern University during my sabbatical leave between January and May of 2018 provided me with the opportunity to conceptualise the current form of the book. My conversations with Berna Turam and the late Jeff Juris were thought-provoking and inspiring. In June 2019, I became a fellow in the summer seminar 'Communism: Return to the New Commons?' facilitated by Étienne Balibar at the Institute for Critical Social Inquiry (ICSI) at The New School. I benefited immensely from the stimulating discussions and side conversations with Balibar and other participants which allowed me to develop radical democracy and the commons as one of the core ideas in the book.

I am grateful to Alpaslan Özerdem and Ahmet Erdi Öztürk, editors of the *Edinburgh Studies on Modern Turkey*, for welcoming this book into their series. Emma House and Isobel Birks at Edinburgh University Press were always encouraging and supportive and made the publication process seamless. Bülent Batuman, Camilo Tamayo Gomez, Derya Özkaya and Gamze Evcimen read and commented on various chapters or their early incarnations. I am thankful for their time and insightful interventions. Barış Ünlü read the entire manuscript with scrupulous attention, like a dedicated editor, for which I am much obliged.

The Ağartan, Aydın and Ünaldı families availed a warm and welcoming home during my research trips to Turkey. My daughters Saba and Neva accommodated my capricious absences (in mind and body) and unprovoked mood swings while they were busy growing up. My ~~wife~~ fellow-traveller and partner-in-crime Tuba remained the biggest support (emotional and more) that kept me going. If it wasn't for the 'brutal awakenings' each morning when she would whisper into my ear: 'wake up. This book won't write itself', it might indeed not have been written at all. It is to her that the book is dedicated.

I would be terribly remiss if I did not recognise the brave, bright-minded and big-hearted activists with whom I crossed paths during this project. They accepted me into their meetings, welcomed me to their events and spent hours with me to share their experiences, hopes and disillusionments. They were – and still are – the embodiment of 'freedom dreamers' in a country where dreaming has always come with a heavy price. It is my hope that they accept this book as a token of my deepest appreciation of their inspiring and admirable courage, perseverance, moral clarity and generosity.

1

INTRODUCTION

It has been ten long years, and yet I still vividly remember strolling through a carnival-like Gezi Park occupied by activists from all walks of life in Istanbul and then watching the TV with rage as it was violently recaptured by the police. Later I witnessed and shared their euphoria when scores of passionate people began to assemble for long forum meetings in neighbourhood parks. The whole experience was a roller coaster of collective emotions unleashed within just a few head-spinning weeks. At the end of that summer of discontent in 2013, I was more than ready to join the enthusiastic chorus to welcome the birth of a new Turkey. The book I set out to write was going to prove without a single doubt that what happened in Istanbul's Gezi Park that summer was yet another blaze in the wildfires scorching the planet in search for a better one – in Zuccotti, Tahrir, Syntagma and others. Keeping company with protests 'kicking off everywhere' to declare daringly that 'a different world *is* possible' and on its way, the revolution had once again 'winked at us', this time in a small promenade at the heart of my beloved Istanbul.

Gezi: The Making of a New Political Community in Turkey is not that book. After all these years since the first spark was kindled in Seattle in 1999, when the promises of the new wave of global movements all but turned into one big disillusion in transforming political structures and overhauling social relations, that book and her comrades are yet to be written. 'What disillusionment?' you may ask. Not only the Gezi protests but none of these movements that were demanding bread, freedom, justice and dignity – neither the anti-austerity protests in Europe and North America nor the pro-democracy uprisings in the Middle East, North Africa and East Asia or any others around the world – could institutionalise their political vision into durable governance structures. Although one may contest, as Breines (1989) does convincingly in her analysis of the student mobilisation in the US during the 1960s, the presumption that the success of movements should be defined in terms of their organisation, leadership or other structural qualities, it is hard to deny that the spontaneous, horizontal and leaderless activism in these movements failed to withstand the authoritarian backlash from the political establishment. Looking through the gloom of our times, as widening economic inequality and the rise of xenophobic, homophobic and chauvinistic politics lead to the concentration of power and privilege in the hands of an ever-shrinking few, the anticipation of a radical reorganisation of society, the sound of which had once rung powerfully in streets, squares and parks all over the world, is a distant nostalgia – at least for now.

In light of all this, *Gezi* grapples with the most immediate question: what explains the initial force and subsequent setback of the Gezi protests – as well as that of protests in Tahrir, Syntagma, Puerta del Sol, Zuccotti and many other places in the last decades – in constituting a more egalitarian society and formulating a democratic citizenship in response to what Brown (2019) calls the 'dismantlement of society' and 'dethronement of politics' by neoliberalism? What are the factors underlying the impressive rise of these movements to shake the existing system to its core, only to be followed by their inaptitude in building the foundations of the new world they promised, resulting instead in further social decay and democratic erosion?

Studying the Social Movements – Democracy Nexus in the Twenty-first Century

Gezi is hardly the first book to ask these questions. The relationship between social movements and democracy has been the subject of numerous studies, increasingly so since the turn of the century with the rise of the Zapatistas in Mexico in 1994, and later with the spread of the World Social Forum and her regional sisters following the Seattle protests in 1999. Most of these studies, however, regard social movements as a reaction to something broken in the economic and/or political system. In the same line of argument, the rebellion/ revolt/insurrection itself is taken as the expression of democratic potential already inherent (albeit dormant until that moment of eruption) in the movement (see especially Castells, 2015; Dikeç, 2018; Fominaya, 2014; Mason, 2013; Tuğal, 2016). *Gezi*, on the other hand, brings to the fore imaginaries and practices of a new model of social organisation as it emerged, evolved and disappeared during and in the aftermath of the Gezi protests. As such, the book belongs to a particular genre that emphasises the ways that political activism prefigures and implements practices of democratic citizenship and how these practices shape collective political subjectivities (see especially Blee, 2014; della Porta & Felicetti, 2018; della Porta & Rucht, 2015; Menser, 2018; Sitrin & Azzellini, 2014).

Despite their insightfulness, however, these latter studies fail to see a fundamental feature of the anti-austerity and pro-democracy movements of the twenty-first century: that they comprise three analytically distinct and irreducible yet inextricably inter-connected dynamics that play out simultaneously in the course of a movement. In other words, three modalities of activism in the square movements and occupations of the early 2010s are often overlooked, or otherwise addressed in isolation.

First, regardless of their national context or individual trigger, nowhere was contentious politics carried out in a vacuum – it belonged to a global wave of social unrest that had arisen in response to the extremities of neoliberalism. As such, they shared a *mobilisational* dynamic that conditioned activists' political identity and perseverance as well as the democratic practices and prefigurative politics they carried out. More concretely, globally connected activists and organisers were continuously mobilising in their local contexts, engaging in various forms of contentious politics, such as fighting the police in the streets, occupying squares, holding forum meetings in parks and other public spaces, squatting in abandoned buildings and others, while inspiring and being inspired by other struggles around the world. The ensuing processes of individual and collective political subjectification against oppression and dispossession were directly influenced by the global protest cycle in that conjuncture. Therefore, the radical imagination of a new society and citizenship in these movements was not emerging in a pure/generic form at a random moment in history, but under this constant mobilisation in our 'extraordinary times'.

Second, social movements of the early twenty-first century arose in hyper-politicised urban places (such as streets, squares, neighbourhood parks, squat houses, community gardens and others), each of which reveal in unique ways the *spatiality* of political activism. More specifically, as neoliberalism conditioned the processes of urbanisation and ultimately shaped the ways in which public spaces in the city were perceived and experienced by (and often stolen from) its residents, each of these spaces turned into a site of contestation. It is in these actual physical sites where activists became 'politically sensitised to world situations and their own connection with these wider processes' (Glass, 2008, p. 27). As such, each site maintained a distinct potential for political activism by making certain emancipatory practices and imaginaries possible while inhibiting others. The democratic horizon that defined the movements of the twenty-first century was thus spatially constructed within this complex ensemble of urban spaces.

Third, novel forms and performances of political activism (such as forums, encampments, squatting, creating community gardens and other non-capitalist practices) were *radical democratic* attempts to transform the political and reconstitute the social. They were an appeal to the 'common' as a fresh model of solidarity and democratic citizenship. In other words, while showing an utmost effort to be inclusive of and expansive towards different political identities, the pro-democracy and anti-austerity struggles of the 2000s aimed to transcend their plurality by prefiguring ways to redefine and experience the common as the basis of a new political community. The radical democratic dynamic in these movements, then, propelled people's radical imagination and political horizon towards not just having full control over their social, political and economic resources but towards designing a new, shared and dynamic moral framework around the idea of the common to foster new relations of solidarity, fellowship and mutual trust destroyed by neoliberalism.

Indeed, despite addressing various aspects of the relationship between activism and democratic outcomes, scholarly work on the transformative potential of social movements has to date failed in addressing the ways in which these three dynamics in contemporary movements are juxtaposed. For instance, della Porta's prolific scholarship (2008; 2009, 2014b; 2015; 2020) delves into the relationship between democratic procedures and social movements through deploying traditional analytical tools (such as focus-ing on resources, strategies, frames, repertoires of action, networks, identity construction and so forth). However, her contributions are often silent in offering a more complicated picture of how, for instance, the spatiality of urban sites shape political mobilisation in distinct ways, or what the moti-vating impulse is behind participatory and deliberative enactments in move-ments that drive activists towards the prefiguration of a radically reorganised society. One can make similar assessments of the work by Blee (2014) and Felicetti (2018), although their analyses, unlike those of della Porta, also dismiss the neoliberal condition as the ultimate catalyst that mobilises (and connects) activists from around different parts of the world and nurtures the radicalism in their activism. While Menser (2018), Ofer and Groves (2017), Sitrin (2012), Sitrin and Azzellini (2014) and Szolucha (2016), among oth-ers, underscore the radical character of the discourses and performances of democratic engagement through participation and deliberation, they take only cursory note of internal dynamics and power struggles *within* the movements they analyse and ignore the spatiality of everyday democratic practices. More particularly, Sitrin (2012) focuses on the 'moment' as the upheaval unfolds, along with what motivates and binds people on the street to devise the radical practices they utilise, without necessarily addressing the long-term 'evolution' of this politicisation process after the initial euphoria subsides. Finally, books by Miller (2000), Hoskyns (2014) and Parkinson (2012) introduce the missing spatial aspect of democracy into the discussion of social movements, yet they overlook the radically transformative character of the prefigurative conceptions and imaginations of political community in these movements.

By focusing on the simultaneity of *the mobilisational, spatial* and *radi-cal democratic* dynamics in the movements of the twenty-first century, *Gezi* brings attention to the otherwise invisible 'constitutive' character of these movements in response to the dismantlement of the social under the yoke of neoliberalism. In other words, by way of a critical analysis of these three dynamics as they appeared during and after the Gezi Park protests, *Gezi* aims to fill a gap in the literature to better understand the complex trajectory of contemporary movements and their democratic potential.

Towards a New Approach

Wendy Brown admits in *In the Ruins of Neoliberalism* (2019) to not having paid enough attention in her earlier work *Undoing the Demos* (2015) to neo-liberalism's demonisation of society and to the suffocation of democratic politics under a system of morality that glorifies the individual and family. Given the decay of democratic institutions, smothering of social policy tools and disintegration of solidarity bonds accompanied by the rise of homophobic, xenophobic and chauvinistic visions moving from the fringes to the centre of political debate in recent decades, we would be remiss if we did not acknowledge neoliberalism's success in dismantling the social.

Against such a comprehensive project of destruction, what we see emerging is a form of political activism that goes beyond defence, objection, reaction or explosion, and that nurtures dreams for a new form of freedom and democratic existence. The Zapatista uprising in 1994, Seattle protests in 1999 followed by the emergence of World Social Forum, and finally the Occupy, Arab Spring and other anti-globalisation protests in the wake of the 2008 financial crisis that stretched from Europe to Latin America and from North Africa to East Asia were not solely trying to put a system gone rogue back on track. They were at the same time actively prefiguring and building an alternative world – they still are. Their horizon is not limited to demanding from the political establishment the restoration of their truncated rights and freedoms or their diminished economic prosperity. They have never settled for a 'system update' in which extreme inequalities were redressed. Their emphasis on 'world-making' transforms these protests into pluralistic, horizontal and participatory movements that dream of a shared life and strive to establish it through everyday actions. It is, therefore, imperative to investigate how today's movements imagine and prefigure the future as much as what they object to and revolt against.

In *Gezi*, I demonstrate that during and after the Gezi uprising, activists in Istanbul and other parts of Turkey engaged in a political struggle defined by a constant state of mobilisation in different parks, neighbourhoods and squat houses where various iterations of a horizontal, direct, inclusive, deliberative, consensus-oriented and overall 'radical democratic' organising emerged. This complexity, I argue, turned the movement into something bigger than a mere rebellion due to deepening economic and political tensions: a form of activism that aimed to reimagine and reconstitute society from bottom up in the face of neoliberal assault. In order to better examine the subtle potential of Gezi and other social movements as constitutive processes, *Gezi* introduces two analytical enhancements.

The first of these enhancements concerns the temporality of social movements. The literature has already offered approaches that underline the importance of moving beyond the narrow treatment of time as a binary of 'cycle' or 'long-term change' (see, for instance: Sewell & McAdam, 2001; also see: Sewell, 2005). Inspired by these, and in contrast with explanations that tend to interpret movements as a moment of explosion or eruption following a series of social, political and economic crises, *Gezi* extends the temporal unit of analysis from the moment of eruption as the apex of Gezi Park protests (especially the street clashes and early days of the park's occupation) to its aftermath (including park forums, neighbourhood solidarities and subsequent initiatives for building a national political movement) as one continuous period which I call the 'Gezi Episode'.

Unlike Tilly (2008), who utilises 'episode' as an analytical tool to examine discrete durations of time defined by their distinctiveness based on action repertoires, goals and other parameters within the totality of a given social movement, I use the term as a way to develop a 'continuous' yet 'non-uniform' temporality which assembles spatially fractured yet temporally overlapping forms of activism and processes of politicisation. Such a stretch in the time frame not only prevents the heat of the moment (the 'uprising') from clouding a more sober and critical analysis, it also allows for reconstructing and reassessing a whole period of political mobilisation as an uninterrupted yet many-faceted, multi-phase, contingent and sometimes contradictory constitutive process as opposed to a linear progression of discrete, intermittent and disconnected political events such as a riot, followed by an occupation, followed by a park forum and so forth.

The second analytical enhancement that *Gezi* offers is the utilisation of a broader definition of 'political community' to trace and gauge the constitutive impact of political activism in the face of the destruction of society by neoliberalism. The main premise of this move is that the transformation of the political and reconstitution of the social in an ensemble of urban settings as a part of contentious politics around the radical democratic idea of the common cannot be separated from the search for and making of a new 'people'.

Here, in contrast to conventional interpretations that romanticise it merely as the expression of accentuated bonds among the similar, I define political community as the crystallisation of social relationships and collective human experience in which people with diverse backgrounds, orientations and aspirations engage in a shared way of life to collectively defend, rebuild and reinvent the solidaristic foundations of democracy.

The term political community dates back to ancient Greeks, yet a cursory look at the more recent political theory literature reveals that it often refers to a state/polity-centred social order: a totality of the relationships between citizens and the state, and between citizens themselves (Linklater, 1998). In this narrow definition, political community is depicted as a territorial unity in which the political apparatus has a considerable authority over its constituents who are bound to each other through a shared national identity and a common understanding of collective good. However, this classic approach to understanding political community has become inadequate in addressing the ways in which social relations have recently been transforming. Under neoliberalism, individuals have become 'disaffiliated' (Castel, 2003) from their solidarity connections and 'dis-incorporated' from their support institutions, finding their atomised selves at the mercy of unfettered market relations. The resulting decline of solidaristic ties has led to mounting discontent, eroding the legitimacy of state and traditional mechanisms of political representation. The search for a new and shared moral framework to identify and politically address many pressing questions, including social equity, environmental justice, self-determination, right to the city, immigration and others became unavoidable. Along with it emerged the need to go beyond formal, legalistic, nation-state centric definitions of political community in order to be able to address the emerging complexities in the ways through which citizens identify themselves as political subjects, especially in times of social and political turbulence.

It is for this reason that *Gezi* draws on a revised concept of political community, moving beyond the dichotomy between a legalistic definition of political citizenship (with an emphasis on rights-bearing individuals) and a conservative communitarian interpretation of solidarity between individuals connected through an abstract, static and homogeneous set of normative values around a pre-decided, non-negotiable 'contract'. Unlike the more stylised notions of 'public sphere' or 'civil society', political community defined by activism-guided solidarity embraces the intentional construction of a new 'we' (Özkaya, 2024): one that encompasses social relations through trust, care and mutual responsibility in collective action ridden by conflict and prefiguration. It embraces a common desire for 'recognition', 'belonging', 'willingness to co-exist', 'emancipation' and 'pursuit of social justice' to reflect the plurality of the idea of 'the people' that transcends the reductionist notions of the 'nation' and 'representative democracy'. This reworked definition of community as 'political friendship' provides a strong analytical leverage to evaluate the constitutive capacity of the social movements of the early twenty-first century in remaking the social against neoliberal assault and building a new political architecture through radical grassroots activism around a shared idea of the 'common'.

It is through these contributions that *Gezi* adds a fresh perspective to the study of the nexus between contemporary social movements and democratic change in Turkey, while at the same time reveals the constitutive character of this unique period in Turkish history, the 'Gezi Episode'.

A Word on Methods

Gezi draws on a synthesis of the findings from the field research that I carried out during 2014–16 in Istanbul. It comprises more than twenty in-depth semi-structured interviews and occasional communications with several key activists of the Yoğurtçu Forum – one of the biggest forums that emerged following the expulsion of protestors from Gezi Park in June 2013 – in addition to participatory observations in regular forum meetings, rallies, seminars and other forms of activism. The field research is supported by primary documents (such as brochures, pamphlets, daily newspaper records and social media messages) and secondary literature (books, zines, audio visual material and other digital content) that aim to capture the voices of a broad palette of Gezi activists in building the main narrative of the book.

The research agenda for *Gezi* was initially conceived as an ethnography of the Yoğurtçu Forum, under the assumption that thanks to its size and outreach, an extensive observation and analysis of the 'forum experience' here would reveal the intricacies of the nexus between social movements and democracy in the Turkish context. Yet, as early as the summer of 2014, the Yoğurtçu Forum had begun to shrink and transform. Some of its activists had left the Forum to form smaller neighbourhood solidarities, defence groups, squat houses and other initiatives. It was obvious that neither being immersed in Yoğurtçu nor focusing only on the forum experience would exhaust the richness of the transformative political experimentation because activists were in a constant state of mobilisation, taking various roles simultaneously in more than one initiative emerging in different corners of the city when in pursuit of collectively building something without a prescription. The continuity and disruption throughout different moments of this experience could only be captured by expanding the spatial and temporal units of analysis beyond the confines of the Yoğurtçu Forum. The fragmented, scattered, contingent, ambiguous and even contradictory nature of the entire 'Gezi Episode' thus conditioned the research design itself.

This is why *Gezi* rests more on theoretical pillars than on a case study with an anthropological orientation or ethnographic rigor, in order to grasp the complexities of social movements of the twenty-first century as crystallised in the whole 'Gezi phenomenon'. Following Parkinson (2012, p. 9), the book carves out for itself a meso-level space between normative theory of social movements and purely empirical analysis of contentious politics. Despite that, *Gezi* is still more inductive than deductive thanks to substantiating its conceptual and analytical emphasis through strategic use of empirical data retrieved from interviews and observations that inform the theoretical endeavour. Put differently, by utilising certain apparatuses of empirical research to ground its theoretical discussions in the lived experiences of activists during the Gezi Episode, the book adopts a 'concept-driven' sociological orientation with a 'framework-building' purpose that aims to transcend the unproductive binary of 'data-driven' versus 'theory-driven' scholarship (Zerubavel, 2021). Therefore, *Gezi*'s main contribution should be sought in its conceptual framing to better account for the workings of social movements in the twenty-first century than to uncover the idiosyncrasies of the 'Gezi phenomenon'.

Overview of the Book

Gezi is organised as follows: Chapter 2 opens with a broad, world-historical canvas that frames the material foundations of the global movement cycle of the early 2000s. It sketches the novel characteristics of these movements, particularly how they utilised direct, decentralised, horizontal, autonomous, anti-capitalist practices of deliberation and participation in squares, parks and other urban sites as dominant logics of resistance against neoliberalism. The emergence of the World Social Forum and protest camps along with the spread of communication technologies are of particular interest here to highlight how these novelties transformed numerous social movements at the beginning of the century, including the Arab Spring, Occupy Wall Street and their sister protests all around the world. The chapter then moves on to offer a lens to interpret various cases of contentious politics in Turkey that would pave 'the road to Gezi' as a part of this wave of global movements. It focuses on protests against environmental degradation, privatisation and other market reforms as the authoritarian, conservative neoliberalism under the AKP (Justice and Development Party) regime transformed the urban space for its political and ideological as well as developmental goals. The chapter concludes by bringing under scrutiny the rise of a coalition of dissenting groups in Istanbul which could find ways to wed their distinct grievances under the same struggle that came to be the Gezi uprising in 2013.

Chapter 3 introduces the *mobilisational* dynamic of political activism during and in the wake of the Gezi protests as the first of the three characteristics of contemporary democratic struggles. It provides a brief account of the events that culminated in the uprising, including the occupation of Gezi Park and its aftermath when park forums, neighbourhood solidarities and squat houses emerged (and waned) along with attempts to institutionalise a national political movement. A closer analysis of the Gezi Episode follows, employing a social movements framework to highlight such factors as the composition of participants, organisational forms they built, resources they mobilised, networks they utilised, tactics and strategies they employed, repertoires of action they drew on and the symbols and ideological frames they constructed during the Episode. The final section of this chapter turns – as do the following two chapters – to the question of 'political community' and investigates the ways through which the *mobilisational* dynamic of the Gezi Episode activated dormant sectors of the society to get involved in constant activism as a way of life and created qualitatively new relationships of solidarity.

In Chapter 4, the reader is introduced to the second – *spatial* – dynamic of contemporary democratic struggles through a discussion on the relationship between spatial democracy and social movements, drawing on different experiences from around the world. The focus then shifts to the complexity of the urban space in Istanbul, which, it is argued, fundamentally shaped political mobilisation during the uprising in a multiplicity of politicised urban sites and affected the democratic vision and horizon of the movement throughout the Episode. The chapter demonstrates how streets, squares, parks, buildings and other places formed a fluid constellation of spaces in which various forms of social mobilisation and political interaction conditioned the democratic potential of the political struggle. The spatial analysis also reveals the ambiguous nature of the Gezi Episode with respect to its impact on political community and democratic prospects. It demonstrates that while activists could easily move from one site to another, developing a distinct sense of solidarity around a common political goal, the multiplicity of physical sites also made it harder for activists to find the appropriate mode/balance/scale of politics that would transform dissent into effective and lasting political action.

Chapter 5 focuses on the third dynamic of the social movements of the twenty-first century – that is, the *radical democratic* vision – as it crystallised in the Gezi Episode. The chapter opens up by suggesting that everyday practices of radical democracy in Taksim Square, Gezi Park, neighbourhood parks, squat houses and other urban sites have motivated activists to develop a new sense of political awareness and subjectivity. These everyday practices and enactments of radical democracy were attempts to build a new collectivity to counter the docile conservative, religious, consumer-subject-citizen model that the AKP had imposed during its tenure. They embodied an alternative social project in defiance of traditional representative politics favouring the ballot box. Offering a detailed account of prefigurative political enactments during the Gezi Episode, the chapter concludes that the idea of the 'common' became the cement of a new political community reinforced by radical democratic praxis (ranging from establishing free kitchens, libraries and workshops during the occupation to practices of participation and deliberation in forum meetings) which culminated in the cultivation of new norms of belonging and mutual obligation beyond national will and state-enforced designations and performances of solidarity.

Chapter 6 offers a comprehensive assessment of the rise and demise of the hope for a democratic political community at the confluence of the three dynamics of the Gezi Episode. The first part of the chapter critically revisits the 'on-the-surface' factors that are frequently cited to explain the inability of translating the Gezi experience to a more sustainable and long-term politics. The rest of the chapter contrasts these explanations by highlighting structural (if not contradictory) forces to better capture the trajectory of this political experience. Three such forces are emphasised in the chapter. First, under the *mobilisational* dynamic, constant state of activism in different urban sites simultaneously motivated activists to adopt and enact different political subjectivities at once, which resulted in the volatility of the common identity that nourished the 'Gezi spirit' in the early days of the Episode. Second, as the Episode became even more fragmented under the *spatial* dynamic, there emerged lack of trust, coordination and harmony between politics at different sites. In other words, too many sites began to produce incompatible political visions at different levels or scales, which could not constitute a coherent, unified political vision, making activists more suspicious of the outside of their immediate circle. Third and finally, despite the *radical democratic* orientation towards building a new common at the local scale, the political horizon of the Gezi Episode could not fully shake off its national (and especially parliamentary) ambitions as activists were often drawn into traditional electoral politics whose political grammar was not suitable to express the essence of radical democratic politics. Adding to this, the increasing violence in politics orchestrated and fuelled by the AKP as well as the pressing immediacy of the Kurdish question during important political moments, further deepened these vulnerabilities and prevented the full maturation of the idea of the common as the basis of new political citizenship. The chapter concludes that as prospects for a broader and more comprehensive conceptualisation of democracy, citizenship and political community faded, the vulnerabilities of the Gezi Episode paved the way for a ruthless backlash, state-sponsored violence and ultimately the consolidation of an authoritarian rule.

2

THE ROAD TO GEZİ

In this chapter I locate the social and political developments paving the way for the Gezi Episode within a world-historical canvas that frames the material foundations of global movements since the Seattle protests in 1999. In the first part, the emphasis is on the ways in which these movements came to develop direct, horizontal, autonomous, anti-capitalist practices of participation and deliberation as the primary logic of organising against inequality, marginalisation and dispossession deepened under neoliberal urbanisation. I will then use this framework to interpret contentious politics in Turkey during the early 2000s as an integral part of this movement wave. In the last part, I will focus on Istanbul and tell the story of how two decades of brewing discontent under the AKP regime – in the face of environmental degradation, urban gentrification, market reforms and the gradual rise of an authoritarian rule with conservative Islamic undertones – culminated in a political force that paved the way to the Gezi uprising.

Neoliberal Urbanisation and Global Social Movements

The global social movements of the first two decades of the 2000s cannot be understood without considering the changes in global capitalism since the latter half of the twentieth century. As a panacea to the systemic crisis of capitalism that could no longer be avoided by the late 1970s, hurdles against the global mobility of capital began to be dismantled. This was followed by the erosion of workers' rights and the purchasing power of wages, heralding the annulment of the implicit accord between labour and capital as the main backbone of the social welfare regime in the advanced capitalist world. Developments in electronic communication technologies facilitated the financialisation of capital through integrating national markets into a global network. As the industrial production shifted from the Global North to the Global South, the decline of rural economies accelerated, catalysing migration to urban centres. Meanwhile, consumption-driven growth models led to the expansion of value-chains and of commodification to feed these chains, which deepened dispossession, poverty, inequality and precarity. Several economic crises around the world during the 1990s did not stop governments from implementing tight-belt policies. On the contrary, they adopted an even more aggressive mode of liberalisation for their economies, accompanied by a more oppressive mode of politics to manage the growing discontent by those crushed under these policies. The rise of food prices coupled with ecological destruction only fuelled the anxiety and anger of the masses around the world in the face of growing existential threat. The gradual decline and eventual fall of US hegemonic power, which hampered the system's ability to shore up anti-democratic regimes and bring them into the fold of a unipolar world order, sealed the ultimate collapse of the global status quo established after the Second World War.

As the neoliberal regime consolidated through financialisation, commodification and other market reforms, cities gained a renewed importance as pivotal sites of capital accumulation (Rossi, 2017). Privatisation of public spaces, commercialisation of housing developments, gentrification and urban regeneration programs, courting of international investors and promoting consumerism became the governing principles of this 'growth first' approach in the new era (Mayer, 2016, pp. 65–9). Big capital investments (such as flagship projects for sports and entertainment), prestigious cultural amenities and offerings for the elite and the transformation of cities into sites of capital stock in fixed assets and commanding heights of transnational companies became important facets of neoliberal urbanism (Mayer, 2011, p. 68; Schmid, 2011, pp. 54–5; Thörn et al., 2016, p. 34).

In *Rebel Cities* David Harvey draws attention to the profound impact this process had on social structure. For him, the proliferation of consumption sites and new market niches contributed to intense possessive individualism in the city, which revealed itself in the form of privatised and fragmented sites within the urban space and eventually resulted in polarisation in the distribution of wealth and power (Harvey, 2013, pp. 12–17). This has perpetually destroyed the city 'as a social, political and liveable commons', as a result of which 'ideals of urban identity, citizenship, and belonging, of a coherent urban politics, already threatened by the spreading malaise of the individualistic neoliberal ethic, [have] become much harder to sustain' (Harvey, 2013, p. 80, p. 15).

The destruction of the social under neoliberalism that Harvey portrays has its roots in the ways in which urbanisation took place under capitalism. More than a century ago, Georg Simmel observed a process of 'objectivation' of space and individualisation of urban dwellers leading to disintegration of communal ties, atomisation of the individual and the rise of sentiments of separation, fragmentation, overwhelmed-ness and longing for others (Eckardt, 2015, p. 16). Similarly, Lefebvre detected a 'tendency towards the homogenisation of lifestyles and an engineering and colonisation of daily life' through monotonous labour processes and bureaucratisation of cities (Schmid, 2011, p. 43). For him, this 'complete urbanisation', that is, 'the instrumentalisation of space in economic development and in the reproduction of social relationships' (Stanek, 2011, p. 163) caused alienation through homogenisation and destruction of the specific qualities of urban life. Consequently, the urban lost its character as a space of 'mediation', whereby differences (in value-systems, activities, knowledge among and between ethnic, cultural and social groups) could come into contact, coexist, explore each other and arrive at some form of mutual understanding (Schmid, 2011, pp. 46–8). Echoing Lefebvre, Bookchin underscored how cities under capitalism lost their form as cultural and political entities as their 'functions have changed from ethical arenas with a uniquely humane, civilised form of consociation, free of all blood ties and family loyalties, into immense, overbearing, and anonymous marketplaces' (Bookchin, 2021, p. 209).

It was when the neoliberalisation of the global economy was juxtaposed with these tectonic changes in the very fabric of society under capitalism that a new social movement cycle was triggered with the 1999 Seattle protests of the WTO, although the origins of the cycle can be dated back to the 1994 Zapatista movement in Mexico. As the destruction of lives and livelihoods in every corner of the world reached a tipping point, the emergence of the World

Social Forum in Porto Alegre and the subsequent regional social forums heralded a new beginning for the imagination and creation of an alternative world (Sen & Waterman, 2007; Smith et al., 2014). These ventures undertaken by activist groups, labour unions, environmental groups and other civil society organisations, as well as prominent individuals from academia and politics, were important as they attempted to unite and harmonise at the supranational level otherwise disconnected local and national struggles. The emerging form of activism and those who created it (the 'multitude' in Hardt and Negri's lexicon (2004)) aimed to connect groups, organisations and institutions in a horizontal, rather than vertical, network while at the same time build a structure that could coordinate local, national and global movements in their fight for democracy, equality and justice (Avtur, 2014; Fominaya, 2014).

Although this authentic experience was cut short by rising chauvinism and militarism following the September 11th attacks (Benlisoy, 2012), the revival of protests in the wake of the 2008 economic crisis was testimony that its achievements were not totally lost. By the second decade of the twenty-first century, various forms of political activism were revitalised and new political identities as well as alliances were forged along deep-seated fault lines, which were activated during the worldwide protests. While some of these movements (especially those in the Global North) focused on the impact of anti-austerity measures and were carried out by those who had to endure worsening economic conditions, others were spearheaded by those who, in addition to similar but deeper economic woes, were rising against corrupt governments and authoritarian leaders, mostly in the Global South. Movements stretching from the Arab Spring across many countries in the Middle East and North Africa to the M15/Los Indignados movement in Spain, Catalonia, and the Basque Country (Fominaya, 2020), from the Occupy Wall Street protests in the US and its global offshoots to the Indignant Citizens Movement in Greece, the Umbrella Movement in Hong Kong, *Nuit Debout* in France, and numerous others were spreading like wildfire from Europe to Latin America, from North Africa to East Asia (Ancelovici et al., 2016; Castells, 2015; Mason, 2013). In May of 2013, Gezi Park protests in Istanbul would join this long list.

This time, however, the protests that furthered various iterations and combinations of 'bread, freedom and justice' themes, along with efforts to save the earth from total destruction, showed noticeable differences in their motivations, discourses, methods and visions from the previous anti-globalisation movements and the World Social Forum experience (della Porta, 2015, pp. 173–92; Also see: Smith et al., 2014 ch. 6; Çetinkaya, 2020, p. 41). The main premise of activism was no longer the global coordination of local protests and initiatives, as was primarily the case with the World Social Forum and its offshoots. More importantly, activists involved in these protests were not necessarily a member of an existing political or civil society organisation. On the contrary, they were proudly 'independent' individuals unburdened by established politics who could easily append themselves to horizontal, decentralised, pluralist and direct practices of creative activism in their own localities (Haug & Rucht, 2015).

Although these protests were almost always instigated by a specific reason and took a distinct course due to their unique national contexts, what united them was the realisation by the masses that they would not be able to voice their resentment and carry out an effective opposition through traditional political channels. The heavy reliance on tools of social media helped distinct initiatives inspire and learn from each other and give a common voice (though not always in harmony) to atomised resentments that could not find the means to socialise and institutions to organise in the age of neoliberal individualism. Overwhelmingly anti-capitalist and anti-authoritarian in nature, and with a strong critique of racism, economic injustices and corruption of the political establishment, activists were in favour of a radical and comprehensive transformation of politics (Burawoy, 2018, pp. 23–24; also see: Ancelovici et al., 2016). By emphasising 'real democracy' in theory and practice, they were promoting an alternative political and social existence against conventional, technocratic and market-dominated political logics and apparatuses of representative democracy, or otherwise ineffective forms of organisation disconnected from material realities under the narcotic comfort of union politics dominated by labour aristocracy. Most important of all, they were doing all this by grounding themselves in the city through reclaiming, occupying and transforming various urban spaces.

And this was no coincidence. The fact that urban space had become the primary site of capital accumulation in this neoliberal phase of capitalism had a considerable impact on deepening spatial polarisation and exacerbating social inequalities in the city (Dikeç, 2018; Wacquant, 2007). Under neoliberalism, urban transformation has often pushed up land and real estate prices, which concomitantly led to the affordable housing crisis and displacement from entire metropolitan regions. Intensified processes of dispossession through gentrification, territorial stigmatisation and police violence in the city created sites of marginalisation and exclusion that affected different urban populations in distinct ways, leading to further erosion of the urban fabric (Bailey, 2020; Brenner et al., 2011; Rolnik, 2019; Thörn et al., 2016, pp. 6–8; Wood, 2017, pp. 88–9).

In other words, urban uprisings that were scattered around the world were eruptions of simmering rage in response to a structural and routinised oppression that was reducing life chances, poisoning everyday lives and ending life with impunity (Dikeç, 2018). New sites of segregation and marginalisation under neoliberal urbanisation were emerging as bedrocks of struggles for radical, anti-capitalist alternatives and community building (Coward, 2012). It was no longer only the 'place of work' where tensions and resentments brewed but any urban space could now become a site of demonstration, riot, rally or other form of civil disobedience (Karataşlı, 2020). The city was becoming the primary front of a multi-faceted contentious politics whose form and place have now shifted away formal sites of politics (such as factory fronts, voting polls, civil society organisations, political parties and other established institutions and practices of representative democracy) towards occupations, encampments, forums and other forms of assembly politics, each of which became the loci of empowerment and emancipation.

In this complex matrix of activism, some groups would be fighting against environmental degradation side by side with others resisting the loss of cultural heritage or the increasing commodification and privatisation of urban public spaces. Similarly, while some groups would be organising against deepening economic insecurity and the waning of public services, housing support or other social policy mechanisms in the urban economy, others would take lead in mutual aid initiatives to help the displaced, homeless or immigrants to survive in the increasingly exclusionary city. In other words, while urban spaces were being produced in the shadow of capital under neoliberalism, they were at the same time 'reappropriated in the symbolic vocabulary of liberation' (Keith & Pile, 1993, p. 25).

This vocabulary of new urban activism was rich and original, and its groundedness in the city allowed activists to repurpose some of the tactics of the earlier struggles according to their own circumstances (for an overview of these changes see: Benski et al., 2013, pp. 548–54). First, almost all of these protests began as riots erupting in response to a trigger event that brought the 'business as usual' to an abrupt halt in the city: the destruction of a green area (such as in Gezi Park in Turkey), the murder of an innocent individual at the hands of the police (relating to the Black Lives Matter protests in the US) or a hike in the price of public transportation (relating to the protests in Brazil) could immediately spark protest, drawing many citizens into the streets, spreading protest across the country and provoking similar protests beyond national borders. Second, being directly connected to the space they occupied allowed activists to reclaim and salvage the urban resources that were abducted from the residents of the city, such as privatised public areas, abandoned buildings or closed factories. Similar spatial patterns in the form of occupying spaces and encampments could be seen in London's Parliament Square, Cairo's Tahrir Square; Puerta del Sol in Madrid and Zuccotti Park in New York City, to name a few. These spaces were not only recuperated but also repurposed to build a new community in which members from diverse backgrounds recognised each other's differences yet sought to find what was common to all. Third, and relatedly, a popular and all-encompassing definition of 'we' became the embodiment of all excluded and marginalised segments of the urban population. The 'popular power' in this broad unity was achieved through relying mostly on politics of trust and friendship between individuals who saw themselves not as activists but protagonists who – without erasing their individuality – undertook acts of mutual aid and solidarity, such as creating common libraries, offering free medical care, establishing community kitchens or developing independent and alternative media projects. In this 'prefigurative' politics, the border between social relations and experiences of everyday life and the political movement was blurred. The rejection of representational mechanisms as well as hierarchical political traditions and customs was reinforced by horizontalism and self-management (*autogestión*) as guiding principles of political communication and interaction in people's assemblies. Finally, these movements were often motivated not through a pre-existing ideology or form of action but a vague 'horizon', which could range from mundane activities undertaken on a regular day in a camp to planting the seeds of a radically different society through interacting with activists around the world (Sitrin & Azzellini, 2014, ch. 1 and 2).

This breed of activism that came to life from within this urban experience had immediate implications with respect to the democratic potentiality of anti-austerity and pro-democracy movements. More specifically, a unique 'chain of equivalence' (Laclau & Mouffe, 2001) between different segments of the population materialised in the face of the unravelling of the urban fabric under neoliberal assault, turning local, self-managed, autonomous spaces into sites of collective decision-making and transformative activism (Hoskyns, 2014, p. 67). These sites and practices they embodied would become the pillars of direct or quasi-direct urban democracy through which these movements aimed to build a new political community, which I address in Chapter 5.

It is against this global canvas that Turkey's own experience with urban neoliberalism should be considered as it unfolded in the past decades and paved the way for the Gezi uprisings.

Contesting Neoliberal Urbanisation in Turkey

Although it became more forceful after the AKP came to power at the turn of the century, the reorientation of the economy under the neoliberal phase of capitalism had already been stoking social unrest in Turkey since the 1980s (Ağartan, 2018). Anti-privatisation protests that have been organised and orchestrated mainly by labour unions and confederations, such as the strike of Zonguldak coal miners and their peaceful march to Ankara (Bakioğlu, 2022), were at the forefront of activism in this early period. During the 1990s, however, with the progressive decline in the legitimacy of established institutions (especially unions and political parties) because of their failure in channelling popular discontent, a new breed of activism emerged: one whose content and scope were not confined to national economic or political agendas but rather were spearheaded by individuals and civil society organisations in a broader framework comprising expression of cultural identity, environmental issues, anti-corruption, women's rights and other democratic demands.

The first glimpse of this new wave of activism could be seen in the *Sürekli Aydınlık için Bir Dakika Karanlık* ('One Minute of Darkness for Everlasting Light') protests or in the resistance by villagers in Akkuyu against the construction of a thermal power plant or in Bergama against the opening of gold mines that would use cyanide in its operations, all of which were engraved in collective memory as acts of civil disobedience from the 1990s. With their peaceful and creative methods (the villagers in Bergama carried out their demonstrations half naked, for instance), these protests were heralding the coming of others in the 2000s (Voulvouli, 2011). During this time, and with the rise of platforms where activists and movements around the world could share their experiences and inspire each other (sometimes with the availability of the translation of a book, participating an international event, the online circulation of a newsletter or attending a rally in support of an ongoing activism in another country), activist networks in Turkey became more entrenched in this wave of social movements (Gümrükçü, 2010, pp. 168–9). From the early 2000s onward, Istanbul hosted some of the European Social Forum's meetings, which gave way to 'Istanbul Forums' to become a space for alternative points of view about, as well as for bringing to national and global attention, issues such as the Kurdish question, women's rights, local governance, energy politics, environmental destruction and anti-war mobilisation (Casalucci & Anghelinas, 2010; Romão, 2009; Üstündağ, 2004). At the 2010 European Social Forum, various groups, neighbourhood associations and activists from Turkey could gather to discuss issues such as urban transformation and the right to the city in Istanbul (Çelik & Ergenç, 2018, p. 83). The demonstrations organised by the *DirenIstanbul* (ResistIstanbul) platform during the IMF and World Bank meetings in Istanbul in October 2009, and protests under the umbrella of *Ayaklan Istanbul* (Rebel Istanbul) in support of the occupation of Zuccotti Park during Occupy Wall Street protests were among the prominent instances of activism with global connections. Ecology collectives and other groups would also gain experience in forum politics when they met in 2012 and would later carry their experience into the Gezi Episode (Çelik & Ergenç, 2018, p. 83).

Yet the most memorable protest of this activism cycle in the first decade of the twenty-first century was the seventy-eight day resistance by the workers of the state-owned Turkish Tobacco and Alcoholic Beverages Company (Tütün, Tütün Mamulleri, Tuz ve Alkol İşletmeleri Genel Müdürlüğü, TEKEL) between December 2009 and March 2010. TEKEL workers, along with their families and other supporters, opposed the privatisation of the company and their redeployment with pay cuts, temporary status and truncated labour rights (Bulut, 2010; Türkmen, 2012; Yıkılmaz & Kumlu, 2011).

Following several attempts to negotiate with the government and facing police violence, workers eventually decided to set up a camp site in the Kızılay district in Ankara and stay there as a form of civil disobedience for more than two months. The importance of the TEKEL resistance came not only from its resemblance to other protests in the world, but also from its novelty in occupying a public space and developing spatial practices of solidarity (even across deeply controversial ethnic lines) as a political tactic in Turkey (Batuman, 2013a), which would later be remembered and inspire the methods utilised during the occupation of Gezi Park and its aftermath.

It was, therefore, the confluence of global dynamics and this historical lineage of contentious politics in Turkey that heralded the coming of the Gezi Episode. With neoliberalism penetrating deeper into urban life, sporadic manifestations of discontent were becoming more intense and frequent. More importantly, different spaces in the city where everyday life was taking place (including parks, monuments, the anterior of public buildings such as theatres or schools, subway stations, even balconies), were politicised through demonstrations, rallies and other forms of grassroots mobilisation. A new conception of urban citizenship, as well as a new process of political subjectification, was becoming more visible in the organisation, discourse and practices of these new mobilisations compared with peasant revolts, factory strikes or student movements of the previous era. Amidst all this, Istanbul's new urban condition that emerged from its unique encounters with neoliberal urbanisation amplified and consolidated popular discontent at the dawn of the Gezi uprisings.

Carriers of Urban Discontent in Istanbul, or 'The Road to Gezi'

The move away from the import-substituting national developmental model towards deindustrialisation in favour of finance and the service sector had already been transforming Istanbul into a significant node for economic, cultural and political flows in global networks since the 1980s (Keyder, 1999). But it was not until the AKP's rise to power that the haphazard process of the city's integration into global circles of capital became a coherent, fully fledged project. Similar to other emerging global cities, Istanbul became a destination for sectors such as media, business services, banking and finance, tourism and especially construction, turning the city's urban space into an over-valued commodity. Under the AKP, the reorganisation of state institutions such as the Mass Housing Agency (Toplu Konut İdaresi, TOKI) allowed the clearing of legally dubious settlements in the inner city and its surroundings and opening up of new spaces for corporate and residential development while circumventing legal scrutiny and accountability (Doğru, 2021). New legislations that authorised and catalysed commodification, gentrification, and privatisation of the urban space granted extraordinary powers to municipalities to clear mostly working-class neighbourhoods and squatter towns (*gecekondu*), which had been swallowed and transformed by the city in the past decades. In a short span of time, an aggressive construction endeavour was in full force (Bora, 2021), not only for building new housing units for different segments of the middle class (Keyder, 2010, p. 30) but also for signature (often dubbed 'crazy') projects including the third airport, the third bridge on the Bosporus, new highways, Canal Istanbul, GalataPort, HaydarpaşaPort and others to be carried out by big consortiums close to the AKP (Karaman, 2013; Ünsal & Kuyucu, 2010).

The urban transformation through full commodification of land brought an end to the most prevalent of informal social policies in modern Turkish history, that is, turning a blind eye to illegal land appropriation and housing construction, providing municipal services and eventually issuing legal titles for the soaring housing stock that had sustained an ever-growing migrant population in Istanbul since the 1950s (Buğra & Keyder, 2006; Erman, 2016a, pp. 83–4). As the industrial production within the city was pushed away (Koçak, 2011) and re-organised as small workshops in apartment buildings outside the centre, the newly vacated spaces were transformed into places of leisure, culture and consumption, such as museums, galleries, bars and cafés, to meet the demands of the incoming urban inhabitants while priming the peripheries of the city for the housing and consumption needs of the new middle class and the working poor (Demiral, 2018, pp. 79–84). In parallel with losing its working-class character thanks to the reversal of labour-focused redistribution policies throughout the 1980s (Boratav, 2016), certain sectors of the population began to more intensely feel the impact of soaring informal economy, growing wealth inequality, precarious employment and low wages, and marginalisation, dispossession and displacement (Dikeç, 2018, pp. 191–2), whereas others could enjoy luxurious lifestyles and consumption patterns reminiscent of their global counterparts (Keyder, 2005, 2010, p. 26).

The intensification of spatial differentiation as the city was turning into a vehicle for capital accumulation under neoliberal urbanisation went hand in hand with deeper changes in Istanbul's distinctive social fabric (Erkilet, 2014). Many places, especially the neighbourhoods (*mahalle*s) in which residents experienced, enjoyed and developed a sense of community and ownership of the city, were lost to shopping malls, business towers, high-rise apartments and gated residential complexes in gentrified districts, which catered more to global networks of finance, real estate, advertising, culture and media than to actual communities (Keyder, 2014a; Öktem Ünsal, 2015; Ünsal & Kuyucu, 2010). Countless transformations in the social fabric of the city followed course: the dissolution of reciprocity and mutual communal bonds in *mahalle*s due to increasing isolation in apartment-style residential life; disappearance of small mom-and-pop shops, which in the past would provide the middle class a buffer and flexibility in times of economic hardship; decline in average household income for middle-class families not allowing for cohabitation with the elderly, further transforming family values and straining relations within extended families; an upsurge in the exodus of middle- and lower-middle class families from the city centres due to soaring rents and other costs of livelihood; deepening spatial fragmentation between social classes preventing the building of meaningful contact with each other and development of a mutual sense of 'belonging to/in the city'; increasing educational attainment among the urban youth (in both secular/modern and more pious/conservative families), which intensified generational polarisation in perception and attitude towards public expressions of gender and sexual orientation as well as enjoyment of the pleasures of the city and further fuelled resentment among younger (especially female) individuals; and clustering of vulnerable populations (such as refugees, the poor, internally displaced and others) in certain parts of the city, turning these districts into brewing grounds for crime and social tension, among many others (see, among others: Erder, 2002; Erman, 2016a; Kardeşoğlu, 2022; Şentürk, 2015).

These tectonic changes in the social fabric of the city compounded the disparities between different segments of the urban population with regards to spaces of work, residence, consumption and other practices of everyday life. Under the neoliberal assault on all aspects of the social in favour of a small community of possessive, consumption-motivated, atomised individuals, the city was no longer a place where social, cultural and political differences could form a diverse, inclusive, cosmopolitan identity but a site of contestation where social tensions became more intense (Geniş, 2020; Kurtuluş, 2016). Unsurprisingly, the alienation, discontent and resentment in a 'totally urbanised' Istanbul activated various segments of the urban population to mobilise against their destruction. Below, I identify three such broad groups that became the primary carriers of the brewing discontent in the city and eventually 'paved the road to Gezi'.

The Dispossessed

Among the constituents of the urban opposition who rose up to defend the ecosystem of their lives and livelihoods were those who were pushed away, both physically and socially, from the heart of the city through policies that aimed to turn it into a new site of residence, business, consumption and entertainment for the elite (Ahunbay et al., 2016; İşeri, 2015; Koca et al., 2013; Uşaklıgil, 2014). The residents of neighbourhoods such as Sulukule, Tarlabaşı, 1 Mayıs or Gazi Mahallesi, which hosted residents predominantly of Roma, Alevi or Kurdish background as well as refugees, saw the existing informal social assistance mechanisms vanish and found it harder to avoid or postpone their fall into abject poverty (Işık & Pınarcıoğlu, 2021). Stories about working-class residents – who have been labelled as 'occupiers' or 'criminals' for some time (Aksoy & Güzey Kocataş, 2017; Gedikli, 2021; Uzunçarşılı-Baysal, 2015b) – clashing with the police to resist the demolition of their homes became commonplace in the national media (Erdi-Lelandais, 2014; İşeri, 2015; Koca et al., 2013). Other residents who preferred to make a deal with the municipal government to move to farther corners of the city had to endure new lifestyles in cramped spaces and with long commutes into the city, not to mention the insecurity of becoming debt-bound to pay for the loans and mortgages (Kuyucu, 2020). Most of the public housing initiatives by TOKİ have been beyond the financial reach of those who were forced to leave. For those who eventually moved to these new housing complexes, lower quality in living and social standards, lack of common areas and other problems made their experiences worse (Kuyucu, 2020). The marginalisation of this segment of the working class joined by a lower-tier group within the new middle class was compounded by the intensified atomisation and decline in communal relations with the loss of neighbourhood connections (Erman, 2016a, pp. 85–6; Çavdar, 2021; Uzunçarşılı-Baysal, 2015a, p. 132; for a similar case in Ankara, see Erman, 2016b). These areas of 'urban captivity' (spaces where new forms of poverty, social exclusion and spatial immobility emerged, and where residents became 'the target of the emerging discourse of urgency and urban fear') became hotbeds of xenophobia and other social tensions in the course of urban transformation (Candan & Kolluoğlu, 2008; also see: Demirtaş-Milz, 2020).

In order to shore up the faltering support for its projects and ease the painful consequences of this bitter transformation on its main constituents in former industrial sites and working-class neighbourhoods, the AKP resorted to a mix of poverty alleviation policies, such as charitable aid giving, direct cash transfers, gifts, shopping coupons, distribution of coal and other staples and municipality-run kitchens for the poor (Toplumun Şehircilik Hareketi, 2014; for an overview of the AKP's poverty-reduction policies see Buğra, 2008, pp. 233–46). These initiatives were coupled with an increasingly conservative, populist rhetoric that aimed to stoke feelings of national and religious pride and successfully (at least partially) appeased the most vulnerable sections of the urban population (Karaman, 2013). Nevertheless, these policies could not keep these sections silent and docile towards the Gezi uprisings.

Indeed, that the urban poor were not visible at the forefront of the rebellion in Taksim Square or in the occupation of Gezi Park should not blind us to later research that demonstrated that the composition of the masses during the Gezi Episode was not purely middle class, as it was often portrayed in popular discourse, but involved different groups occupying different positions in the class matrix, including the dispossessed populations around the city (see especially: Bora, 2014, pp. 24, 26, 32–3; Yörük & Yüksel, 2014). More importantly, the dispossessed often chose (or were compelled) to protest in their own neighbourhoods in solidarity with the Gezi protestors during the early days of the uprising. Districts such as Gazi, Nurtepe, 1 Mayıs in Istanbul and others in different parts of the country, which have seen the brunt of displacement, marginalisation and urban transformation, became areas where the most violent clashes with the police took place. The residents of these districts belonged to the most vulnerable segments of the working class, the 'precariat', who had also been severely influenced not just by gentrification but also by the increasingly deteriorating job prospects and working conditions in

the informal sector (Doğan, 2013). That was what made them a natural constituent of the alliance against neoliberal urbanisation.

The Concerned

The second major group in the urban opposition comprised those who resisted
the complete urbanisation of Istanbul on the basis of its environmental consequences and of social justice concerns. This heterogeneous group included,
first and foremost, residents who were witnessing – and raising their voice
against – the ongoing transformation of the city by focusing particularly –
and sometimes solely – on gentrification and other regeneration efforts in their
own neighbourhoods. The discontent among residents in places such as Arnavutköy, Galata, Fener-Balat, Kadıköy and many others was growing in response
to the endless construction activity in their vicinity. Demolition of older buildings (especially cultural and social landmarks) and their replacement with new
and repurposed ones; construction of overpasses and crossings, underground
passages, and subway stations causing traffic, noise and pollution; deforesta-
tion and shrinking of green areas in the city; and heightened anxiety about
security due to changes in the composition of their neighbourhood were all
a constant source of growing resentment in the face of the destruction of the
urban fabric and living spaces (Henden-Şolt, 2019; Kaya-Erdoğan, 2020). This
is why some of the residents decided to join existing initiatives – or form new
ones – to stand against urban transformation.

They were often joined by environmental activists and students whose
cultural capital allowed them to develop an urban consciousness and ability to organise in these neighbourhoods as a propelling force in resistance.
Such activism would often take the form of neighbourhood initiatives, such
as Sulukule Platform, Tarlabaşı Solidarity (Tarlabaşı Dayanışması), Taksim
Solidarity (Taksim Dayanışma), Validebağ Resistance (Validebağ Direnişi) or
Arnavutköy District Initiative (Arnavutköy Semt Girişimi) (Akyıldız, 2015;
Elicin, 2017; Özkaya Günaydın, 2021; Ünsal, 2013; Voulvouli, 2007). Other
initiatives would organise within larger organisations, such as the Union of
Chambers of Turkish Engineers and Architects (Türk Mühendis ve Mimar
Odaları Birliği, TMMOB), Society's Urban Movement (Toplumun Şehircilik
Hareketi, IMECE), or Istanbul Urban Movements (Istanbul Kent Hareketleri)
(Erdi-Lelandais, 2016), all of which aimed to draw attention to policies turning

Istanbul into a construction site. IMECE, for instance, emerged as a grassroots movement in 2007 and has organised itself in the form of 'forums', similar to its European counterparts of the time (IMECE, 2011). There were also organisations, such as Solidaristic Studio (Dayanışmacı Atölye) and Urban Movements (Kent Hareketleri), which aimed to develop alternative sustainable and equitable development plans as well as provide assistance to resistance movements at the local level (Rittersberger-Tılıç, 2015, pp. 90–1).

All these initiatives and forms of resistance addressed a broad palette of issues ranging from dispossession and forced displacement of residents, wealth/property transfer from public/individuals to corporate groups, anti-democratic and illegal policy implementation by local government and the exclusion of the public from participating in decision-making processes, especially those with environmental consequences (such as the depletion of water reserves and other natural resources) and historical/cultural issues, particularly the destruction of sites of historical and cultural importance, such as the Emek movie theatre in Beyoğlu or historic vegetable gardens in Yedikule (Öktem Ünsal, 2015; Ünsal, 2014; Ünsal & Kuyucu, 2010). Although they could not successfully coalesce their separate agendas and local protests into a broader front of environmental activism before the Gezi uprising, it was the culmination of their resentments that would find a unified expression when bulldozers entered Gezi Park to destroy one of the last remaining green areas in the city.

The Ambivalent

The third group among the bearers of urban discontent in Istanbul in the 1990s and 2000s can be loosely defined as the 'new middle class' – a malleable category that makes the picture more complicated and analysis difficult.[1] Members of this group in Turkey – similar to their counterparts around the world – were often imagined to be young, college-educated individuals working as white-collar professionals in branches of big national and global corporations in sectors such as technology, media, finance, accounting, marketing, insurance, consultancy and real estate. They also included university students aspiring to join the ranks of the former, and whose credentials and ability to speak at least one foreign language endowed them with social and cultural capital to fit into the consumerist urban lifestyle shaped by global trends in the media and cultural industry (Belbağ et al., 2019; Üner & Güngördü, 2016).

The high self-regard of the new middle class based on their professional and educational qualifications was accompanied by a sense of entitlement to better living standards, political freedoms and cultural flexibility, similar to their counterparts in wealthier societies (Keyder, 2013b, 2014b). Meanwhile, their numbers kept rising with new universities mushrooming all over the country, and with the intensification of migration to bigger cities, especially Istanbul (Rutz & Balkan, 2010).

Changes in the composition of the workforce in the country, and more noticeably in Istanbul, as a result of the decline of the formal sector and the deindustrialisation of the urban economy during the 1990s and early 2000s, were reflected in new urban patterns (Demiral, 2018; Yıldırım, 2018). As Keyder summarises it: 'the new apartments in high rises represented a transition to more modern dwellings by the new service-sector employed generations whose parents lived in the ramshackle neighbourhoods of former *gecekondu*s. Expansion of credit allowed them to invest in new residences as well as the modern conveniences of apartment living' (Keyder, 2010, p. 32). Indeed, while those employed in industrial or construction jobs and in the lower tier service sector were continuously being driven towards the periphery of the city, this emerging segment of the middle class was taking up residence either in gentrified districts of the inner city (mostly along the hills of the Bosporus) or in the gated communities within the newly cleared spaces in the Northern Forests region, reflecting their desire for a life away from the chaos of the city centre (Candan & Kolluoğlu, 2008; Öktem, 2011). With the construction boom gaining speed from 2005 onwards (Bora, 2021), new residential colonies expanded towards farther corners of the city, including Göktürk-Kemerburgaz, Zekeriyaköy-Demirciköy, Bahçeşehir and Büyükçekmece on the European side and Beykoz, Çekmeköy-Dudullu and Ömerli on the Anatolian side (Öktem, 2011). This expansion became possible by (and also reinforced) the group's mobility in the city thanks to the infrastructural developments in the form of new roads, underground tunnels and enhanced public transportation that connected the two main axes (Büyükdere-Maslak and Altunizade-Kozyatağı) on both sides of the city.

From a cursory perspective, this glowing new middle class would be expected to support the urban transformation, which found its expression in the gentrification of neighbourhoods, clearing of *gecekondu*s or other urban renewal undertakings due to the unique political subjectivity emerging from their ambivalent class position in global capitalism (Evcimen, 2019). Indeed, the whole process could have been interpreted by this group as a chance to get rid of migrants, refugees, sex workers, the Roma and the poor from their beloved city. It was this very group – at least some segments of it – who had adapted to, if not wholeheartedly supported, the gentrification of historical districts such as Fener-Balat, Galata and Cihangir so that they could move in and 'restore' their neighbourhoods to their nostalgic past (Şen, 2011). According to studies conducted in the early 2000s, the new occupants of these places as well as those of the new gated communities reported that they chose these 'hygienic' spaces to be able to keep themselves away from the 'undesirable' groups, especially internally displaced Kurds from the South-East, but also other rural migrants who lived traditional, religious lifestyles and who had become more visible with the rise of political Islam since the mid-1990s (Aydın, 2012). These 'liberated zones' corresponded to this group's need and desire to live comfortably and securely among a homogenised community of elites outside 'provincialised (*taşralaşmış*) Istanbul' brought about by the 'invasion of the dark crowds' (Bali, 2020; Geniş, 2007).

Nevertheless, three factors complicated this picture and changed the way in which the new middle class experienced social and spatial tensions in the city under neoliberal urbanisation.

UNKEPT PROMISES

The first of these factors was the deepening economic insecurity among some members of this group in more precarious segments of the employment ladder, such as call centre workers, mid-level managerial staff or non-tenure university instructors. Similarly to their counterparts almost everywhere in the world (Lorey, 2015 ch. 1; Standing, 2016; Vatansever, 2018), despite working to the point of exhaustion the lack of financial security due to soaring indebtedness in home and credit card loans was making it impossible for them to reap the material rewards and other benefits they believed were promised to them in this 'new gilded age'. The deepening precarity was creating ever-growing concern among white-collar professionals about losing their status, fuelling resentment as their future looked ever bleaker and the assurances that were fed to them in the education system, media and all aspects of life did not seem to materialise. The intensity of fear of losing one's job – or having a hard time finding one despite the hype about how well their education and skills would serve them – was mounting to an existential crisis (Bora et al., 2011; Vatansever & Gezici Yalçın, 2015; Yılmaz Şener, 2018; Yücesan-Özdemir, 2014).

All this was in fact a symptom of a deeper stratification within the new middle class: while it was expanding as an umbrella category through educational attainments, availability of white-collar service jobs and spread of consumption-oriented lifestyles, the polarisation within the category was widening. More specifically, high-level managerial ranks were rising even more in terms of their wealth and opportunities available to them while middle and lower ranks of the white-collar professionals were showing signs of proletarianisation (Özden & Bekmen, 2015, p. 101; Sunar, 2018, p. 18; Uca, 2016). This could be observed no better than in the new spatial segmentation in the city: while the opportunity of living in spacious apartments in gated communities had progressively expanded for a broad segment of white-collar professionals (Aydın, 2012), the richer tier of the group was often concentrated in gentrified districts of the old city or in luxurious residential complexes with their own shopping malls, parks and other recreational amenities on the outskirts of the city. The more modest segments of the group tried to replicate this spatial experience (mostly with the help of the availability of loans and under intense media campaigns pumping the idea of real-estate ownership) in similar apartment buildings and gated, multi-storey apartment complexes (*sites*) in farther corners of the city (Eraydın, 2008; Geniş, 2007; Keyder, 2013c; Kurtuluş, 2003, 2011; Öktem, 2011). Meanwhile, the explosion in this style of housing not only made the divisions within the new middle class more visible but also, and more importantly, destroyed social relations and sense of community or urban citizenry through dividing and severing ties between individuals/ families, preventing any possibility of social and political mobilisation and making these populations subject to intensive government regulation and control (Akay, 2015, pp. 52–4; Çavdar, 2016a, pp. 52–3).

That the residential spaces inhabited by modest white-collar professionals and small business owners were different from the ones that richer groups owned (such as Kemer Country or Beykoz Konakları) added more fuel to the alienation and resentment of the former (Tanülkü, 2012). The contradiction between being employed in state-of-the-art plazas and not being able to enjoy the neighbourhoods in which these plazas were situated (due to the fact that the whole neighbourhood, if not the whole city, was in service of the owners and CEOs of these plazas, or they were for the consumption of tourists, leaving little if any meaningful space for employees to use parks, green areas and other public places outside the corporate world) deepened this already painful spatial experience and turned the white collar employee into a resentful, dissident, political subject (Vatansever, 2018, p. 212). It was this process of the proletarianisation of the new middle class and further precarisation of the working class (including those who sold their intellectual labour) that became one of the principal factors that eventually paved the way for the Gezi uprising (Bürkev, 2013, pp. 29–44).

DEVALUATION OF EXPERTISE AND DE-STATUSING

The second factor that brought the white-collar professionals to the forefront of the urban revolt in Istanbul was their loss of status, or what Vatansever calls 'income-status disequilibrium' – when this group realised that their expertise could not take them too far in their career (Vatansever, 2018, p. 184). This was especially the case among those employed in the public sector, such as architects, urban planners and other experts in municipality governments who had to witness corruption, clientelism and favouritism, which devalued their education and experience. They often found themselves powerless when their expertise was being instrumentalised under urban transformation forced upon them by political elites who courted the needs of global capital instead of focusing on the good of the public and the needs and priorities of the city. Architects, urban planners, cultural heritage and conservation professionals working for local municipalities found themselves in a bind between their public mission and what they saw as the increasingly neoliberal, authoritarian, marketised implementations of urban planning, which was deepening their alienation (Penpecioğlu & Taşan-Kok, 2020). Those in the private sector, too, often complained about the disrespect they had to endure when they attempted to put into practice what they were trained for: creativity, flexibility, autonomy and taking initiatives or risks in decision making and implementation (Farro & Demirhisar, 2014, pp. 179–80; Yılmaz Şener, 2018, p. 254; also see: Kömürcüoğlu, 2015).

Numerous interviews conducted with teachers, lawyers, engineers, academics and other white-collar professionals demonstrated that the perception of decline in status made them increasingly alienated and resentful (Penpecioğlu & Taşan-Kok, 2020; Sunar, 2018, p. 19; also see: Evcimen, 2019). They were expressing as their source of discontent not only the deteriorating working conditions (such as the growing subcontracted forms of employment instead of direct state employment with protection and benefits) but also widespread nepotism, which prevented the qualified from advancing in their career (Bora et al., 2011, pp. 205–6). The latter often appeared in the form of discrimination at work against those who were not 'one of them' (that is, someone connected to the AKP), along with rumours about cheating at public servant admission exams, all of which were planting seeds of bitterness among white-collar professionals ('Bizim İçin Gezi, Çocuklarımıza Anlatacağımız Sivil Bir Devrim', 2013, p. 33). Feelings of victimhood, helplessness, weakness and self-blame were commonplace because the nature of white-collar employment under neoliberalism (uncertain, atomised, coercive practices) prevented these people from expressing their growing resentment through collective organisation, such as political parties or unions. It was by the end of the first decade of the 2000s that associations, union branches and solidarity groups began to be formed to defend and support call-centre employees, plaza workers, non-tenured instructors in private and foundation-owned universities, information and communication workers and others (Bora et al., 2011, pp. 68–71). Despite all that, as recently as 2020, a majority of young people in Turkey, regardless of their political affiliation, did not believe that their prospective employment would come through merit-based hiring, and an overwhelming majority of them preferred to move abroad in search of freedom and opportunity (Sosyal Demokrasi Vakfı, 2020; Tol & Alemdaroğlu, 2020).

THE DIVIDE

A third factor that enlisted some white-collar professionals for urban resistance was a deeper social fault line, the activation of which led to further fractures within the urban middle class in Turkey. Since coming to power in 2002, the AKP has successfully nurtured a loyal strand among the new white-collars workers who, unlike the entrepreneurs of the small and medium size businesses (infamously dubbed 'Anatolian Tigers') that emerged in different parts of the country during the 1990s (Keyman & Koyuncu Lorasdağı, 2010), comprised young and educated pious men and women joining the ranks of the salariat in public and private sectors (especially in such fields as media, finance and education) after receiving degrees mostly from the newly founded universities across the country (Akçaoğlu, 2018; Çavdar, 2019; Erdik, 2017; Özet, 2019). Growing up with stories of previous generations having been discriminated against under the strict imposition of Kemalist secularism in everyday life (from not allowing female students with a headscarf to enter university campuses to preventing employees in the public sector from reaching higher managerial positions because of their openly pious lives), this new breed of college graduates could now find a spot for themselves in every layer of public and private bureaucracy. They could also enjoy new freedoms of self-expression and public lifestyle, including living in their new residential communities, such as Başakşehir and Merkezefendi Kiptaş Homes, which – with their separate swimming pools and other amenities for men and women, for instance – offered a conservative Islamic lifestyle for its residents (Aydın, 2012). It was also in this period that one could observe the proliferation of private schools with religious curricula, extravagant mosques, spaces of culture, art and leisure that offered a commodified taste of Islamic/Ottoman civilisation, shopping malls marketing global brands and other conveniences the city could offer (Balkan & Öncü, 2018). This was, in Şengül's words, 'a double process of commodification and aggressive conservatism' (Şengül, 2015) unfolding to refashion neoliberal urban distinction in line with Islamic characteristics (Tuğal, 2021). The result was a bourgeoning urban lifestyle that evoked the kind of housing, consumption and recreation patterns enjoyed by the more secular sectors of the new middle class, only with a conservative twist (Çavdar, 2019, 2010; Erdik, 2017; Kurtuluş, 2012; Seni, 2013).

Reconciling their consumerism (with respect to of what they wore, where they dined, how they decorated their homes, and so on) with religious values (Akçaoğlu, 2018; Belbağ et al., 2019; Türküsev, 2015), members of this breed of the new middle class were hardly distinguishable from their secular counterparts in the city, with one big exception: their social mobility was faster and more visible thanks to the proliferation of new businesses loyal to the AKP as well as rampant favouritism and nepotism in the public sector, especially thanks to the newly established proximity to power through the AKP's local organisations (Doğan, 2016, pp. 208–9). The higher they climbed up in the social ladder and the more dominant they became as a social group, the more they adhered to 'social closure' and 'spatial exclusion', especially in their interactions with Kurds, the Roma, rural immigrants and refugees. This could be observed in gated communities like Başakşehir, where the rich conservative residents did not want to keep around those who reminded them of the 'old habits and life styles' that did not conform with the new lives they had adopted (Özet, 2019).

The implications of this bifurcation within the new middle class can best be traced through the increasingly conservative character of neoliberal urbanisation in Istanbul. One obvious expression of this effort – carried out mostly by AKP-controlled municipalities (metropolitan and smaller) and faith-based organisations with full government support behind them – was the increase in number, centrality and functionality of mosques in daily life as spaces not just of worship but also of socialisation, education and cultural activities (Batuman, 2018, ch. 2). The same intent could also be seen in the organisation of events, such as big fast-breaking events in Ramadan during which separate spaces were reserved for men and women, or in renaming streets, parks and public venues after notable historical Ottoman and Islamic figures (Batuman, 2018, pp. 90–2). Mega projects (always emphasised for their grand dimensions) and extravagant mosques (such as the Çamlıca mosque) were presented as homage to the long-lost grandiosity of the Ottoman Empire and an attempt to revive the glory of that era (Ünal Çınar, 2012, pp. 92–5).

In the Taksim district where Gezi Park is located, four related projects revealed the Islamist colour in neoliberal urbanisation in the hands of the AKP: pedestrianisation of Taksim Square (which demolished historical neighbourhoods in the Beyoğlu district, similar to what had happened in Sulukule, Fener-Balat and Tarlabaşı in earlier projects), resurrection of the late Ottoman-era artillery barracks (Topçu Kışlası) in Gezi Park in the form of a shopping mall and high-end residences, demolition of Atatürk Cultural Centre (Atatürk Kültür Merkezi, AKM – a symbolic building representing the nation's aspiration for adopting secular, modern and Western culture) and construction of a grand mosque at the centre of Taksim square, the idea of which had enchanted conservative Islamic fantasies since the establishment of the Turkish Republic as an act of reconquering Istanbul and reinstating its alleged Islamic character.

The master plan originally included demolishing Gezi Park, but court cases brought by TMMOB stalled the process. Without waiting for a court order and legal clarity, the municipality began to build a construction site around the park by the winter of 2013 and started removing shop owners and tenants from the buildings owned by the Istanbul Metropolitan Municipality. This move triggered unrest among other shop owners in the area, who knew that their time was coming, and mobilised Taksim Solidarity (Taksim Dayanışması), a platform that had brought together around eighty NGOs, political groups and professional organisations to resist the urban transformation efforts in the area and which would become the central actor to kindle the fire that would become the Gezi uprising (Atalay, 2013).

Policies and steps such as limitations on serving alcohol in restaurants or the closure of historical sites of Western-style entertainment and leisure (such as the Emek movie theatre) were complemented by other and increasingly oppressive moves that aimed at socially engineering the lives of the urban population. Starting by taking full control of the media and silencing the opposition or any dissident voice from political organisations or civil society initiatives, the AKP government took many steps towards creating a repressive environment, which included: introducing legislation and regulations regarding abortion access; converting public schools to *imam hatip* schools with more conservative religious contents in their curricula; fostering an oppressive social milieu that harboured increasingly discriminatory rhetoric against women, LGBTQIA+ individuals, Kurds, Alevis and others who refused to conform to conservative Sunni Islamist restrictions in their lives; and directly intervening into people's private lives, especially through condemning commentary about presumed immorality of unmarried young couples living together and appearing in public. Adding to all these, attempts to curtail citizens' right to assembly and demonstration in public places through police violence during May Day or pride marches, and overall malevolent, vengeful and arrogant rhetoric adopted by Erdoğan, were all constituents of an increasingly authoritarian regime that utilised Istanbul as a political apparatus for a broader social transformation.

The refashioning of Istanbul's façade and tampering with its social fabric, then, was another attempt by the AKP to manufacture an alternative memory of a romanticised era with a vengeance towards the constitutive ethos of the Republic that had envisioned a secular and Westernised foundation and future for the new nation (Tokdoğan, 2018, ch. 4). It was through the erasure of the habits, patterns and symbols of modern, Western orientation from everyday life and the privatisation of public spaces that a predominantly (if not exclusively) Islamic identity was forced upon Istanbul in general and Taksim in particular, further undermining the cosmopolitan diversity that the district historically harboured (Batuman, 2018, pp. 128–31; Çavdar, 2016b).

It is safe to argue, then, that the AKP's neoliberal urbanisation project in Istanbul in general and the attempt to demolish Gezi Park to build a shopping–residence complex in particular, was not only a move towards turning the city and its public domains into privatised spaces for capital accumulation. It was also a key part of the social engineering efforts that tampered with the urban fabric to court the expectations of the more conservative segment of the middle class in the city (Karaman, 2013). Put differently, what lay behind the AKP's enthusiastic catering to the demands of the more conservative segments of the new middle class and the college-educated youth (Avcı, 2012, p. 254) was the reorganisation of urban life along conservative, Islamist lines. From grand mosques (Çavdar, 2020) to great malls, the motivation behind the AKP's construction frenzy was to create a new 'community' of pious employees and consumers, and replace the Western, secular ethos that underlay the foundations of the Republic (Ünal Çınar, 2012, ch. 4.). With the support of this new group, neoliberal urban transformation in the hands of the AKP became an act of rewriting history and monopolising the narrative about being a Turk, Muslim, citizen and an Istanbul resident (*Istanbullu*). Behind the seemingly straightforward undertaking of the re-production of space at the heart of Taksim Square in the form of a profitable development project was a well-choreographed spatial strategy of stoking 'structural nostalgia' in the imagery of Istanbul as an Islamic city that belonged to the devout only (Harmanşah, 2014). Any alternative interpretation that fell outside this narrative was marginalised if not criminalised, and progressively expelled from the definition of desirable citizen (Rivas-Alonso, 2015, pp. 236–8).

It was against this backdrop that the defiance and resentment of the secular and Westernised segments of the new middle class became more visible as they helplessly witnessed the façade of their 'global city' getting painted with increasingly conservative and Islamist hues. The omnipresence of Islam in every corner of the public space was interpreted as attacks on an urban lifestyle they longed for. Their already deepening *political exclusion* (due to not being a part of the inner circles of the political establishment or influence politics through traditional electoral mechanisms, not to mention self-censorship for fear of persecution) and *social exclusion* (due to the intensification of religious conservatism in social practices and official discourse demonising modern, secular, Western lifestyles) were now compounded by *spatial exclusion* (due to fast-paced changes that destroyed the urban environment as well as the very social fabric, rhythms and memories in order to refashion urban life with Islamic codes), which intensified their alienation and frustration. The more they realised the deepening precarity in their status and material conditions, the stronger they felt the urge to stand up against this development, which was engulfing the city and truncating their social habitat. In Keyder's words, 'they wanted to defend public space against neoliberal incursion, and they refused to live under the authoritarian guidance of a self-appointed father of the country' (Keyder, 2013a). As an anonymous activist who was interviewed in the earlier stages of the Gezi rebellion put it: 'I was at the point of "enough is enough"' (Altunok, 2013). The mode of survival and gasping for air in the midst of a repressive political regime solidified in the city was what made the masses turn Gezi Park into the last bastion where they could fight back.

* * *

All in all, the urban discontent that paved the way for the Gezi Episode was a symptom of Istanbul's 'complete urbanisation'. It was the culmination of isolated, small-scale expressions of resentment, rage and resistance that turned into forceful protests pursued by, among others, the dispossessed urban poor, ecologically conscious groups and the declining secular, Westernised segments of the new middle class, all of whom could bring in tune each other's distinct issues, demands and motivations. Suffering under Erdoğan's regime became a unifying experience, breeding anger in many corners of the city and eventually galvanising many segments of the society towards action. Seemingly disconnected backlashes against the twin processes of neoliberal urbanisation and Islamisation of the urban life morphed into a collective defence of the city: resistance against ecological destruction and material insecurity and the protection of urban historical heritage and common spaces against neoliberal Islamic utopias of this peculiar urbanisation (Harmanşah, 2014). It was in this context that we arrive at the Gezi Episode when the first glimpses of transforming the political and reconstituting the social began to appear.

Note

1. For an overview of the early debates on the emergence of a new middle class in Turkey, see (Bora, 2014). For more sceptical analyses see (Boratav, 2013; Bürkev, 2013; Saraçoğlu, 2015; Tonak, 2013).

3

MOBILISATIONAL DEMOCRACY: THE GEZİ EPISODE AS SOCIAL MOVEMENT

Having revisited in the previous chapter how the road to the Gezi Episode was paved by a confluence of peculiar developments and conditions under neoliberal urbanisation in Istanbul, I now turn to the Episode itself. Any analysis of political activism and democratic practices it cultivates requires a world-historical lens to interpret its impact because a unique form of contentious politics to reconstitute the social in the face of neoliberal destruction has been 'kicking off everywhere' (Mason, 2013). Therefore, this chapter offers a social movements analysis of the Gezi Episode to discuss the first of the three dynamics of contemporary movements: the *mobilisational* dynamic that conditioned activists' political subjectivity and overall experience with radical democracy and eventually led to the emergence of what I call 'fluid political identities'.

The Gezi Episode: A Non-chronometric Chronicle

Despite the inevitably chronological style in the narration of the events in this section, contentious politics during the Gezi Episode did not advance as a linear succession with one form of activism ending to be followed by another. What is presented below as a 'phase' is based on the prominent mode of activism that defines the core character of that phase rather than the temporality of the events. In other words, various modalities of activism were interpenetrating throughout the course of the Episode without following a sequential order, although some of these modalities appeared as the dominant or hegemonic

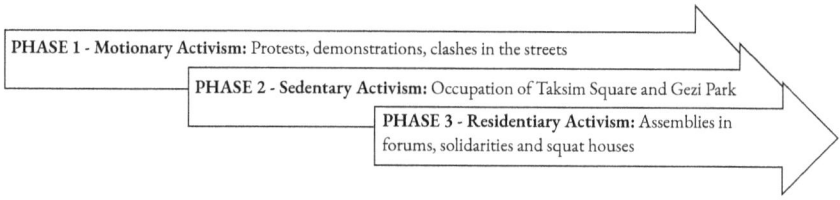

Figure 3.1 Three Phases of the Gezi Episode

form during certain periods. Riots, rallies, occupations, forums, workshops, canvassing for elections, organising in a national movement and other types of politics would exist side by side and in resonance on the streets, in public parks, neighbourhoods or buildings. Hence, despite the phraseology, the Episode should not be understood as a chain of discrete and successive forms of mobilisation but as coexisting and constantly interacting, interpenetrating and resonating political processes.

Phase 1: Motionary Activism

The beginning of the Gezi Episode can be traced back to the last days of May 2013 when a handful of environmental activists in Istanbul began clashing with the police to stop the demolishment of Gezi Park. A series of developments had preceded these clashes: when the Cultural Assets Preservation Board (Kültür Varlıklarını Koruma Kurulu) of Istanbul gave a decision in favour of Taksim Solidarity (Taksim Dayanışması)[1] following the latter's appeal to annul the pedestrianisation project that included the re-building of a historic artillery barracks (Topçu Kışlası) on the exact location of the park, then Prime Minister Erdoğan replied: 'We will build the Topçu barracks. The board refused it. We will refuse the refusal' (Vardar, 2013), as if to give a glimpse of what was to happen in the coming weeks and months. His threats led to the approval of the project by the High Council for Protection of Cultural and Natural Assets (Kültür ve Tabiat Varlıklarını Koruma Yüksek Kurulu) in March 2013. While the legal proceedings were still under way following Taksim Solidarity's renewed appeal in court, bulldozers appeared at Gezi Park to demolish parts of its surrounding wall and remove nearby trees. These preparations prompted peaceful demonstrations by environmentalist groups responding to Taksim Solidarity's call to defend the park. In order to prevent a surprise incursion, some of these groups began camping in the park (Elicin, 2014, p. 154). It was during these days that news about the sale of a historical and still-functioning public harbour in Beşiktaş to a nearby hotel and the opening ceremony for the construction of the third bridge on the Bosporus fuelled resentment among activists (Fresko, 2013).

The number of protestors in the park rose to almost 1000 in the span of a couple of days. During periods of relative calm, small concerts and forum meetings were held. Meanwhile, the police launched offensives on the park, often at dawn, using excessive force with water cannons and tear gas, burning tents and chasing away the campers. These skirmishes barely made the national news, but it was also during these last days of May 2013 when the famous photos of deputy Sırrı Süreyya Önder putting himself in front of a bulldozer to stop the removal of the trees, and especially of one of the peaceful protestors – dubbed 'Lady in Red' (*Kırmızılı Kadın*) – being cruelly gassed by the police appeared on social media. More images of police setting tents ablaze and callously mazing or gassing peaceful protestors, washing them away with powerful water cannons and detaining journalists reporting the riot began to circulate like wildfire on social media and other communication platforms. It was these images that became the straw that broke the camel's back and kindled the explosion that would become one of the most memorable anti-government uprisings in Turkish history.

Intense clashes took place on the main avenues and smaller streets that connected to Gezi Park as the police tried to prevent protestors from entering Taksim Square, which had been unconstitutionally closed to May Day celebrations just weeks earlier. The inhumane treatment of the protestors by the police instigated disbelief, rage and defiance, resulting in more people joining the rebellion (Koloğlu et al., 2015; Özgür, 2013; Uluğ & Acar, 2014). Given the lack of experience among most of the protestors, the guerrilla style clashes with the police came as a surprise to many, although the presence of several radical leftist groups whose familiarity with urban combat with security forces helped sustain and fortify the resistance on the streets. Even so, attempts by these militant groups as well as other organisations to claim ownership of the protests were thwarted by the masses who were becoming more diverse every day (Cassano, 2013). Multiple identities could find a place for themselves in this heterogeneous mass. Soccer fans, nationalists, Kemalists, feminists, LGBTQIA+

and politically unaffiliated individuals (most of whom were disinterested in and disenfranchised from politics in the past era) who belonged to different professions, age groups, political orientations, ethnic backgrounds and other identity markers could be seen in the streets. Young, middle-class, professional women were at the forefront as they were among the most affected by the AKP's social engineering project, which infringed on their lives, tried to curb their reproductive rights and imposed an overall conservative mode of life.

Not surprisingly, and similar to their counterparts in other parts of the world (Castells, 2015), protestors relied heavily on social media and wireless communication. Residents in neighbourhoods, as well as some businesses, shared their Wi-Fi passwords to help protestors remain connected and inform each other about the state of the clashes.[2] These and other spontaneous enactments of solidarity and mutual care that did not emerge from pre-existing relations or fellow membership in political organisations would sow the seeds of respect, trust and camaraderie to flourish in the coming days and weeks of the Episode. It was in this phase that the protestors began to transform into activists and adopt a new lexicon that included such terms as 'militant', 'barricades' and 'resistance'. It was also in this phase that humour became a way to deal with fear and despair, but most importantly became a method of perceiving and conceptualising the world now defined by the sheer violence from the state. Witty expressions on walls or phone screens served as small and scattered 'bits of ideology' around which the young protestors mobilised (Yalçıntaş, 2015).

The police finally retreated from Gezi Park on June 1 and protestors began to settle in different parts of the park. Despite losing its steam and primacy inside and around the park, the 'motionary form of activism' would continue as occasional skirmishes at the barricades erected to stop the police from attacking the camp. Meanwhile, clashes continued in other districts in Istanbul, such as the Gazi neighbourhood and Beşiktaş (where Dolmabahçe Mosque served as a make-shift emergency room for the wounded protestors), as well as in other cities, including Ankara, Izmir, Antakya and Eskişehir.[3]

Indeed, while a 'sedentary form of activism' was slowly moving to the centre of politics, starting with the occupation of Gezi Park, the motionary form (rallying, chanting slogans, actively clashing with the police, and so on) that dominated the first phase of the Episode never fully ceased. In the year following the occupation, for instance, people were on the streets again for commemoration of those who died during the clashes. There were also protests against corruption and media centres because of their biased coverage or otherwise indifference to the rebellion or passing of certain legislation, such as one on regulating the internet, or against the government's neglect that caused the death of more than 400 miners in Soma. Women's Day celebrations, May Day celebrations and many other dates, incidents and developments became occasions for active mobilisation, which were almost always met with brutal police force and immediate closure of Gezi Park to avoid its potential re-occupation (Soğukdere, 2014).

The unceasing escalation of symbolic violence emanating from Erdoğan's mouth was partly to blame for the permanence of the 'street mode' even when sedentary activism was becoming more prominent as the Gezi Episode unfolded. Despite efforts by the then president, speaker of the prime minister's office and governor of Istanbul to de-escalate the tensions and appease the protestors, Erdoğan never ceased his divisive and offensive rhetoric. The glorification of the police's harsh treatment of the protestors, calling protestors 'marauders' (*çapulcu*) or 'extremists some of whom were implicated in terrorism', pitting a narrow interpretation of national will (i.e. electoral majority) against democratic criticism about the erosion of rights kept street activism alive. This is why the Gezi uprisings were often described as 'dignity riots' to underline that the protestors were demanding respect in the face of Erdoğan's arrogant, dismissive and authoritarian political style (İnsel, 2014). Meanwhile, the latter's unfounded allegations against activists for consuming alcohol in Dolmabahçe Mosque or attacking women wearing headscarves, furthering unfounded claims about protests being supported by foreign entities, such as the 'interest rate lobby', and various other iterations of conspiracy that from the prime minister's mouth were broadcast daily. Amidst all this, something spectacular was happening inside Gezi Park.

Phase 2: Sedentary Activism

When the dust settled and a host of groups began occupying the park on June 1, the mosaic of the resistance became clearer in this new phase of the Episode. As *Der Spiegel* reported, protests were 'drawing more than students and intellectuals. Families with children, women in headscarves, men in suits, hipsters in sneakers, pharmacists, tea-house proprietors – all are taking to the streets to register their displeasure' (Gezer et al., 2013) Another journalist observed that 'flags of the environmentalist movement, rainbow banners, flags of Atatürk, of Che Guevara, of different trade unions, all adorn the Gezi park' (Letsch, 2013). Indeed, the long list of the park's new occupants included urban grassroots organisations and neighbourhood associations, various socialist political parties, radical left groups and platforms, environmentalist groups, soccer fans of the prominent Istanbul clubs (who could set aside their long-standing antagonisms) and various groups who identified as Kemalist nationalist, LGBTQIA+, feminist and more ('GENAR'ın yaptığı Gezi Parkı anketi', 2013; Konda, 2013; Özcimbit, 2013). In this colourful crowd, there were artists and celebrities, employees in precarious service-sector jobs, members of trade unions, confederations, chambers and associations (although they were not there to officially represent their organisations), the youth divisions of political parties, university and high school students, white-collar professionals, such as academics, journalists, doctors, lawyers, architects and city planners, anti-capitalist Muslims (a group of pious Muslim individuals who fervently criticised Erdoğan's and the AKP's arrogance and greed disguised behind Islam at the expense of the poor), several deputies of the parliament and mostly politically non-affiliated citizens (Ercan-Bilgiç & Kafkaslı, 2013; Kibar & Tatari, 2013a; Konda, 2014; Ruccio, 2013; Uluğ & Acar, 2014). Each group installed a tent or put tables, banners, posters and flags in a specific part of the park and turned the occupation into a big outdoor festival.

In addition to the complexity and diversity of the camp residents, the overwhelmingly young profile of Gezi Park's occupants has drawn great popular and scholarly interest (see for instance: Gümüş & Yılmaz, 2015). As a category that cuts across all the above-mentioned social groups, most of these young men and women self-reported they belonged to more Westernised, secular, urban sectors of the society (İplikçi, 2013). While they were often portrayed as 'apolitical', such characterisations disguised the deep discontent and resentment they held towards the AKP's socially conservative policies and Erdoğan's paternalistic discourse and authoritarian actions (Ercan-Bilgiç & Kafkaslı, 2013; 'GENAR'ın yaptığı Gezi Parkı anketi', 2013; Keyder, 2013a; Konda, 2013). True, traditional politics did not entice or excite them, yet they were still well aware that it had real repercussions and significant (negative) consequences on their lives. With the occupation of Gezi Park, they realised that it was possible (in fact necessary) for them to actively engage in politics, except in their own terms.

Much ink has been spilled on these two weeks in the park as its occupants were metamorphosing into radical activists and turning the park into a political laboratory. Parts of Beyoğlu were 'emancipated' from the state's (and capital's) dominion to be repurposed as vegetable gardens, groves or living quarters for the homeless, refugees or activists. In the park, although the peaceful occupation could occasionally be interrupted by police intervention, concerts and other recreational activities, such as yoga, chess or soccer, movie screenings, activities for children as well as informative workshops on a variety of topics became commonplace (Mashallah Team, 2013). A library and a makeshift clinic were established immediately after the park was occupied. Meanwhile, donations including food, toiletries and other needs were piling up as food stations – dubbed 'Çapulcu Café' – started distributing food free of charge. Indeed, money transactions were not allowed in the park, and street vendors were driven out of the park on the second day of the occupation. Anti-capitalist Muslims would hold Friday prayers encircled by other occupants providing security. The park even celebrated a *kandil* (a holy night in Islam) together although the majority of the residents did not identify as religious. Crews of volunteers worked in shifts for keeping the park clean. All the while, barricades surrounded the park, and activists (both men and women, some of whom were as young as sixteen) took turns as 'guards' while others provided food and other necessities (Atayurt, 2013, pp. 27–8). There was a media centre that hosted Gezi Mail (Gezi Postası), Gezi Radio (Gezi Radyo) and later Çapulcu TV to serve as the voice of the park commune. Humour as a symptom of 'disproportionate intelligence' remained strong in graffities, banners, slogans and satirical songs. A new term 'chapulling' was invented with which activists (and their sympathisers in different corners of the world) re-appropriated the term *çapulcu* gifted to them by Erdoğan ('Gezi Parkı Eylemleri Yepyeni Bir Fiil Yarattı', 2013).

Most importantly, all this activism in the park turned it into a space of interaction, communication and debate among as few as two or three people hanging out in a small corner to hundreds in bigger forums. Crowded assemblies sometimes lasted well into the night, and participants utilised special communication protocols, reminiscent of their counterparts around the world, and respected each other's sometimes hard-to-swallow opinions (Kibar & Tatari, 2013a, pp. 62–7). Early interviews with activists as well as observations by embedded journalists revealed that themes such as diversity, tolerance, peaceful coexistence, community, feeling of freedom and incessant hope for a better future would often emerge in these forum meetings as the shared time and space among the occupants in the park continued to expand (Güven, 2013).

It should be noted that none of these events or developments were planned, organised, directed or dictated by Taksim Solidarity, which made the first call to resist the removal of the trees that sparked the protests. The organisation was never seen as, nor did it ever claim to be, the leader of the movement or the representative of all the people or groups in the park. On the contrary, there were times that Taksim Solidarity could not capture or connect with the emerging sentiments of the diverse, unorganised and unaffiliated activists as they collectively decided their subsequent moves (Z. U., personal communication, 16 July 2015).

From the earliest days of the occupation, there were groups who tried to dominate the discourse emerging from the park and steer the movement towards their own interpretation of what this uprising was about and how it needed to be advanced. Facing a backlash, their proposed emphasis on the Turkish flag or tired references, symbols and slogans of patriotism (which have long been shared by the Turkish left, including some socialist variations) were quickly rejected by the diverse park community, who did not let the movement be swallowed into a chauvinistic discourse (M. C. B., personal communication, 10 July 2015). There were times – especially in the early days of the occupation – when contentious issues resolved themselves almost organically. In one such instance, the Kurdish group wanted to put up a poster of Abdullah Öcalan (the imprisoned founder of the Kurdistan Workers' Party (PKK), an armed guerrilla movement seeking autonomy and rights for Kurds in Turkey) on their stand when members of a self-identified socialist group with ultranationalist sensitivities verbally harassed them, but eventually the two groups reconciled. In another instance, the use of sexist and homophobic language at forum meetings, in chants, slogans and casual conversations was reprimanded by LGBTQIA+ and feminist groups, which, once again resulted in the members of the community respecting these complaints and modifying their behaviour accordingly. Other issues in distributing resources or providing safety in the camp were all sorted out as individuals and groups continuously engaged in constructive interactions (Atayurt, 2013, p. 28). This peaceful co-existence of diverse groups and their demands in the park – and leaderless, horizontal, non-hierarchical character of the occupation – would be a source of admiration and pride, even long after the park was forcibly evacuated.

Meanwhile, long forum meetings took place in the park to discuss the road ahead as the government and Erdoğan were growing impatient with the now two-week long occupation (Tufekci, 2017, ch. 3). Amidst disagreements and confusion among the occupiers with respect to leaving or staying in the park (one option being to end the occupation and keep one symbolic tent in the park), the police launched an offensive on the occupiers with tear gas and water cannons on the night of 15 June and then closed the park, heralding a new chapter in the Gezi rebellion.

Phase 3: Residentiary Activism

The expulsion of the protestors from Gezi Park set off the third phase in the Gezi Episode when activists refused to simply retire to their homes but instead continued to congregate to discuss the future of the rebellion. At the beginning, two major public parks on both sides of Istanbul became the new gathering spaces because of their size, popularity and proximity to the main axes and networks of transportation in the city: Abbasağa Park on the European side and Yoğurtçu Park on the Anatolian side. In the span of a few weeks, as many as thirty-eight park forums and assemblies emerged in different neighbourhoods of Istanbul (Akçalı, 2018; Ramazanoğulları, 2022). At one point in July and August of 2013, as many as sixty park forums were meeting in different neighbourhoods in Istanbul and around the country.[4] Taking their cues and inspiration not just from the Gezi occupation but also from previous global experiences such as the World Social Forum and its regional offsprings, these public gatherings became yet another instance of a global wave of radical politics, ranging from autonomous municipalities in Latin America (Baiocchi, 2005) to popular committees in Egypt and assemblies in Athens and Barcelona (Özer, 2014), to encampments in Belarus (Naumov, 2015) and many others.

During the initial forum meetings in Abbasağa and Yoğurtçu parks (situated in prominent middle-class districts, Beşiktaş and Kadıköy, respectively) residents joined others with whom they shared a connection and a concern about the future of the city and country. In their most active moments, about 1000 people participated in these assemblies, congregating almost every night (M. C. B., personal communication, 10 July 2015). Occasional protests and rallies against police violence or to commemorate the young protestors who died during the heyday of the uprisings were still taking place, but the centre of gravity of politics was shifting to neighbourhood parks where long meetings among residents were taking place on such issues as the state of democracy, freedoms, rights, media legislation and urban transformation, among others (Roos, 2013).

Some of the characteristics of the second phase of the Gezi Episode continued into the third phase, too. For instance, the very idea of occupying and appropriating a space for activism would prevail in squat houses. Similar to the occupation of Gezi Park, in big park forums, too, participants continued to use hand gestures, sitting arrangements, loose moderation or facilitation and other communication protocols to ensure diversity, inclusivity and democratic participation (Tufekci, 2017, p. 74). Almost every night, occasional participants and more regular activists either gathered to share their views on wide-ranging issues or hosted guests (including policy experts, artists, journalists, scholars and politicians) to learn about various topics. Workshops and thematic sub-committees – similar to those in Gezi Park – were also emerging. Not just in these small committees and workshops, but even in larger general assemblies, consensus (rather than majority rule) was often the preferred method of decision-making and political action. Issues addressed in these forums and committees included national, global or even politico-philosophical questions, yet these progressively gave way to smaller, local topics concerning the district or surrounding neighbourhoods. It was with this transition that the composition and the character of the activists began to diverge from earlier iterations of the forum experience: instead of a handful of 'courageous vigilant militants' on the street or 'adventurous festive campers' in Gezi Park, the park forums and neighbourhood solidarities were now increasingly composed of residents focusing on the more immediate issues concerning them and their place of residence. In other words, activism in this phase of the Episode was becoming more localised and democratised, if not also a bit uniform and 'tamed', especially as attempts by more 'edgy' political groups and individuals to 'capture' the helm of the movement were thwarted. It was also in this phase that efforts to organise a national political movement emerged as a counter (or complementary) tendency to the ongoing localisation in activism in neighbourhood solidarities and squat houses. I will address the ambivalent nature of this dual tendency in Chapter 6.

The Gezi Episode: A Social Movements Perspective

To make better sense of the Gezi Episode as a constellation of interpenetrating modes of activism, I offer, in this section, a social movements approach that highlights the characteristics of the above-mentioned phases. Without getting into the intricate evolution of competing perspectives within the social movements literature (see Edwards, 2014, for a succinct and comprehensive review), and using them somewhat eclectically, I am focusing on four sets of parameters to assess the Gezi Episode in terms of its impact on the emerging political community, and hence on the efforts to reconstitute the social in the face of neoliberal assault: (a) participants, organisations, resources and other constituents of a movement; (b) networks and other relational mechanisms; (c) political processes and other environmental mechanisms; and (d) frames, identity and other cognitive mechanisms.

Participants, Organisations, Resources

One of the critical benchmarks utilised in conventional analyses to assess a social movement is the extent to which the said movement is 'organised', that is, whether or not the movement could establish itself as – or rely on – a professional, centralised, well-resourced social movement organisation (SMO) with a stable bureaucracy and full-time paid staff to convince 'conscience constituents' for support. In this setting, movements structured as organisations harvest and mobilise resources, such as people, money, social capital (including education, skills and connections), infrastructure, leadership and other forms of public support for their cause (Edwards, 2014, pp. 44, 56–7).

Similar to other global movements at the turn of the twenty-first century, it is hard to find a mature organisation directly involved in mobilising resources to maintain the movement during the Gezi Episode. Although Taksim Solidarity was active in raising consciousness about the urban transformation project in Taksim, it could not be considered as a stable SMO consistently mobilising resources for the movement. During the early days

Table 3.1 A Social Movements Analysis of the Gezi Episode

	Phase 1	Phase 2	Phase 3
Primary Spaces	Streets	Gezi Park	Public parks, neighbourhoods, buildings
Participants	Amorphous crowd of the urban discontented from all walks of life and political identities	Same crowd joined by others; groups now more recognisable due to spatial arrangements	Residents of neighbourhoods where parks are located; activists occupying squat houses
Organisations, Resources	Taksim Solidarity most visible at the beginning yet not in leadership position; donations, ad-hoc support mechanisms provided to protestors as needed	Words of solidarity from some labour unions, oppositional political parties, professional associations but no formal organisation emerging from the camp; Taksim Solidarity becoming less relevant; donations mobilised independently	Assemblies, forums, squat houses resembling local organisations and social centres; neighbourhood residents volunteering time and resources; expertise shared by members of professional associations
Repertoires of Action	Clashes on the street, humour on the move	Occupation, encampments; practices of radical democracy	Radical democratic practices now more regularised; occupation only in squat houses; beginnings of national-scale and election-oriented politics
Relational Mechanisms	Social media, other digital platforms for instant communication; Taksim Solidarity's network of individuals and civil society groups calling for action; networks of transnational solidarity	Social media continue to be primary network, supported by new online TV, radio and others; physical space becoming important in establishing new connections, cross-fertilisation; initiatives such as Müştereklerimiz attempting to coordinate separate initiatives as Taksim Solidarity's influence wanes	Social media continues to be primary network, increasingly for sharing information about events; initiatives to coordinate isolated local activism (such as 'parks are ours') not always effective; networks becoming less diverse with localisation; squat houses have limited success with extending their connections to the local residents

Environmental Mechanisms	Discontent towards the AKP, Erdoğan and overall urban transformation; police violence; cracks within the ruling elite; similar uprisings in the world as inspiration	Cracks within the ruling elite growing wider, Erdoğan escalating tensions strengthening Gezi as a legitimate political force and beacon of hope; continuing global support fortifying the movement's prestige and legitimacy	Escalating state violence and rising authoritarianism making activism difficult and risky; national parliamentary and presidential elections starting to dictate the terms of politics on increasingly localised activism, causing tensions, divergences, divisions
Cognitive Mechanisms	Slogans, images, social media posts (often humorous) emphasise the park, trees, environment; discourse evolving towards democracy, justice, defence of modern lifestyle, right to dissent, 'real democracy', anti-authoritarianism; broadening the struggle through 'everywhere is Taksim, resistance everywhere' (*her yer Taksim ber yer direniş*); counter narrative from the ruling elite, presenting protestors as disruptive, unpatriotic *çapulcu*	Expressions of victory, collective joy, hope; reappropriating *çapulcu*; emphasis on the park and the Gezi spirit emerging from the occupation; diversity, harmony, common as the basis of co-existence; less about defence than building a new life; counter frames from the ruling elite, presenting the occupation as being against 'national will' and development of the country	Symbols, slogans, references becoming more localised, more detached; missing a master ideological frame that connects different experiences

of the Episode, this loose-knit umbrella organisation, along with personalities such as deputy Sırrı Süreyya Önder and a handful of artists and celebrities, gave voice to the revolt against the demolition of the park in Phase 1, but there was no particular spokesperson of the movement, which, similar to other movements in the world, hailed horizontal networks, non-hierarchical relations and overall structureless mobilisation as 'the new organisation' (İplikçi, 2013). Indeed, Gezi and her global sisters took pride in defying the traditional understanding of organisation built around a vertical hierarchy with a leader chaperoning the movement. Similarly, while proudly carrying their identities as LGBTQIA+ or a feminist or a fan of a soccer team, it was the individuals, rather than their organisations or associations, who were actively involved in street clashes and protests. A broad palette of discontented individuals turned into an amorphous crowd, a 'multitude', during street activism in this phase.

Despite the impression it gave as the voice of the Gezi Park occupants (especially during the negotiations with the government in critical moments), Taksim Solidarity began to further lose its primacy in Phase 2. As politics was taking different forms and new directions, it became difficult, if not impossible, for Taksim Solidarity to even attempt to guide or coordinate political activism in the park, let alone offer centralised resource mobilisation. While various unions, municipalities and other organisations showed institutional support to the camp community, the occupiers were mostly self-reliant and depended on outside donations from independent individuals. The park itself became a resource in the form of a critical space for political experimentation (della Porta & Piazza, 2008, p. 33) as well as value and norm construction, adding to the strength of the movement. Meanwhile, the diversity of the camp increased as the regular residents of the occupation were joined by more white-collar professionals, university students and political organisations, most of whom were making daily trips to the park, sometimes with their children. Having a designated location in the park, the groups within the amorphous multitude became more visible, adding to the richness of politics emerging from the park.

After Gezi Park was dispersed and as park forums emerged in Phase 3 (which were later to be joined by smaller neighbourhood forums and squat houses), members of various organisations and associations, such as lawyers, engineers, journalists, unionists, politicians and university professors began to appear more frequently in special events and informative workshops offering their 'social capital' as a resource. Once again, these individuals did not act in the capacity of an official representative from organisations and associations such as TMMOB, the Turkish Medical Association (Türk Tabipler Birliği, TTB) or the Turkish Bar Association (Türkiye Barolar Birliği, TBB) but instead brought their expertise into the movement through personal commitment. Meanwhile, neighbourhood solidarities and squat houses were turning into informal SMOs (some of which were calling themselves 'social centres' or 'community homes') as they began to sever ties with bigger park forums and create their own loosely structured assemblies, which prioritised mobilising local resources and residents for local issues.

Repertoires of Action

For Tilly, 'repertoire of action' is 'a cultural notion where you have collective learning going on through interaction and you have the residues of this historical process of struggle showing up as constraint on how people relate to each other next time they make claims' (quoted in Edwards, 2014, p. 203). During the Gezi Episode, too, there emerged various claim-making practices, performances and processes that had their precursors in previous instances of contention, especially in anti-privatisation protests such as the TEKEL resistance, pro-secularism rallies, such *Cumhuriyet Mitingleri* (Republican Rallies) and anti-corruption protests, such as *Sürekli Aydınlık için Bir Dakika Karanlık* (One Minute of Darkness for Everlasting Light). While the overarching theme during the Gezi Episode was a 'right to the city' against authoritarian neoliberal urbanisation, the principal method of action could be summed up as 'community as politics and political action' (Breines, 1989). Despite the continuity through its different phases, one can still find variations in the emerging repertoires during the Episode, drawing on a mix of novel and traditional acts of contention.

In the first phase, activism was confined to street clashes and protests that necessarily involved acts of violence. Calls for joining the uprising on social media drew thousands of people to the streets all over the country. Clashing with the police, building barricades and using all possible means of urban combat were complemented by humour expressed in graffiti or circulated through social media. Threats of strikes by trade unions and confederations in support of the protestors would not materialise until the early days of Phase 2. It was also in this phase that the movement's political centre of gravity shifted to Gezi Park and the action repertoire began to diversify. In fact, the occupation came to build its own unique action repertoire (Kolluoğlu, 2020; also see: McCurdy et al., 2016) through creative productions and performances of music, art and theatre but also through a free library, kitchen, infirmary, media centre, yoga sessions, park clean-up tasks and recreational activities for children, not to mention numerous forum sessions and other meetings facilitating interaction and engagement in the camp. The emerging politics in the park found its radicalism within this novel repertoire: creative, improvised, inspiring and enticing enactments of everyday life in the camp allowed a new experimentation with horizontalism and a whole new host of repertoire of radical leftist protest culture. By heavily relying on social media to coordinate their activism, activists transcended the 'politics as we know it'. It was at this stage that the movements began to set free a new generation of activists from the heavy weight and limitations of former, historical struggles and concepts of success or failure.

The prefigurative and radical nature of politics was carried into the third phase when park forums and neighbourhood solidarities emerged following the Gezi occupation. This time, however, activism was taking place in a more 'calendar-ised' fashion, in the form of regular meetings, informative workshops or gatherings for event planning. While camping was no longer the preferred method, squat houses continued the occupation-based and 'life as politics' style activism.

Relational Mechanisms: Networks

A better assessment of the rise and maturation of a social movement involves looking beyond the individual activist (and her material interests, rational thoughts or emotions) or the organisation (and its structure or capacity to mobilise resources), and focusing instead on the 'relations' that surround the movement and connect individual activists and organisations to each other in a network structure (Edwards, 2014, p. 71). These informal, interpersonal ties emerge along a shared collective identity and steer activists into a collective understanding of the problem and why it needs to be addressed – a state of consciousness that goes beyond material interests of individuals or groups, or the potential of SMOs involved. In other words, a network is not simply a recruitment channel, nor is it yet another mechanism that provides a movement with resources. Rather it allows activists to establish affective bonds with each other and shape their position, allegiance and collective will to mobilise together, which all affect forms of solidarity, trust, meaning, ritual and shared opinions in the course of activism (Edwards, 2014, pp. 72–3).

Aside from the transnational activist networks to which the Gezi uprising became deeply connected via electronic communication platforms, which I will address later in this chapter, the Gezi Episode can be seen as a period of establishing new and refashioning old movement networks in Turkey, especially on the left side of political spectrum. Along with Taksim Solidarity, the most visible formal network of organisations that appeared in the Episode, ad hoc and more elusive networks emerged among activists using various digital platforms and social media tools. 'Hashtags' became the primary mode of acquiring and sharing information about the state of the street clashes, including the location of the police, Wi-Fi passwords that could be used in certain neighbourhoods or the contact information of lawyers, doctors and other volunteers. These momentary and volatile webs of information would also bring national and global support to people on the street, expanding the networks of solidarity and immediately incorporating the rebellion into the constellation of struggles all over the world.

With the occupation of Gezi Park in the second phase, physical space, in addition to virtual communication networks, became an important medium for interaction and establishing connections among activists. Physical proximity and constant interaction in the park facilitated what della Porta and Piazza (2008) call 'cross-fertilisation' among different groups through workshops, concerts, forum meetings and recreational activities, consolidating these informal relations. Through video broadcasts via the internet, the park community could connect with the rest of the country and the world, further expanding these networks. Groups such as Müştereklerimiz (Our Commons), which had been cultivating local and transnational connections on issues such as environmental degradation and refugees during rampant urbanisation under the AKP, found themselves in a good position to mobilise the activists in the park.

With the recalibration of politics in park forums, neighbourhood solidarities, squat houses and other initiatives during the third phase of the Gezi Episode, more local information-sharing networks on social media began to disseminate announcements or invitations to events, rallies and protests in certain locations. Initiatives, such as the 'Parks are Ours' (*Parklar Bizim*) blog, emerged to coordinate these increasingly localised networks, despite being short-lived and with limited success. Social media accounts of park forums, neighbourhood solidarities and squat houses contained denser information about the local issues that were of concern to them, while keeping informed about other groups. Initially, smaller forums kept representatives in larger park forums to sync their activism, yet these attempts would not yield satisfactory outcomes. As we will see in Chapter 6, it was partly the frustration regarding the lack of coordination between local initiatives that fuelled efforts to build a locally connected national movement, Birleşik Haziran ('United June'), a political initiative that brought together certain leftist parties, groups and individuals with the aim to establish a national movement in the wake of the Gezi uprising.

Environmental Mechanisms: Political Processes and Opportunity Structures

In order to move beyond a myopic understanding of movements as one-off (or a series of discrete) explosions, it is necessary to bring into the analysis the broader external political ecosystem that harbours the relations between the state and other institutions and political actors. This is necessary to see whether this very ecosystem is conducive for the success (or even for the emergence) of a 'sustained opposition to elites and authority' (Edwards, 2014, pp. 4–5). In other words, the conception of a movement's success cannot be confined to focusing on its 'internal' constitution (that is, resources, people and networks it comprises) but should also address 'the world around it' (Edwards, 2014, pp. 78–80). It is within this political matrix that 'opportunities' (including elections, changes in the legal system, alignments or divisions among elites, openness or closedness of the regime to democratic demands, the presence of independent centres of power, influential actors as allies and any other decisive changes) may emerge and make the time ripe for the changes the movement seeks to effect (Edwards, 2014, pp. 81, 83–7).

Chapter 2 addressed in detail the broader social, political and economic processes that made up the fundamental pillars of the political context from which the Gezi rebellion was born. One can identify more specific political processes and opportunities (or misfortunes) that emerged during the Gezi Episode. In the first phase, when physical violence perpetrated by the police against peaceful protestors during the street clashes was complemented with the 'silent violence' (Coşar & Yücesan-Özdemir, 2012) of the government targeting Taksim as the symbol of the modern and secular nation, a political window became available: the overwhelming support to resist the AKP's model of neoliberal urbanisation made alliances possible between various groups across the political spectrum, especially among leftist factions but also among some from the liberal wing of the intelligentsia, which in the past had offered its support for the AKP. Meanwhile, Erdoğan's legitimacy and hegemonic power took a hit following a corruption scandal in 2013, which itself was a result of the ongoing rift with the Gülen Movement (Öztürk, 2021, pp. 120–1). Finally, the fact that world-shattering protests, such as the Occupy Wall Street and the Arab Spring, were still fresh in the memory and continued to inspire movements around the world also provided a favourable political context for the Gezi rebellion's transformation into a fully-fledged movement and a chance to take its place in the global movement cycle of the 2010s.

In the second phase, when it became clear that the occupation of Gezi Park was not going to end anytime soon, negotiations began to take place between Taksim Solidarity and members of the political establishment, especially with the mayor, governor and spokespersons of the government, turning the movement into a legitimate political actor. These meetings could be interpreted as a sign of cracks among the political elite, as the much calmer and reasonable rhetoric adopted by them was in sharp contrast with Erdoğan's divisive and domineering attitude, further conferring legitimacy on the occupation and the overall movement. The longer the occupation lasted, the more support and prestige it gained, especially in its staunch defiance of Erdoğan's personality. So much so that Erdoğan needed to congregate 'Respect to National Will' rallies to consolidate the support of his constituency. Meanwhile, continuing global support as well as the ongoing street clashes in other parts of the city and the country that were upholding the occupation were further encouraging cross-fertilisation within the park between unlikely groups (such as the Kurds, Kemalists, anti-capitalist Muslims and many factions of the left) and turning the occupation into a collective 'space of hope'.

In the third phase of the Gezi Episode, when park forums, neighbourhood solidarities and squat houses became central in the overall mobilisation, local politics became more relevant and effective in shaping the course of the movement, which I will discuss in Chapter 5. However, the national stage did not lose its primacy in politics. The June 2015 general elections, which did not end in favour for the AKP's prospects as the governing party, were followed by increasing urban violence in the form of explosions and attacks in Suruç, Ankara, Istanbul, Diyarbakır and other places, claiming hundreds of lives in less than two years (Diken, 2016). The government's decision to end what is colloquially referred to as the 'peace process' with Kurdish guerrillas followed by another election in November of the same year in the midst of fear, uncertainty and social tensions gave Erdoğan the majority he and his party sought for. The ongoing political instability deepened with the failed coup attempt by the Gülenist movement in 2016, which helped Erdoğan completely transform the political system and consolidate his authoritarian rule. As we will see in Chapter 6, the primacy of this political context effectively brought an end to the Gezi Episode, exposing its vulnerability and weakness as a transformative political process.

Cognitive Mechanisms: Frames, Symbols, Meanings

Social movements cannot simply be defined or understood by objective and material conditions (such as available resources, composition of activists) or by the social, historical and political contexts in which they find themselves – they also carry a subjective component with which activists give meaning to their actions and develop a shared sense of purpose and solidarity. This symbolic construction of conflict is a contemplative process of diagnosing problems that motivate activists to interpret the world around them and eventually initiate or join contentious politics (della Porta & Piazza, 2008, p. 57). It is in this process that 'frames' (elements of a cognitive map in which various narratives, ranging from the necessity or legitimacy of the protest to strategies for success, from norms and values that inform the movement to the interpretation of historical events, coexist as a coherent scheme) are activated in order to collectively reflect on, memorialise and communicate convincing and unifying symbols (Edwards, 2014, pp. 91–5). While they constantly evolve, expand and are reconstituted through negotiations and contestations during the course of a movement, these frames become essential components of collective identity, solidarity and emerging political community.

Similar to the other social movements of the 2010s in which competing frames spread mostly through online communication platforms that circumvented the state-controlled mass-media, a host of frames, symbols and narratives circulated during the Gezi Episode in the form of slogans, banners and social media posts. In the first phase, while clashes with the police were taking place in the streets of Taksim, the originally peaceful environmentalist stance of 'saving the trees' in Gezi Park turned into frames of injustice due to Erdoğan's defiance and the shocking heavy-handedness of the police. Images of disproportional use of force helped activists weave a story of the uprising in which they could connect this 'physical' violence with the many instances of 'symbolic' violence that had been perpetrated on citizens (but particularly on women) for more than a decade under the AKP, encouraging more participation from those who were not initially in Gezi Park. Photos and drawings of trees, gas cannisters, riot vans, even penguins (to criticise mainstream media for not covering the protests in the early days of clashes but instead continuing their regular coverage, as was the case with CNN Turk which broadcasted a documentary on penguins) became the main frames that memorialised this period.

These sentiments resonated not only in different parts of Istanbul and the rest of the country but also in the global diaspora (Başer, 2015) as if to attest to the popular slogan 'everywhere is Taksim, resistance everywhere'. The expansion of this frame that transcended the actual physical space of contestation was not only a consequence of the growing approval of the riots, but more importantly because it was in line with the 'zeitgeist' of the period: calls for justice, right to dissent, anti-authoritarianism, right to the city and defence of all forms of life (both human and non-human) helped expand the fronts of the resistance from defending trees to demanding 'real democracy' and liberation. The popular phrase 'it's not just about a few trees' became one of the main punch lines of the first phase of the Episode.

The political establishment was quick to strike back with counter narratives by accusing activists of being disingenuous about the park or the environment in general, and of acting against the interests of the nation by obstructing economic progress. It was in the early days of Phase 2 of the Gezi Episode that Erdoğan uttered the word *çapulcu* to denigrate the protestors. The timing was not surprising since the protestors (now resolute occupants of the park) were claiming and appropriating the space that 'did not belong to them', and consequently graduated from being merely 'unruly' to relentless 'thieves' and 'looters'. However, the effort to pit the nation (*millet*) against the *çapulcu* to delegitimise the latter failed as the emerging Gezi community (occupiers and their supporters and sympathisers all around the nation and the world) quickly adopted and re-appropriated the term as a strong weapon in this war of symbols (Carvin, 2013; Uluğ & Acar, 2019).

The initial euphoric joy of 'victory' with the police retreating from Gezi Park morphed into 'hope' for a new, ethically imperative and possible future, and began to shape the cognitive–emotional universe of the movement from which the 'Gezi spirit' emerged as the pillar of the new collective identity and political community in the making. The diversity, harmony and novelty of the political experimentations in the park were the culmination of the shift in emphasis from environmental concerns and resistance against police violence to a desire for building a new citizenship, a new grammar of belonging and a better community. The radical method for achieving this goal was the 'common': the idea of sharing resources, establishing collective ownership and building a mutual future, the roots of which – reminiscent of the roots of a tree – would grow in the park and spread out to the rest of the country.

In the third phase of the Episode when the occupants of Gezi Park took refuge in other parks of the city, later to be joined by thousands more in many districts of Istanbul and other cities, the dominant frame of narrative began to shift towards the 'local'. Local slogans, local symbols to emphasise the importance of or to call to action for local issues – such as 'Don't Touch My School' (*Okuluma Dokunma*) campaigns against the possible conversion of a public school to a religious school, or Northern Forests Defence (*Kuzey Ormanları Savunması*) drawing attention to the attack on 'Istanbul's lungs' – came to replace the national and global frames. In addition to being able to closely follow each other on social media platforms, initiatives such as the *Parklar Bizim* blog tried to keep the local and separate mobilisations emerging in various park forums, solidarities and squat houses connected to each other. Yet, with the waning of captivating and uniting 'master' frames, it became difficult to harmonise parallel (and sometimes competing) narratives at local and national levels.

The Transformation of the Activist

The close examination of the Gezi Episode through the lenses of social movements analysis reveals two aspects of the mobilisational dynamic of the global movement cycle of the 2010s as it pertains to the transformation of the activist and emergence of new forms of collective identity in contentious politics.

Translocal Connections and Solidarities

While being autonomous in planning, organising and executing different forms of activism (ranging from protests and rallies to encampments and assemblies) in their own contexts, activists from around the world enthused, educated and supported each other, connecting through a sprawling 'logic of aggregation' (Juris, 2004, 2012; also see: Graeber, 2002). According to Tufekci, these activists had already created and utilised translocal networks and communities 'rooted in friendship and solidarity networks that have been built over decades of travel, digital connectivity, solidarity, friendship, and even strife' (Tufekci, 2017, p. 86). Indeed, as early as the first World Social Forum meetings, there was a growing 'interest in connecting local settings to larger networks, and most protest groups have quickly forged connections with translocal counterparts through interpersonal and online networks [. . . which] have produced both tensions and adaptations as different generations of activists learn to work together' (Smith et al., 2014, ch. 6).

Following the footsteps of their predecessors, movements of the 2010s developed common ideals, used similar methods (such as encampments) and created similar solidarity forms through keeping informed about each other's experiences in different parts of the world (Id, 2011). According to Hard and Negri, the geographical expansion of these movements took 'the form of an international cycle of struggles in which revolts spread from one local context to another like a contagious disease through the communication of common practices and desires' (Hardt and Negri, 2004, p. 213). While each of the local struggles in this global network was unique, a wide circulation of democratic imaginaries was taking place across borders through the connected activism of 'rooted cosmopolitans and transnational activists' (Tarrow, 2005, ch. 3). Each local movement interpreted and translated the contents of the global revolts through the prism of their own political and social cleavages. In other words, as both inspiration and trigger, global struggles activated existing social fault lines and shaped the very grammar of local struggles: ideas, imaginations, practices and any other forms and performances that emerged from different movements around the world were projected onto the local context (Castells,

2015) and produced 'common conduct, habits, and performativity [as the] symptoms of the common dreams, common desires, common ways of life, and common potential' (Hardt & Negri, 2004, pp. 212–13; also see: Wisniewska, 2017). In the process, a widely shared repertoire of collective action and democratic experiments encouraged local activists to replicate these experiences with messages of support between New York City, Tahrir, Athens, Tel Aviv, Istanbul and many others (Genç, 2018, p. 73). This translocal character bestowed upon activists the ability to create a 'unity of practice', a broad form of 'solidarity across differences' (Buck-Morss, 2013a, p. 67, 2013b).

The Gezi Episode is a good portrayal of how learning various tools, models and strategies from other social movements around the world serves as the building blocks of a new political community. It was not only the outpouring of support, expressed both in social media and through the international mainstream media, or in the form of rallies and demonstrations in different cities around the world, that was a sign of global solidarity (Karakatsanis, 2019; Kilkenny, 2013). Protests on the streets of Taksim, the occupation of Gezi Park, emerging park forums, neighbourhood solidarities and squat houses in Istanbul and beyond were quite reminiscent of those around the world (Özer, 2014). Slogans, tactics and organisational forms and practices that appeared at any stage of the Episode were inspired by – and themselves inspired – other uprisings around the time they were happening, as if they were a 'product of a global cultural convergence of protester aspirations and practices' (Tufekci, 2017, p. xv).

This diffusion of knowledge and experience had already started in the early 2000s, when activists from Turkey began attending regional social forums in Europe and learning practical skills, such as preparing durable banners or how to medically help those affected by pepper gas (Yıldırım & Gümrükçü, 2017, pp. 398–9). This 'know-how' would later be critical during street clashes in Taksim and beyond. The very idea of occupying a public space was also an inspiration from global movements of the period. During the occupation of Gezi Park and later in big park forums, communication protocols (hand gestures, rotation, facilitation etc.) were adapted from various Occupy movements from around the world. Yet the best examples of such connections and enactments of solidarity during the Gezi Episode could be seen in how squat houses kept their translocal connections. There were times, for instance, when the occupants of the Yeldeğirmeni squat house in Kadıköy would host guests from Greece and share squatting experiences, especially on building trust and support among the local community. There were also events when squat houses, neighbourhood solidarities and other platforms from various European cities would join their Turkish counterparts in Istanbul (Fırat et al., 2021, pp. 18–19). These and other interactions helped Gezi activists envision a political community beyond the borders of the nation-state in which solidarity frameworks and other imageries of a democratic society were built in connection with global as much as local and national allegiances.

Yet, the shared grammar of political activism, common repertoire of actions or the globally allied vision for the future did not fully erase the local dynamics and peculiar historical tensions that culminated in the Gezi rebellion. On the contrary, the protests were framed and acted upon by participants and supporters with respect to existing social cleavages that conditioned the country's political landscape for decades, but especially under the AKP rule whose ascent to power, as we saw earlier, infused elements of neoliberalism into the very fabric of society along with a flavour of Islamist authoritarianism (Gürcan & Peker, 2015). What the activists during the Gezi Episode achieved was to borrow various modes of collective action from global social movements and translate them into a language of grievance at the local context that told a uniquely Turkish story. The result was, borrowing from Douzinas, 'an extraordinary metamorphosis shared by people in different parts of the world, which has changed them from obedient subjects of law to resisting subjectivities' (Douzinas, 2014, p. 79).

Normalising Politics / Activism as Everyday Life

The second way in which the mobilisational dynamic of the anti-austerity and pro-democracy movements of the 2010s shaped the formation of political community came from the very nature of the political subjectivities these very movements brought about. As Samaddar (2012, p. 140) points out, one of the effects that social movements have on politics is that they reinforce relations of trust in a community, and hence facilitate the emergence of democratic spirit. For Blee, too, activism 'creates space in civic life for ideas and actions that exist nowhere else, encouraging people to envision how the world can be transformed into something better [. . .] It gives activists a sense of common purpose' (Blee, 2014, p. 134). Ultimately, constant mobilisation in social movements shapes the activists' ideology and allows them 'to imagine possibilities for changing the world—not abstractly, but in terms of their own actions [. . .] Collective political imagination [becomes] a way that activist groups define the reach and limits of what's possible' (Blee, 2014, p. 85).

The evolving – if unstable – nature of the social movements of the 2010s gave collective activism a dynamic character, keeping activists constantly vigilant and ready to mobilise and able to adapt to unpredictable turns. As Rutland puts it: 'the formation of movements, and especially the success that movements sometimes attain in changing certain power relations, appears to be a process that involves and alters the constitution of activist-subjects. Bound together, the subject and the socio-political context are changed together, or not at all' (Rutland, 2013, p. 1001). In the movements of the 2010s, this co-constitutive relationship between the activist and social movement unleashed a transformative energy, opening up the way for 'activism as a way of life', which ultimately shaped the process of politicisation and emerging collective identity in the community. Constant mobilisation and direct action on the streets, then in the parks and elsewhere paved the way for the 'normalisation' of street (and later park, forum and neighbourhood) politics, reinforced collective identity and solidarity, and eventually steered people into a political community of 'insurgent citizens' (Holston, 2009) or 'activist citizens' (Isin, 2009). Extrapolating from Lichterman's analysis of social movements of another era (Lichterman, 1996), it is safe to argue that the contemporary movements strived to find a way to remain plural around a common goal, without eroding the particularities of constituting individuals and groups, which made the emerging political community different from the conventional, fraternal understandings of community.

Once again, these dynamics could be observed in the Gezi Episode, especially during the occupation of Gezi Park and later in park forums, neighbourhood solidarities and squat houses. If anything, the Gezi Episode, and especially the forum experience in various assemblies, woke up the politically dormant to engage in activism. This meant being constantly active in the street (and later in the park, neighbourhood or squat house) where individuals were involved in, learned about and undertook different forms of politics, ranging from violent street clashes to organising workshops, movie screenings or establishing 'money-free' exchange zones. First the streets, then Gezi Park, and neighbourhoods and squat houses became 'spaces of encounter' for the oppressed of all creeds, where people could stand together, interact with each other and develop a common language of struggle during the Gezi Episode (Altınay, 2014, p. 304). Embodied and performative experiences (Butler, 2015) of solidarity through everyday activism continuously energised previously inactive individuals and groups and united them around a new collective identity against what they framed as oppression from a mutual political enemy.

As activism became an everyday practice, the transformation of the activist could best be observed in four areas.

Enlightenment

First, activists became progressively better informed based on the political experiences and interactions from the very first days of the Gezi Episode. Even at the height of the street clashes, activists became more conscious and 'enlightened' about the ways that the AKP government was destroying the city in line with a relentlessly neoliberal rationality or about how brutally the police could respond to peaceful acts of dissent, or about different facets of the pressing issues in society, especially those of women, LGBTQIA+ individuals or refugees (A. D., personal communication, 10 July 2015). The enlightenment process in the street extended to park forums and beyond, especially when these spaces became places where knowledge on particular issues (mostly local but broader, too) was produced, shared, discussed and acted upon by the very occupants, participants and residents. As one of the Yoğurtçu Forum activists indicated during an interview:

> Yoğurtçu educated activists. It helped create networks among people. It also served as a school for activists. They now continue doing politics in smaller groups or bigger ones. They now know what to do, how to act if Gezi happens again and if they find themselves in the streets again. Yoğurtçu taught people how to do politics, whom to trust, and how to get together. (M. C. B., personal communication, 29 June 2016)

Another activist shared this belief and expressed that the Gezi Episode in general, and Yoğurtçu Forum in particular, helped raise:

> political consciousness among the indignant people who came out of their homes during the Gezi uprising. Even those who are no longer actively

participating in any political activism will 'recall' what they have gained in terms of what they can do, with whom they can come side by side, and how powerfully they can resist with others. (Y. O., personal communication, 30 June 2015)

Some activists even believed that the growing awareness about the issues that the Gezi rebellion unveiled for the majority of the population might have resulted in Turkish activists becoming conscious of one of the most burning cleavages in the society, that is, the ethnic strife around the demands of the Kurdish liberation movement, because the experiences that Turks accumulated during the Episode (first-hand police brutality, radical democratic practices, co-existence in diversity and so on) resembled those the Kurds had experienced for decades (Z. U., personal communication, 16 July 2015).

EMPOWERMENT

The impact of constant mobilisation on shaping the political subjectivity of the Gezi activists could also been seen in the ways that they were 'empowered' by being directly involved in any form of activism. In addition to being more informed (about issues in the neighbourhood, city, country or the world), activists were also taking initiative to address these issues and contribute to their solutions. From the early days of the protests, Gezi activists began to realise that they could be in command of their own political destiny. Being out in the streets, then utilising parks and other spaces for political activism to transform the conditions of their lives was a source of self-confidence, self-realisation and harmony with others coming from the effort to build something collectively. The resulting experience was, similar to what Breines observed in the student movements of the 1960s, no less than 'a feeling of omnipotence', 'a sense of power and energy' and deepening belief in 'collectivity and coherence' (Breines, 1989, p. 32).

During my fieldwork, an activist jokingly disparaged me when I used the word 'activist' in our interview to describe him and other Yoğurtçu Forum participants, and said: 'I'll get mad at you if you call me an activist'. For him, there were two types of 'activists' in a movement: the first type would think and talk a lot about issues but would not get involved in active struggle to address them. The second type would run around and execute whatever orders he or she would receive, like a foot soldier. However, he saw himself and other members of the Yoğurtçu Forum as different from both types since they were 'radical organisers' who themselves were realising, formulating and executing what needed to be done (M. C. B., personal communication, 10 July 2015). Their direct involvement in activism in many different capacities during the Gezi Episode helped them overcome their immobilising pessimism about the possibility of social change and to confront their own 'apolitical' and 'anti-political' attitude (O. S., personal communication, 11 August 2015).

Indeed, activists during the Gezi Episode found their own unique ways to contribute to the emerging and constantly changing forms of solidarity without being instructed by a what would be a central command unit (Fırat, 2013, p. 38). As one of the activists told me: 'I realised the extent of what I could do', referring to how she overcame the fear of police violence or getting arrested while defending a grove from being turned into a construction site (S. A., personal communication, 13 July 2015). The longer they stayed and mobilised in public spaces, the more normalised it became for the activists to engage in political action with others: they felt emancipated from their chains of atomisation, not hesitating to take initiatives and risks, which was both liberating and reassuring because they were not alone and powerless (Demirok et al., 2013, p. 129). They were also, as one of my interviewees from the Yoğurtçu Forum put it, no longer a 'calendar activist', someone who would attend a protest or an event organised for certain days of symbolic importance (such as May Day): 'In the past, I was a mere participant (*katılımcı*). Now I am the subject (*özne*); I am what the task is (*İşin kendisiyim*)' (A. D., personal communication, 4 August 2016). This new state of being was precious for her: she felt more courageous, passionate and empowered as she saw her opinions and actions being valued by others and that she could be influential in shaping the course of activism (also see: Kömürcü, 2014).

EMPATHY

In addition to becoming enlightened and empowered, the transformative impact on Gezi activists of constant mobilisation in different corners of the city included developing compassion towards other groups and learning to empathise with the issues they had to endure. One of the activists made the observation that she no longer felt privileged or protected by virtue of being an ethnic, middle-class Turk and came to the realisation that it was not just historically marginalised groups such as Kurds, Alevis, non-Muslim minorities or others but '[we], too, are among the oppressed' (S. A., personal communication, 13 July 2015). This feeling of turning into a 'minority' was widespread among the protestors at the beginning of the Gezi Episode (Arslanalp, 2014). Yet, numerous interviews with activists during the occupation of Gezi Park revealed that instead of settling with this imposed status, activists chose to connect with each other, dropping their prejudices or indifference towards even the most unlikely groups, especially when they needed to mobilise in solidarity during clashes with the police or taking initiatives in the park (İplikçi, 2013; Uluğ & Acar, 2014). Constant mobilisation and different forms of collective activism allowed activists of all different traits to be exposed to different opinions and attitudes and learn about the lives and struggles of others around them.

This could be clearly seen in the changing relations between the Turkish and Kurdish groups during the Gezi occupation and later in park forums. On social media, numerous tweets and posts circulated in which Turkish activists themselves and those who sympathised with the uprising confessed that they felt deceived regarding the Kurdish question in Turkey because of the state propaganda they had been fed by the mainstream media for years. Akçalı writes about witnessing an instance in one of the early meetings in the Yoğurtçu Forum when a group of young Turks thuggishly confronted a Kurdish group, accusing them of being 'terrorists' and intimidating the participants of the meeting. Eventually the facilitators successfully negotiated peace between the two groups, and the latter could cordially converse with each other (Akçalı, 2018, p. 330). One of the Yoğurtçu Forum activists I interviewed told me how he felt that the rally in Kadıköy to protest the murder of Medeni Yıldırım by the armed forces in Diyarbakır's Lice district turned out to be a spectacular moment when Turks openly recognised and overwhelmingly opposed the state violence against Kurds in the south-eastern regions of the country. This, for him, was testament to the dictum that 'the peoples make peace on the streets (*halklar sokakta barışır*)' (S. B., personal communication, 10 July 2015).

A similar process of 'political friendship' took place among different factions of the radical left. In the early days of the clashes, the overall sentiment was that 'a person who witnessed those days, and that sense of solidarity and togetherness, could never remain the same' ('Bunu Yaşayan Aynı Kalamaz', 2013). Indeed, one of the Yoğurtçu Forum activists shared with me that her social life and networks changed during her involvement with the Yoğurtçu Forum, which brought her new friendships while taking others away. In one instance, she began to socialise with people belonging to different left organisations and political factions with whom she would now 'sit together, discuss and disagree' about many things. According to her, they learned 'to trust each other', unencumbered by the 'weight' of past divisions (A. D., personal communication, 4 August 2016). This camaraderie would later extend to other political initiatives she became involved in, such as the Birleşik Haziran movement. For A.D., the solidarity that was created during the forum days made the Birleşik Haziran movement stronger:

> We [those who came from Yoğurtçu Forum] have this affection [*muhabbet*] towards each other from the forum days, and we learned to stay together. We do not know any other type of politics [than being in solidarity]. When other groups [in Birleşik Haziran] act with their old habits [of prioritising their petit interests in small cliques] we try to pull them back to solidarity, to being in common. (A. D., personal communication, 4 August 2016)

EUPHORIA

Finally, the joy and excitement emerging from collective activism was another symptom of the transformation that activists often reported during the course of the Gezi Episode. The highest level of euphoria could be seen during the unprecedented enactments of solidarity among the protestors and their supporters in the early days of street clashes. Numerous protestors shared their stories of experiencing and revelling in support and solidarity in these days: stories of people donating food and other resources to the protestors, or of women having never felt this level of safety and camaraderie in crowds, surrounded by people with whom they would hardly imagine being together for a common cause, and many others (see, for instance, İplikçi, 2013, p. 24; Uluğ & Acar, 2014, pp. 36–7, 134, among others). Later, when the police retreated and Gezi Park was occupied, the feeling of freedom and liberation that came from 'having successfully carried out a people's revolt and overcome state repression' became the source of elation and solidarity (Özgür, 2013, p. 34). The overall carnivalesque character of the mobilisation roaming from the streets to parks to squat houses gave goosebumps, even tears of joy, to its protagonists, similar to other examples from around the world (see, for instance: della Porta, 2015, pp. 194–5). In Tufekci's words: 'this mélange of community, rebellion, and altruism create[d] a special moment, a sense of sacredness, among the protesters' (Tufekci, 2017, p. 94). Despite the level of exhaustion and the extent of the toll due to busy agendas and the ever-increasing tempo of (over-)commitment to the movement (which was fundamentally different from simply being a rank-and-file member in an organisation), activism in the streets, forums and squat houses gave activists a deep sense of satisfaction and made them feel that they were 'in the right place and among the right people' (A. D., personal communication, 4 August 2016; Y. S., personal communication, 13 July 2015).

'Fluid Political Identities' and the New Political Community

Given these transformative experiences – animated by the mobilisational dynamic – through which activists perceive their activism and the very movement in which they take part, how does this novel, complex collective identity shape the emerging political community to counter the neoliberal destruction of the social? It is to this question that I now turn.

According to Glass, activists do not only do 'resource work' in which they generate and mobilise resources for the maintenance of the movement. The also engage in 'identity work' through which they 'frame' the identity of the activist group or organisation they belong to and 'place' themselves in that picture (Glass, 2008, pp. 16–17). This identity work is crucial for a social movement because: 'collective action cannot occur in the absence of a "we" characterised by common traits and specific solidarity [. . .] A collective actor cannot exist without reference to experiences, symbols and myths which form the basis of its individuality' (della Porta & Diani, 2006, pp. 94, 106).

And yet, collective identity is always in flux and in progress, if not in tension, for it does not simply emerge from – or reflect – the social location or structural position of individuals or groups, but is rather produced through, around and during constant mobilisation within a social, political and cultural matrix (della Porta, 2015, pp. 81–5, 94–5). The solidarity and community imagined and built around this collective identity are not static, either, as they change through constant mobilisation across various urban spaces in the course of a social movement. This is why the mobilisational dynamic of social movements strongly affects the ways in which activists define themselves, their activism and the world around them while protesting on the streets, forming assemblies in parks or squatting abandoned buildings. In other words, the unique politicisation process carried out by the mobilisational dynamic – which draws on trans-local networks and their shared frames, repertoires and experiences of austerity, injustice, authoritarianism and other grievances – paves the way for the emergence of what I call 'fluid political identities'.

The way I operationalise the term 'fluidity' in describing these activist identities is different from what McDonald calls 'fluidarity'. The latter emphasises the public expression of multiple temporal experiences that an individual activist undergoes instantly and simultaneously in various networks relying mostly on electronic communication infrastructure (Mcdonald, 2002). 'Fluidity' is different from mere connection or co-operation or collaboration in a network between fully established, static nodes as in the World Social Forum or other global and regional forums of the early 2000s, which were a loose federation of already established groups and organisations. The fluidity of an activist's political identity also has less to do with the 'cross-fertilisation of networks of activist groups' (della Porta & Piazza, 2008) or mere 'diffusion' of ideas (della Porta, 2017) than the emergence of a permeable, nomadic, flexible identity as the core of the activist-citizen's envisioning and taking active part in building a new political community. It underscores the formation of common traits or a shared sense of 'we-ness' among diverse participants that emerges in the process of mobilisation. In this political formation, each activist who is now a unique political subject in the multitude 'denies politics as a separate sphere' but rather sees it as the expression of everything (Kioupkiolis & Katsambekis, 2014, p. 6).

The distinctiveness of this political identity in contemporary social movements is that it often emerges from loose social ties and short-term engagements, rather than strong, durable and stable collective bonds, which leads to weaker identification with existing social organisations such as unions, political parties, associations and others. The fluidity of an activist's identity, then, comes from the fragmented nature of these 'light communities' (della Porta,

2015, pp. 162–4) in which identities are shaped and reshaped not through interaction with similar-minded members in a strictly-defined organisation or a movement, but through the interaction of individuals and groups whose political maturation involved different sets of capacities, priorities and approaches developed in different contexts. Moreover, and extending Lichterman's analysis of an earlier era, political identities under constant mobilisation oscillate between individualistic and communitarian motives, expectations, concerns and priorities (Lichterman, 1996, p. 24). This pushes activists to reinvent their political activism beyond traditional methods, forms and ideologies and to reinterpret their commitment to each other and 'to the cause' in accordance with the populist nature of contemporary movements, as crystallised in the slogan 'we are the 99 percent'.

One of the signature characteristics of the global social movements that emerged in the 2010s was that actors/activists/participants could simultaneously exist in different urban sites while assuming different roles, capacities and statuses in specific political formations and spaces. Developing a 'nomadic' character (Hoskyns, 2014, p. 119), these groups – often comprised (as we saw in Chapter 2) of middle-class professionals, environmentalists and other concerned urbanites, most of whom had a deep sense of urban consciousness and were well connected to global circuits of ideas – assembled following the 'logic of aggregation' (Juris, 2012) and possessed the flexibility, experience and skills with which they could produce multiple forms of politics simultaneously. They could at once be a precarious labourer on a picket line, a re-tweeter or re-poster on social media, a marching protestor on the street, a watchman at the barricades, an orator in a rally in a square seized from the police, a librarian of an ad hoc 'revolution library' in an encampment in an occupied park, a volunteer cook in a squat house, a banner designer or an accountant in a neighbourhood forum or a district representative in a national political movement.

During the Gezi Episode, too, activists simultaneously took part in multiple initiatives, assumed different activist roles and embodied different political identities simultaneously. In their professional lives they could have been all different types of white-collar professionals (or students, artists and so on), but in the park or behind the barricade they would become whatever the 'multitude' needed at that moment (İplikçi, 2013, p. 16). Even at the heyday of park forums and neighbourhood meetings, activists would easily be mobilised for collective street demonstrations (such as protesting the murder of protestors by the police, or rallying in solidarity with Palestine) or individual acts of protests, such as the 'standing man' (*duran adam*) protest, which was initiated by a choreographer where he and others remained immobile for hours facing the Turkish flags hanging from the Atatürk Cultural Centre (Atatürk Kültür Merkezi, AKM) in Taksim after the banners on its façade were cleared by the police and the square was closed to public demonstrations. Similarly, an organiser busy with canvassing the residents of a neighbourhood for a local issue or with preparations for a movie screening or other art event in the squatter house, would still attend – and sometimes act as a liaison for – larger forum meetings in Yoğurtçu or Abbasağa parks.

Indeed, the creative energy in activism would find its expression among activists in different settings and modalities. Although the overall politics that was emerging from the Episode was predicated on rejecting electoral politics in favour of a radical alternative, there were instances when activists chose to engage in traditional politics at the local or national level, as if they were a lobby group, youth section of a political party or members of a civil society organisation. One activist, for instance, who was a member of Yoğurtçu Forum while also attending to Yeldeğirmeni squat house, did not mind taking active part in the 'After 10' (*10dan sonra*) initiative during the national election campaign in June 2015, developing electoral strategies to influence voter decision (Z. U., personal communication, 16 July 2015). Many of those Yoğurtçu activists took various active roles in the foundation of the Birleşik Haziran movement while continuing to engage in other non-traditional forms of politics throughout the Episode (M. C. B., personal communication, 29 June 2016; A. D., personal communication, August 4, 2016). In other words, activists during the Gezi Episode, similar to their counterparts in other movements across the world, developed a capacity to mobilise constantly (as a way of living their everyday life) while being politically active in multiple spaces and at multiple levels simultaneously, without finding any contradiction in this shift between scales.

Following Said and More's analysis of the Arab uprisings, we can argue that constant mobilisation during the Gezi Episode activated at least three forms of different, yet related, political agency: first, activists 'lived and experienced the revolution' and as such they became, in an ethnographical sense, the agents of immediate mobilisation by clashing with the police, cooking in the kitchen, tending the common garden, and so on. Second, they 'engage[d] with and manage[d] the political struggles while the revolution [was] ongoing'. In other words, they were the agents who thought about and implemented political tactics, made political calculations and responded to the immediate calls of daily politics. Third, activists 'perceive[d] the revolution in a philosophical and historical way or in the larger social sense' (Said & Moore, 2021). Put differently, they reflected back on broader questions of community, solidarity and collective existence in plurality but also engaged in self-reflection both during the experience as it was unfolding and in its aftermath. Even more importantly, all these three modes of political activism could co-exist thanks to the fluidity that enabled activists to flow from one site to another, from one responsibility to another and from one radical democratic act to another.

Therefore, one cannot speak of a finalised and uniform 'Gezi spirit' for it was a patchwork of distinct motivations, interpretations and identities coexisting in harmony yet continually 'negotiated, tested, modified, reconfirmed' under constant mobilisation (Özkırımlı, 2014). A broad range of groups, especially those who previously could not make claim to public appearance (LGBTQIA+ individuals, women, the displaced and so on), could find a place in the streets of Taksim, in Gezi Park and later in forums, solidarities and squat houses. A novel performance of citizenship emerged when militant/insurgent/ activist citizens of the Gezi Episode took part in various communities at once, developing capacities and networks of solidarity at various degrees of local, national and transnational levels. 'Being there'ness, the dialogue and togetherness helped them constitute a politics of the body in all its multiplicity and diversity (Gambetti, 2014), a form of harmony in fluidity that could only be possible in the complexity of the city. Their constant mobilisation in various urban sites conditioned the ways in which they interpreted their own role in reconstituting the social against neoliberal destruction.

In the next chapter we will see the spatial implications of these fluid political engagements in Istanbul's peculiar urban settings. The unique political forms these engagements assumed (i.e. the assemblist character of radical democratic politics) and how they in turn shaped the object of activism (i.e. the common) will be addressed in Chapter 5.

Notes

1. Taksim Solidarity was a platform that brought together around eighty NGOs, political groups and professional organisations as well as individuals to resist the urban transformation in the Taksim area. Chambers, unions, confederations and bar associations had representatives on the platform, although it was relatively unknown to the public until the Gezi protests. The platform organised against and informed people about other steps of the transformation efforts in this historical area, such as the closing of the Emek movie theatre, pedestrianisation of Taksim Square and revitalisation of Topçu artillery barracks in the form of a high-end residence and shopping mall, claiming that the nature of the overall constellation of projects ignored not just the history, identity and memories of the area but also were not pedestrian/resident friendly (Elicin, 2017; Fırat, 2013).

2. Some of the entries posted in one of the most popular blogs in Turkey, *ekşisözlük*, during these days helped spread this information widely. See (*31 mayıs 2013 taksim gezi parkı polis saldırısı*, 2013).

3. According to the Ministry of Internal Affairs, 2.5 million people in 79 of the 81 cities joined protests in support of the Gezi Park rebellion (Şardan, 2013).

4. Voluntary reporting from some of these early forum meetings appeared on a blog until October 2013: 'Parklar Bizim' (Parks are Ours), http://parklarbizim. blogspot.com/ (accessed: 21 February 2023)

4

SPATIAL DEMOCRACY: THE GEZİ EPISODE AS URBAN INSURGENCY

The previous chapter discussed the *mobilisational* aspect of the Gezi Epi-sode by highlighting the ways that dissident voices against neoliberal destruction of the social could unite and unleash their democratic energies in a state of constant mobilisation and in alliance with other movements around the world. But what role does urban space play in uniting, harmonising and amplifying activists' resentments and aspirations for a radically democratic political community? What is in the city that conditions activists' political consciousness and subjectivity, intensifies the fluidity of their political identity and allows them to engage in a diverse set of politics in different places? This chapter delves into the *spatiality* of the Gezi Episode as the second dynamic of contemporary social movements. It discusses how urban space was further fragmented into spatial units ('sites') under constant activism and how each fragment complemented (or contradicted) others with its unique capacity for nurturing radical democracy to rewrite the terms of a shared vision of solidarity and political community.

Space and Contemporary Urban Movements

The spatiality of urban politics, democratic practices and identity formation has long been a theme within the prolific field that focuses on the relationship between politics, democracy and the city (see, for instance, Barnett, 2014; Hoffman, 2014; Magnusson, 2014; Mostafavi, 2017; Parkinson, 2012). This is not surprising. Space maintains an inextricable connection to contentious politics as the locus for holding, attracting, practicing and generating political power (Turam, 2013, 2015). According to Tilly, 'everyday spatial distributions, proximities, and routines of potential participants in contention affect the extent and character of their mobilisation', which, in return, 'transforms the political significance of sites and spatial routines' (Tilly, 2003, p. 221). For Mouffe, it is only when social movements take place in physical space that they develop a 'productive space of conflict' (Miessen & Mouffe, 2012, pp. 72–4). Juris, too, suggests that while the 'logic of aggregation' could flourish on different forms of electronic communication as the primary organising rationality behind contemporary movements, it is within physical spaces that the viral flow of information builds affective solidarity, sociality and eventually an alternative political experience among individuals (Juris, 2012, p. 268).

Yet, space is not merely a static location that hosts and nurtures (or inhibits) social movements but is itself 'subject to transformation as a consequence of the very social action that [it] shape[s]' (Sewell, 2001, p. 55). It is key to the constitution of political subjectivities and collectivities (Massey, 1995, pp. 284–5) by allowing groups and communities to 'colonise' their place through unique rituals and practices (Hoskyns, 2014, p. 97). In this process, space enables the emergence of a collective identity around which activists imagine and execute their political projects, which in turn restructures the 'meanings, uses, and strategic valence' of the very space they occupy (Sewell, 2001, p. 55). Furthermore, space is capable of simultaneously holding multiple identities in a fixed location (such as in a general assembly in a forum) and fragmenting the shared identity of dissenting actors in multiple places (such as when smaller neighbourhood collectives branch out from the general assembly) (Çetin, 2016, p. 199). This dual process creates an 'ecology of subjectivities' (Coward, 2012, p. 473) and shapes the nature of emerging contentious politics.

Complicating this picture even more, Lefebvre reminds us that there is not one but multiple social spaces that 'interpenetrate one another and/or superimpose themselves upon one another' (Lefebvre, 1991, p. 86). This is especially true for multi-faceted and fragmented public space in the urban setting in which many forms of social interactions can take place – a quality that makes the physical proximity/mobility/scale of different locations important for collective action. Each locale or site in the city, in its own way, offers unique starting points, transitory stations and final destinations for different forms of mobilisation (strikes, marches, sit-ins, occupations, forums and the like), sometimes thanks to their symbolic importance (as a site of commemoration, or of mockery of government ceremonies, for instance) or their functional attributes (where, for instance, government functions are targeted by protestors) (Tilly, 2000). When people march on streets, occupy a square or reclaim an abandoned building, they create a complex topography of politicisation as they – consciously or unconsciously – deploy distinct spatial strategies and tactics to challenge relations of domination and oppression in these sites (Soja, 2000, p. 352). More importantly, the scale and physical infrastructure of an urban site, resources it holds and visibility or vulnerability it confers on its inhabitants become constitutive of the plurality of political subjectivities that assemble in that very site and of the parameters of activism they produce, articulate and pursue. In other words, the material fabric of each distinct urban site shapes the types and possible strategies of the political struggle, forms of solidarity it produces and the potential it carries as a 'counterpublic' (Warner, 2005) in which alternative political imaginations flourish.

Below, by way of analysing the spatiality of the Gezi Episode, I unpack the term 'urban space' and investigate how political processes traversed (and were conditioned by) different sites in Istanbul and generated various forms of political empowerment and solidarity, as well as political deadlock, weakness or incompatible visions. Similar to other movements in the global cycle of the twenty-first century in which the city was the locus of political mobilisation, multiple forms of territorial activism emerged during the Gezi Episode, too, as residents felt under attack by neoliberal urbanisation and collaborated over attainment of their jeopardised freedoms, rights and livelihoods (Turam, 2017). The spatiality of urban politics played out in unique ways in different locales and sites in Istanbul and produced distinct configurations of political power and democratic horizon. Here, too, an ensemble of contentious politics took place at different sites in which activists resisted attempts 'to redefine the dominant meanings of the city [. . .] where (most of) those who participate in collective action live[d] or spen[t] their daily lives' (Thörn et al., 2016, p. 31).

In the next section, I will first take a bird's eye view of the streets of Taksim and Beşiktaş to examine how violent clashes with police shaped the political motivations of the masses at the hight of the Gezi uprising. I will then wander around the camp where novel experiences of a communal life emerged unexpectedly from the occupation of Gezi Park. The next stop will be the inner veins of Istanbul where activists, following their expulsion from Gezi Park, gathered in neighbourhood parks and established forums and solidarities to deliberate on social and political issues and undertake (often) mundane tasks but also collectively conceive, prefigure and act on the future. My final destination in this expedition will be buildings to demonstrate how deeply diverse politics – from anarchist experiences in squat houses to preparations for a parliamentary election – could emerge from within built environments. The whole journey will demonstrate the ways in which site-specific urban rhythms (Lefebvre, 2013) and spatial routines (Sewell, 2001) during the Gezi Episode produced particular forms and repertoires of activism and experiences of solidarity as activists moved between urban sites almost instantaneously in pursuit of 'emancipatory visions'.

One caveat is that although it is tempting to think of the spatiality of the Gezi Episode as a temporal lineup of spaces in which activism in one urban site dies down and is replaced by another form of politics in another site, this was not the case. A condition similar to the non-chronometry of mobilisation we discussed in Chapter 3 could be detected as the spatial dynamic of the Episode was unfolding: while certain sites became more prominent and visible in certain moments and with certain 'modalities' of political mobilisation (streets during protests, Taksim Square and Gezi Park during the occupation, neighbourhoods and parks following the dispersion of the camp and rise of assemblies, or buildings during squatting, two national elections in 2015 and the birth of Birleşik Haziran as a political movement), none of these sites and activisms they nurtured necessarily followed a chronological or a hierarchical order in which one form of political mobilisation (and associated political imagination) subsided to allow another to rise. What emerged was not a single space but 'several and relatively autonomous spaces where different forms of hegemonic articulation [were] at work' (Prentoulis & Thomassen, 2013, p. 226). Different forms of political activism co-existed, informing, complementing and co-constituting each other in different spaces of Istanbul.

Distinct forms of struggle, subjectivities, imaginations, utopias and awareness emerged as activists simultaneously pursued different forms of politics in an ensemble of urban spaces.

Spaces of the Gezi Episode

Streets

'The street is where movement takes place', writes Lefebvre in *The Urban Revolution*, 'the interaction without which urban life would not exist' (Lefebvre, 2003, p. 18). The street is also a space for marches, rallies, demonstrations – it is a space for crowds in motion. The word 'street politics' evokes images of a slow, steady, seemingly uniform (despite the possibility of a variety of intriguing banners and slogans) flow or of a battleground where defiant (and often loud) bodies in motion sometimes clash with security forces or adversaries as in the conventional depiction of riots or revolutions. Contention on the street can range from ordinary labour strikes to more colourful and diverse protests, such as feminist marches or pride rallies. Issues voiced on streets often involve higher-level politics (such as protesting an authoritarian government, demanding better working conditions or condemning homophobia, police violence and so forth), but smaller local concerns also trigger street activism (such as resisting the construction of a gas pipeline in a neighbourhood). Either way, the street is the space of 'disruptive' politics – both in the sense of disrupting the typical, accustomed rhythms of the city and challenging the undisputed normative framework of state machinery. While the street can be, using Marxist terminology, where the 'revolutionary situation' is materialised, it does not automatically transform crowds into mature political subjects endowed with constitutive power. Crowds on the street, following Jodi Dean, are not political yet, that is, the formation of their political subjectivity is not complete, but they are a *potential* for collective politics (Dean, 2016). This volatility further deepens the tension-laden character of the street and makes it both unpredictable (the protest can always descend into vandalism or violence) and vulnerable (the crowd can be blocked, redirected or dispersed by the police), further destabilising the politics emerging from within it.

As we saw in the discussion on the 'motionary activism' phase of the Gezi Episode in Chapter 3, the very first spaces that hosted transformative political processes – which began with chaos, scrimmage and violence – were the

streets around Taksim Square, and later those in Beşiktaş, Dolmabahçe and
Gazi Mahallesi in Istanbul, progressively spilling over into the whole country.
Political mobilisation during this phase of the Episode first materialised on the
street orchestrated by the masses who stood up against militarised law enforcement and their riot vans (popularised as TOMA, official Turkish acronym for
'Intervention Vehicle against Social Incidents'), threw gas cannons back to the
police and tended those affected by tear gas with special water solutions. The
intensity and exuberance of the active clashes on the streets stemmed – at least
partly – from the fact that the area was regarded as one of the last remaining
green areas in the face of the construction frenzy in the city, and the last bastion of a modern, secular and diverse lifestyle to defend against the increasingly
authoritarian Islamist government, as discussed in Chapter 2.

This made the streets inclusive of numerous and sometimes conflicting
activist modalities: rage, tension, apprehension, frustration and intimidation,
but also love, admiration, camaraderie, hope, resistance and, of course, solidarity became rapidly floating sources of motivation. In that sense, the streets
of Taksim and Beşiktaş hosted the 'big bang' moment of a robust ecology of
political subjects in-the-making where new spaces were soon to emerge (or at
least appear as a possibility) for alternative politics in defence of the social.

Although they moved and acted in some form of bodily cohesion, activists
had not yet transformed their mobilisation into a more abstract, creative and
prefigurative politics, except maybe for witty and captivating slogans and graffiti. In terms of the spatiality of politics during the height of the clashes, protestors were collectively trespassing and even 'liberating from the police' various
streets of Taksim, yet they were not necessarily appropriating or 'occupying' it
as a space of collective existence, a space of 'we'. Except for allowing the crowds
to improvise the division of labour and take momentary decisions for survival,
the streets of the Gezi Episode were not yet conducive to a political community with a rich depository of abstract ideas or creative interactions for a new
society. Barricades were erected to defend a particular area from an imminent
police attack, but not yet to build a new 'common' within it.

And yet, it was the direct and violent confrontations on the street that not
only raised the visibility of the movement (and desirability of the cause) but
also kindled in the protesters a sense of togetherness and potential to collectively imagine a different politics. The action on the street opened up a space

for 'side-by-side-ness', 'shoulder-to-shoulder-ness' – in the true sense of the words – for those from all walks of life (Özgür, 2013). It was again on the sidewalks and roads where they were pursued, maced and gassed by the apparatuses of state repression, the memorialisation of which, as moments of injustice, violence, martyrdom and victory, would later fortify a collective identity and solidarity throughout the Episode. This was experienced most intensely in this 'motionary phase' of the Episode as 'other streets' in different parts of the city (and the country) connected/identified/associated with the 'first street' through the slogan 'everywhere is Taksim, resistance everywhere'.

The importance of the street on the politicisation of the activists during the Episode did not come from being merely remembered as the site of glorious and heroic moments of collective resistance against police brutality. Streets (and activism they hosted) were also reconsidered and reimagined – especially in park forums, neighbourhood solidarities and squat houses where self-reflection meetings took place – as a potential refuge for reinvigorating activism in times of dormancy (S. B., personal communication, 10 July 2015). These reflections and deliberations transformed street activism into various and novel forms, such as the GasMan (*GazdanAdam*) and ForumFest festivals or 'Earth Tables' (*Yeryüzü Sofraları*) as outdoor fast-breaking dinners (*iftar*) to protest the lavish meals in luxurious hotels during the month of Ramadan, in addition to commemorations and rallies where activists could forge a strong sense of mobilisation and solidarity. In other words, the accumulated political experience on the streets transformed the individual and collective consciousness of the activists and broadened their political imagination, which in turn transformed the streets and their political potential.

Taksim Square / Gezi Park

Contentious politics takes a different turn when streets calm down and activists settle in an open public space, such as a square (as in Tahrir or Syntagma) or a park (as in Zuccotti), often around a monument or a place with historical or cultural significance, drawing on (and reinforcing) the latter's symbolic power. In Istanbul, too, a new form of spatial politics began to emerge when protestors congregated first in Taksim Square and then in the adjacent Gezi Park, forming and embodying a spatial concentration with 'dual-foci' during the two weeks of occupation. While political subjectification of the crowds had already been under way during clashes on the streets and behind barricades, a peculiar politicisation process was set in motion in this new spatial setting defined by – somewhat paradoxically – the openness and visibility of the square and orderliness and partial shelter of the park (Batuman, 2013b). It was here in the square/park that the shared discontent and frustration that initially assembled groups of otherwise politically unaffiliated and loosely (if at all) connected individuals as a mass were being translated into a discourse of courage, victory and solidarity as the foundations of a new political modality and subjectivity.

With the threat of street violence subsiding, more people were attracted to Gezi Park, curious about or willing to participate in daily activities of the camp, enriching the multitude and paving the way for more 'shared intimacy' and 'unforgettable moments' among activists. The overwhelming majority of the activists concentrated in the square/park were not previously affiliated with any political group or organisation (Uluğ & Acar, 2014). In this 'sedentary phase of activism', new interactions (whose seeds had already been sown while the activists were in 'survival mode' during street mobilisation) between the occupants became the first steps towards a new form of collectivity, transforming the square/park into a different form of 'resist-space' (Çetin, 2016) and opening it up for a more stable and intensified form of solidarity.

Although the square/park offered a less vulnerable space for establishing this new type of solidarity than the street thanks to its stable and steady presence, the possibility that the occupation could always be purged by the police, or that the campers would be forced to leave due to physical or weather conditions, added some level of precarity to the emerging politics. Moreover, the fact that many activists in the park did not belong to a political organisation and lacked conventional organisational skills (Konda, 2014, pp. 14–17) as well as the necessary historical or contemporary reservoir of knowledge (except maybe the inspiration they could draw from infamous cases, such as the Paris Commune) regarding mechanisms, rules and institutions of survival in an occupation, made the camp even more volatile for political engagement. While this precarity helped keep the mobilisational dynamic of the Episode alive in this phase, it progressively subsided and the campsite adopted more established patterns of producing and reproducing life with routine – even banal – spatial functions of maintenance (such as picking up the trash, distributing food, maintaining the library, and so on) that required collective organisation and division of labour. Parts of the square/park became functional as they were designated as library, infirmary, kitchen, and miscellaneous spaces for concerts, sports, yoga, childcare and forum meetings.

Yet this spatial pattern was producing much more than a mere sense of 'colourfulness' and 'vibrancy' in the park, as it was mostly depicted by sympathisers, for a different type of harmony was now emerging from the occupation: not the harmony of moving bodies clashing with police on the street, but of daily practices (eating, sleeping, talking, dancing, cooking, cleaning together in addition to discussing political matters), which complemented each other and fomented a sense of togetherness. According to Batuman, the architecture of the space became an important factor in shaping this occupation-based activism. The degree of openness of the public space (whether square versus pedestrian zone) or the layout of the 'street furniture' (benches, steps, walls, shades) could allow certain activities (protest, sustenance and recreation) while inhibiting others (Batuman, 2018, p. 124).

In the following two weeks, there emerged within Gezi Park spaces that touched and interpenetrated each other, and the activists occupying these spaces were being transformed into individuals with fluid roles and political identities through joining and then disconnecting from these spaces depending on how they utilised (or became a part of) the latter's functions (Karakaş, 2018). The emerging and constantly evolving spatial patterns of interaction facilitated 'a kind of federalist mode of assembly, enabling encounters between different sections, groups and identities who could thereby relate positively to each other, in the first step towards recomposition' (Karakayalı & Yaka, 2014, p. 124). As a place of 'freedom, plurality, anonymity, adventure, entertainment, romance, and commerce' (Benhabib, 2013), the square/park became a site of deliberation and communication as well as socialisation through constitutive, proto-political daily acts of existence. As such, being in (and remaking, repurposing) Gezi Park itself became a political statement: defending and reviving a green space as a way of fighting against the commodification of land, gentrification of the city and theft of the commons.

In other words, the transition from street protests to occupation of the square and encampment in the park signalled the emergence of a new and broader logic of political engagement. As Batuman (2018: 132) observed, the park became a 'constitutive void', an empty space of possibility that allowed different groups with various (sometimes conflicting) agendas to be together and act on their issues side by side. The emerging political community in this political space devised and experimented with methods that prioritised direct, participatory, consensus-driven political engagement in order to tackle issues ranging from the most basic and mundane ('how are we going to collect the trash?') to the most intricate even philosophical ('how are we going to build a new life together?'). In this process, following Balibar's analysis, people were becoming a political category producing politics under the shared banner of equality, freedom and solidarity (mentioned in Dikeç & Swyngedouw, 2017). Eventually, the square/park morphed into a 'power-less' (in terms of the non-presence of state authority) yet not a 'powerless' (in terms of lacking power) space where inhabitants claimed and exercised collective authority.

In that sense, the inability of Taksim Solidarity to orchestrate the occupation and encampment turned out to be a blessing. The park and the square imposed their own conditions of social existence on the activists/occupiers when different stands, workshops, a kitchen, library, infirmary and later yoga areas, vegetable gardens, movie areas, media centres, among other things, began to appear almost organically and out of necessity, without the intervention of any central commanding heights. It was the necessities of occupying a space and surviving in it that conditioned the course of politics.

All in all, thanks to their unique spatiality, Taksim Square and Gezi Park became sites where radical imagination of a new and dynamic political community began to be seriously experimented with for the first time during the Gezi Episode. The plural, participatory, prefigurative and radical democratic activism emerging from the square/park transformed the 'protestor' on the street and the 'occupant' and 'visitor' in the park into political subjects (Batuman, 2018, pp. 136–7). This novel democratic experience incubated in this distinct setting paved the way for a more stable and coordination-based activism in which individuals assumed multiple responsibilities and identities, which they would later carry into their loose allegiances to and flexible engagements with park forums, neighbourhood solidarities and squat houses in different parts of the city.

Public Park Forums and Neighbourhood Solidarities

At some point during contemporary urban uprisings, the multitude in the square/park retreats to (and penetrates into) the inner veins of the city, either by force (police dispersing/clearing the camp site) or by choice when certain groups separate from the main assembly. As we saw in Chapter 3, during the Gezi Episode two big forums – Abbasağa Park forum on the European side and Yoğurtçu Park forum on the Anatolian side of the city – emerged after the police raided the camp in Gezi Park. The unique experiences and novel political practices developed during the two weeks in Gezi Park were carried over into these major parks, yet with one notable difference: activists no longer occupied or camped in the parks but would come to forum meetings and other activities and then leave.

As the imminent danger of police violence subsided, more people began to join these forums in numerous public parks scattered across the city and became involved in the committees and workshops emerging from them. In this 'residentiary phase' of activism (when it was primarily the residents of a locality who were involved in activism), despite being designed as a site of rec-reation, the park was – once more – transformed into a site of politics through debates, discussions, vigils and other forms of political acts. Yet, these two functions (recreation and politics) did not sit in contradiction: rather, the park retained its recreational aspect in harmony with the 'political spirit' carried over from the occupation of Gezi Park. Film screenings, plays, concerts, pic-nics, *Yeryüzü Sofraları* during Ramadan, conversations with political or cul-tural public figures as well as with experts on certain topics, and other activities all contributed to the joy of collective existence with a political twist, blurring the difference between politics and recreation. Issues addressed in these meet-ings included national, global and sometimes even philosophical questions. However, unlike Gezi Park, which became a symbol and major signifier of national resistance during the Gezi Episode (despite the fact that the area's his-torical, cultural and urban characteristics left a stamp on the form of politics that emerged in the park), political activism in these public parks was becom-ing increasingly 'localised', especially as the actual residents of the neighbour-hoods and districts in which these parks were located began to join the forums, carrying with them agendas and issues concerning their community. The idea of organising in the neighbourhoods and 'embracing/appropriating the space in which we lived' was overshadowing broader, more general proposals, such as 'extending the movement to the rural parts of the country' (Bakçay, 2013).

As politics in these forums slowly lost its defensive character and constant vigilance inherited from Taksim Square and Gezi Park, a new type of political agency and subjectivity began to emerge. Although principles of direct, horizontal, diverse and consensus-based political action were brought from Gezi Park into these other parks, the overarching feeling in the forums was no longer occupying a public space through camping but intentionally reappropriating/utilising this space in service of imagining a novel form of politics. While the forum in the park was still open and visible, and bodies were still vulnerable to outside threats as they were during the occupation of Gezi Park, political activism in the park was becoming more structured, coordinated and systematised with pre-planned meetings and scheduled activities. Participants – the composition of whom was becoming increasingly predictable – began to assume more stable (though never obvious, static or formal) roles and responsibilities. Over time, politics in the forums began to look and feel more routine and less ambitious (if not disenchanted) with regard to the 'motionary phase' of the Episode (defined by confrontational character and survival urgency), which faded as the main propeller of activism.

Despite this common trait, however, the spatial and historical features of the neighbourhood also left their mark on the character of the politics emerging from specific park forums. For instance, the forum in Cihangir Park – a historically non-Muslim neighbourhood that had seen the worst of the gentrification driving away low-income residents as well as students and trans sex workers – would bring to the fore these elements in formulating its radical democratic politics (Atılgan, 2013). Similarly, the overall activist dynamism in forums in Okmeydanı and Nurtepe (both relatively low income, blue-collar neighbourhoods with a considerable Alevi population) or the forum in Kartal (which used to be known as 'little Moscow' or 'communist nursery' in the 1970s thanks to the Alevi and Kurdish communities settling there to work in the burgeoning factories) stood in stark contrast with forums in Maçka (one of the most expensive neighbourhoods whose residents were among the most fervent supporters of secular, Westernised lifestyles), in Sarıyer (another upper middle-class neighbourhood that had seen the environmental consequences – along with increasing real estate value – of the AKP's 'crazy projects' such as the third bridge on the Bosporus and the Istanbul Airport), or in Etiler (a well-off neighbourhood whose residents often have higher than average educational level due to the proximity to Boğaziçi University) (Atılgan, 2013; Bakçay, 2013; Baysal, 2013; Çuhadar, 2013; Dinler, 2013; Gülün, 2013; Karakaş, 2013; Kibar & Tatari, 2013b; Özdemir, 2013).

Although big park forums never turned into fully bureaucratic social movement organisations or completely lost their creative and prefigurative character, and could still hang onto their direct, horizontal, pluralist and consensus-oriented radical democratic principles, they began to lose their initial appeal to the activists who were eager and excited to continue their mission after being forcefully expelled from Gezi Park. One of the main reasons for the fading interest in the forums was that activists and other participants were increasingly disillusioned by 'a lot of talk but no action' that had been going on in the parks (O. B., personal communication, 10 August 2015). In Yoğurtçu Forum, for instance, some established political groups (especially leftist groups such as the Turkish Communist Party, TKP, and some hard-core Kemalists) tried to impose on the crowd their 'ready-made political analyses and solutions', alienating those who were yearning for a different politics (Z. U., personal communication, 16 July 2015). As this attempt failed time and again, they left the group altogether, causing loss of interest and diversity, turning the forum into a place where the like-minded enjoyed the pleasure of always being on the same page.

As a result, big park forums saw a progressive decline in the number of participants following the initial euphoria of the summer of 2013. During my field work in Yoğurtçu Forum from 2014 to 2016, where the attendance dramatically fell from hundreds of participants to 15–20, the need to address the issue had become more pressing (M. C. B., personal communication, 29 June 2016). And yet, a paradoxical situation emerged for the activists who felt the urgency to tackle the diminishing impact and relevance of park forums. On the one hand, in line with the overall tendency, issues tackled in the forums were becoming increasingly local. In the Yoğurtçu Forum, for instance, issues concerning the Kadıköy district (such as the rehabilitation of *Kurbağalıdere* brook which passes through the district) became the centre of political activism. On the other hand, the forum could become 'alive' again only when its – what its participants defined as – 'calling power' (*çağrı gücü*) was activated in relation to some form of street action triggered by issues that were anything but local (more on *çağrı gücü* in Chapter 5). Protesting the escalation of Israel's violence against Palestinians, commemorating the death of Berkin Elvan (a 15-year-old boy who was hit on the head by a tear-gas canister fired by the police during the heyday of the uprising in the Okmeydanı district of Istanbul) after he was in a coma for months or protesting the murder of Medeni Yıldırım (who was killed by soldiers while protesting the construction of a new police station in the Lice district of Diyarbakır) were moments when Yoğurtçu Forum could reach out to (and mobilise) hundreds of people and would replenish its 'prestige' with the attendance to the forum soaring again following such a protest or an event.

In other words, tensions emerging from the way spatiality of politics in public parks played itself out, that is, how the evolution of politics in the forum towards more localisation was in stark contrast with the increasing need to 'return to streets' for mobilising the masses, began to be seriously felt by the political community: politics that was localised in a 'real (physical) space' of the local park was increasingly in conflict with the 'higher-level politics' of an 'imagined national space'. The incompatibility of issues tackled in the forum, and the mismatch between the scale, discourse and vision of political activism appropriate for local and national spaces began to condition the imagination, horizon and potential of the political community, a theme to which I will return in Chapter 6.

Over time, the number of activists who felt that larger forums were not suitable for addressing pressing local matters soared (A. D., personal communication, 4 August 2016). That the primacy of the local gained more currency among an increasing number of activists, a trend exacerbated by the surfacing of ideological disagreements and personal animosities, further diminished the power of big forums in holding distinct groups together within a broad political frame. Heated disputes regarding the scale of politics and the appropriateness of the space to address the issues at hand sometimes led to controversial break-ups. In the case of Yoğurtçu Forum, the diversity and plurality took a hit when participation declined, leaving the forum with a small number of similar-minded people while intensifying the proliferation of smaller neighbourhood solidarities.

The beginnings of the above-mentioned shift in scale, scope and locus of spatial politics with the branching off of small neighbourhood solidarities from bigger forums can be traced all the way back to the occupation of Gezi Park, and later to Abbasağa and Yoğurtçu Parks, when many activists gravitated towards developing creative forms of activism on particular issues through sub-committees and study groups. In Yoğurtçu Forum, for instance, many work-shops and thematic groups were established in the first couple of weeks (Y. L., personal communication, 16 July 2014). Yet these early groups were consid-ered to be complementary to, and in harmony with, the broader (and what was believed to be mutual) political vision rising from the park. In some cases, some of these sub-committees or study groups would report back to the larger forum that would ensure coordination in the broader movement. Neighbour-hood solidarities that broke off from big park forums, such as Abbasağa and Yoğurtçu, however, were often an expression of the growing 'disenchantment' with the forums' inability to address what some activists considered to be the 'real issues' that affected the lives of the residents in that neighbourhood. It was the pressing problems and urgent matters concerning the place where they were located that made activists believe these neighbourhood solidarities had to be the primary focus.

Any local issue could become a vehicle to promote and mobilise a critical, dissenting politics. For instance, efforts to prevent a neighbourhood school from closure or conversion into a religious school, such as the 'Don't Touch My School' (*Okuluma Dokunma*) campaigns or resisting the demolition of public woods or forests, the most famous of which was the Validebağ grove, could easily garner support from residents for successful political mobilisation. In other words, as the residentiary phase of activism gained more prominence, the scale and the centre of politics shifted to local even more and began to lose its anonymity and improvisational character that had empowered the diverse crowds at the beginning of the Episode. This shift not only changed the num-ber and composition of the activists involved in this political mobilisation but also fundamentally shaped their sense of belonging and political subjectivity. It would be unthinkable that such a shift in the process of politicisation would not be influenced by the physical conditions of, and the social relations within, the space it occupied. As Kuryel and Fırat put it:

> As the scale got smaller, the number of participants and distances bridged
> decreased. Local initiatives served as excuses to get together with familiar faces

rather than places to encounter strangers. The ever-changing face of the crowd gave way to existing proximities within communities. (Kuryel & Fırat, 2020).

Buildings: Squat Houses and Others

It was not only open spaces, such as squares or parks, but also buildings and other built environments that played a crucial role in producing unique forms and processes of politicisation during the Gezi Episode. Among these, squat houses had a special place.

Squatting has long been a part of urban social movements through creating autonomous spaces where private property and other fundamental principles of capitalism were questioned (and suspended) and where radical and prefigurative political imagination could materialise in real life despite facing the danger of state persecution for its unlawful nature (Rittersberger-Tılıç, 2015, pp. 87–8). In squat houses, life and politics fuse into a new mode of social organisation, and alternative ways of existence emerging from this experience become tangible expressions of the very critique of (and opposition to) the established social and political order. The underlying defiance (appropriating a built-space through extra-legal means) ascribes a romantic, almost 'Quixotic', character to squatting. The anarchist, autonomist and socialist roots of squatting have to date provided numerous historical and wide-ranging geographical examples to draw on for activists all over the world (Vasudevan, 2023).

During the Gezi Episode, partly because of the impossibility of continuing outdoor meetings due to weather conditions, two buildings located in two neighbourhoods in the Kadıköy district were occupied: Don Kişot Social Centre and Caferağa Community House (Kural, 2013; Yılmaz et al., 2020). These were run-down, abandoned buildings in these neighbourhoods, which were struggling with the impact of gentrification (Resneck, 2014). Their occupation by activists reignited the thrill and enthusiasm that accompanied the feelings of occupying a space, rejecting authoritarianism and rebuilding the world, all of which ran deep during the early days of the Gezi occupation, yet progressively declined afterwards at forum meetings in public parks and neighbourhood gatherings. In that sense, as was the case with the occupation of Gezi Park, squatting was a performative act of direct political confrontation with the system: it was not solely reclaiming ownership and socialising a space but also awakening, inspiring and organising the public to demand democratic, equal, inclusive collective existence against the exclusion and discrimination of privatised, compartmentalised, commodified life (Gezen, 2014).

Most of the groups and individuals that established these squat houses in Kadıköy broke off from the Yoğurtçu Forum mainly because they realised that the spatial characteristics of parks in general, and the politics emerging from there in particular, were not conducive to the total transformation of life and building the social relations of which they were dreaming. The very characteristics of political mobilisation in the park (such as meeting on specified schedules, discussing pre-decided topics, carrying out pre-determined tasks for organising events, developing calculated methods and strategies) were giving way to a certain type of politicisation that would not suit squat houses. Daily needs and practical tasks of survival in the house necessitated direct, horizontal, participatory and often improvised acts, which in turn paved the way for intimate collectivity and served as the foundation of shared political imagination (Yılmaz et al., 2020). In all decisions and actions in the house – from determining the needs of the house to establishing relations with the residents of the neighbourhood, from organising events to deciding about the house's political stance on various issues – voluntarism, consensus and solidarity were at the forefront. The distinction between life and politics became blurred as these two were being reformulated on the principle of building the 'common' (Sandıkçı & Yılmaz, 2014; Ülger et al., 2014).

The way that the houses were organised internally also became an important factor in the type of politics emerging from the squatting experience. In accordance with its claim to be a 'social centre', Don Kişot squat house, for instance, had spaces in it designated to certain workshops, movie screenings or repurposed as a library, in addition to more intimate spaces for eating, cooking or simply hanging out, including a larger room for throwing a party for kids. The walls would display art from local artists or otherwise would depict current events, such as pictures of Berkin Elvan and other Gezi 'martyrs'. There was a room reserved for women only, and a small vegetable garden was created on the roof. Activities in the house were geared towards building community, which even included hosting a wedding (Fırat et al., 2021).

While they were imagining and constructing the political along the principles of autonomy and self-governance, activists in squat houses would at times breach the local and national political frame to reach out to their global counterparts (Koç, 2015, pp. 181–3; Rittersberger-Tılıç, 2015). Yet beyond providing the activists with merely a sanctuary for nurturing their translocal links, these squat houses were first and foremost a point of contact with the residents of the neighbourhoods they were in (Araman, 2013). This was especially important as a close relationship was developing between the squat house (and its occupants) and the neighbourhood: on the one hand, activists in the squat house saw their conception of politics being shaped in line with the issues, needs and expectations (but also with the dominant characteristics and tendencies) of the neighbourhood and formulated their political action following the feedback they received. Over time, squat houses became a more integral part of the neighbourhood, acting as a resource for residents, helping them with their issues and needs, or otherwise acting as a space of solidarity around issues concerning the neighbourhood (Fırat et al., 2021). These would include initiatives like organising birthday parties for kids, 'Ashura Days' (*Aşure Günleri* – a day of commemoration in Islam), 'shop local' campaigns, events for raising awareness for alcoholism, and others (O. S., personal communication, 11 August 2015). On the other hand, they could instil the idea of a 'different world' in the hearts and minds of the residents with whom they constantly interacted through film screenings, workshops, small charity bazaars, and other forms that would offer them an alternative radical perspective of co-existence in the neighbourhood (Yılmaz et al., 2020). In other words, the squat house became a space of political encounter at the heart of the city that had the potential to transform both the occupants of the house and residents of the neighbourhood.

As spaces of politics, squat houses were an important part of the politicisation of the activists during the Gezi Episode, yet they were hardly the only built environments that became political. As early as the fall of 2013, one of the cultural locations in Kadıköy district, Barış Manço Cultural Centre, began hosting forum and committee meetings. This and the other buildings – some of which were designed as residential or commercial spaces, while others served as arts, culture or sports complexes – became the loci of a different form of politics than that of the neighbourhood or park politics due to their enclosed nature and not being an organic extension of city flows, unlike a street, square or park.

The possibilities of politics and the contours of emerging political identities as well as the horizon of political imagination in a building are conditioned by its architectural, infrastructural and functional characteristics. Moreover, while the rigidity of the built environment gives a sense of order, its adaptability to variable politics through 'altering' or 'repurposing' its structure is weak. The political imagination in this space is often confined to the physical limits of the room in which the fixed form of the space dictates the course of the political process rather than the other way around. What emerges is a new type of political mobilisation and experience identified with abstract thinking and planned deliberations instead of freely experimenting with the space and prefiguratively repurposing its physical set up as the inspiration for direct political action.

During the Gezi Episode, too, moving into a building (unless it was a squat house) disconnected forum activists from the natural environment. Meetings in these buildings were often much smaller in number than those in a park or on a street. But more important than losing numbers, when Yoğurtçu and other forums began to meet in Barış Manço Cultural Centre and other buildings, they lost their visibility in the demarcated and hardwired space. The loss of visibility to the public led to further deterioration in diversity and plurality because only those who were previously informed of a meeting at that specific time and place were able to take part in the process despite the availability of social media as communication tools to reach out to a broader audience. The politicisation process and its outcomes emerging from such a setting (which were confined to those who already knew each other, and did not allow for any surprise encounters, contingencies or flexibility for unforeseen incidences) was in sharp contrast with the ways in which activists were used to conducting politics (that is, in the open, haphazardly, side by side with 'strangers', responding to the practical needs of the moment, and so on) during the protests on the streets, or in the campsite during the occupation of Gezi Park, or in a neighbourhood park.

It was ironic that Barış Manço Cultural Centre would later become home to many meetings of Birleşik Haziran which tried to establish itself as a national political movement to transform the energy rising from the Gezi rebellion (more on Birleşik Haziran in Chapter 6). The irony was due to the fact that by catering to Birleşik Haziran, the building would become the space of returning to 'politics as usual', that is, the loss of authenticity and uniqueness of the Gezi Episode that arose as early as the very first clashes on the streets of Taksim. It was this disillusionment with politics that had drawn the activists into the streets in the first place. Limited in its scope and performative or prefigurative possibilities, the spatiality of politics enacted in a room or a building weakened the mobilisational dynamic of politics that it enjoyed outside, and it morphed into performances and intellectual (if not didactic) practices for the more privileged who could 'fit in there' – which became yet another factor for possible suspicion, intimidation and probable exclusion of diverse groups and individuals.

The Implications of the Spatiality of the Gezi Episode for a New Political Community

The previous chapter laid out how the mobilisational dynamic of the Gezi Episode galvanised various social groups to engage in different yet complementary forms of political activism to oppose neoliberal urbanisation. This state of constant mobilisation, along with deepening translocal connections with other movements around the world, conferred on activists 'fluid' political identities with which they could join – and disconnect from – different forms of activism, enabling new and strengthening existing bonds of solidarity among each other. The spatiality of the Gezi Episode discussed in this chapter confirmed yet complicated this picture by demonstrating that the urban setting in which this political mobilisation took place was not uniform or monolithic, but rather taking place in a spatial matrix composed of distinct sites, such as streets, squares, parks, neighbourhoods and buildings. During the Gezi Episode, a particular constellation of 'space-activism-subjectivity' would emerge in each site, which – with its unique spatial characteristics – would foster a particular form of political mobilisation (and hence nurture a particular form of political imagination) while inhibiting others. In this process, urban sites in which different modes of political activism took place made the emerging political identities among activists more tangible and sensory but also more fluid. As new forms of camaraderie were experienced in real space, the sites themselves became 'fluid spaces': assemblies of political subjects who knew the city and its needs and problems by heart and who became part of the struggle to build common counterspaces against neoliberal urbanisation by making themselves available in different capacities in different places.

The fluidity of space in this political process emerged in two ways: on the one hand, an urban site could hold the power to attract and assemble – in line with its spatial characteristics and with the political possibilities it availed – political subjects with diverse set of capacity, status and political visions. That is, activists whose political subjectification took different forms as they moved from one space to another during the Episode could overcome their differences and disagreements as they joined the political struggle at a site and adapted themselves to the needs and expectations of the political mobilisation (and emerging political imaginations) in this particular site. On the other hand, as these activists could appear in any of these 'space-activism-subjectivity' constellations almost instantaneously thanks to their increasingly flexible political identities, they could intensify the relations and connections between the sites of the movement and synchronise their politics. For instance, during the Gezi Episode the same activist could go through different stages of political subjectification by appearing almost simultaneously on the streets of Taksim (as a protestor), in Gezi Park (as a medic), in Yeldeğirmeni squat house (as a washer in the kitchen), in one or more of the neighbourhood solidarities in Kadıköy (as the person in charge of the social media account) and in Barış Manço Centre (as a delegate for the Birleşik Haziran movement). What emerged from this was an assemblage in which various instances of political mobilisation against neoliberal urbanisation were realised by activists whose political subjectification and emerging identities transformed and were being transformed by these very sites.

What does this spatial fluidity mean for the emerging political community? If community is a spatial experience rather than an extension of allegedly 'natural' relations and traditional bonds (Blokland, 2012), then many experiences of political activism during the Gezi Episode heralded the possibility for the emergence of a unique political community: one that was made up of political subjects who could travel from one urban site to another and adapt (and contribute) to the particular form of political struggle in each site while at the same time being shaped (and demarcated) by the political horizons these sites offered. This was a dynamic community that formed and dissolved almost instantaneously and existed in multiple scales and spaces as it occupied, embodied and travelled through different urban sites, each of which fostered (or hindered) certain types of emancipatory vision. During the Gezi Episode, political subjects joined and left many such communities, contributing to the recognition and implementation of an array of different political imaginations (and utopias) while at the same time being transformed by these visions. These sites, in other words, became immanent spaces 'for nurturing political subjectivation, mediating political encounter, staging interruption and experimentally producing new forms of democratisation that prefigure radical imaginaries of what urban democratic being-in-common might be all about' (Dikeç & Swyngedouw, 2017, p. 3). In this process, activists not only found no contradiction in belonging to multiple spaces and their politics at once, but they also became more flexible in accepting and tolerating different political views as they flowed from one space to another as a part of the ongoing mobilisation, paving the way for a peculiar sense of solidarity and common purpose around the idea of a collectively inhabitable city. These spaces, in one way or other, 'transform[ed] otherwise unconnected people into a "commun-ity"' (Gambetti, 2009, p. 106).

Focusing on the nuances in the relationship between urban sites and the characteristics of activism they enable, and on the fluidity of the political actors, which allows them to easily traverse through – if not simultaneously exist within – different sites, helps us understand what binds different participants or activists together or prevents them from building those bounds, which ultimately determines the character of the emerging political community and urban citizenship. During the Gezi Episode, it was in these spaces that the movement nurtured many dreams and visions for a democratic future and negotiated 'the terms of the common' as the basis of reconstituting the social against the neoliberal assault on society. In the next chapter, I will delve deeper into the characteristics of these 'emancipatory visions' emerging in the fluid spaces of the Gezi Episode, transcending what emerged as an urban defence into a broader community-building agenda around the idea of 'the common'.

5

RADICAL DEMOCRACY: THE GEZİ EPISODE AS BUILDING THE COMMON

What kind of politics was likely to emerge from this intense experience of urban insurgency in Istanbul? What model of community could one expect when constant political mobilisation as a part of a global wave of radical activism guided and nurtured a new sense of solidarity in a variety of politicised sites in the city? In this chapter, I turn to the third dynamic of the global movement wave of the early 2010s that aimed to reconstitute the social in the face of neoliberal assault on the city and its diverse urban population: *radical democracy*. I argue that in our current juncture democracy gets 'radicalised' when practices, expressions and enactments of a new form of solidarity and citizenship do not emerge in a void but as a continuous and globally connected mobilisation in different corners of the city. The Gezi Episode is no different. First, as we saw in Chapter 3, the contentious politics during the Episode belonged to a global movement cycle guided by questions of recognition, democracy, urban sustainability and ecological survival as well as those of inequality and dispossession. This particular mode of mobilisation shaped activists' identity as well as their perception of others and politics in general. Second, as discussed in Chapter 4, it was the spaces of everyday life in the city that became lines of defence against the destruction of the political and dismantlement of the social. As Istanbul was becoming a site of coercive capital accumulation under neoliberal urbanisation, the loci of social conflict diffused into the veins of the city, which in turn shaped practices of contestation, resistance and imaginaries for a new society (Kapsali & Tsavdaroglou, 2016). In other words, it was only when the radical democratic imagination of 'peaceful co-existence in diversity and plurality' rhymed with these two dynamics (*mobilisational* and *spatial*) that the cultivation of a new model of belonging, solidarity and urban citizenship became a possibility in the Gezi Episode. It was at the heart of the co-constitutive relationship between direct, horizontal, consensus-driven, emancipatory practices of radical democracy on the one hand, and the emergence of the 'insurgent/militant' citizen as the essential constituent of a new political community on the other that we find 'the common'.

Radical Democracy and Contemporary Social Movements

Radical Democracy

Radical democracy can be defined as 'a normative political project which brings together a series of contingent demands and identities in order to challenge relations of domination and oppression' (Howarth & Roussos, 2022, p. 3). In the context of social movements, radical democracy comprises a body of anticapitalist practices around principles of horizontalism, pluralism, autonomy and direct action without a central structure or leadership, rather than making claims for the rectification of the system. It is the operating mode of diverse groups who redefine the idea of 'organisation' as coming together, collaborating and collectively taking decisions in the course of contentious politics. A unique type of active citizenry is thus born 'through successful democratic political activism, where citizens see their engagements as contributing to their own and societies' self-constitution' (Dahlberg, 2013).

It is important to highlight that the values, practices and organisational forms of radical democracy of the recent wave of social movements were not only different from the methods, principles and institutions of representative liberal democracy. They were also different from pure deliberations, mental exercises or abstract formulations for 'radicalising' democracy in 'regular times'. Rather, they emerged as concrete solutions to urgent needs of the community (food kitchens, infirmaries, childcare centres and others) to remedy the damages inflicted by neoliberal urbanisation. While offering a critique 'of the suspension of political practice and participation [and] of the cementing of political inequality' (Volk, 2021, p. 439), these practices were the very ways of self-organising and social reproduction on the ground

(Howarth & Roussos, 2022, p. 4). The radical democratic character of contentious politics thus revealed the 'constitutive' capacity of the demos to replace an old, oppressive, dysfunctional social order with a collectively imagined one (Celikates, 2021, pp. 129–30). In other words, with their direct, participatory and deliberative style of politics, horizontal organisation and consensual decision-making, contemporary social movements aimed to revolutionise the social, political, and economic order in which democracy was re-appropriated, re-invented and radicalised according to the needs of the community at a particular place and time.

During the occupations of squares in Athens and Spain, for instance, 'autonomy' and 'direct democracy' were often contrasted not just against parliamentary politics but also against traditional leftist and formal union politics (Prentoulis & Thomassen, 2013). In other places, too, the rise of 'popular power' meant that people rejected hierarchical structures while deliberating among and taking care of themselves. They were not mere rank-and-file in existing organisations but organisers and protagonists who, engaging in a thick politics of trust and friendship as their guiding principle of activism, would pursue an autonomous yet inclusive type of politics to prefigure a new community (Sitrin & Azzellini, 2014, ch. 1). Different variations and combinations of initiatives including autonomous workers' councils, participatory budgeting, neighbourhood committees, encampments, debate facilitation groups, rejection of electoral politics and numerous mutual aid initiatives (soup kitchens, barter exchanges, cooperatives) emerged over a broad geography, including various iterations of Occupy Wall Street in the US and beyond (Press, 2013; Szolucha, 2016), in Brazil (Baiocchi, 2005), Spain (Nez, 2016), Greece (Oikonomakis & Ross, 2016), Argentina (Sitrin, 2012), Venezuela (Sitrin & Azzellini, 2014), South Korea (Lee, 2022), Egypt (Olivier, 2014) and other regions in the Middle East and North Africa during the Arab Spring (Brownlee & Ghiabi, 2016). What united all these different experiences was the widely shared belief among activists that existing systems of political participation would not bring about true liberation. They needed a different, more organic principle of composition.

Assembly

The *assembly* emerged to respond to this need in social movements, both as the means and the end, and the method and theory of radical democracy.

Collective decision-making in open and participatory spaces regarding every-day needs of the community turned assemblies into the locus as well as the primary motor of self-governance. Occupying a square, erecting camps in a park, and collectively 'grounding' democracy – on which the assembly was predicated – became a material force behind and a concrete experience of a 'future in the present' (della Porta, 2014a, p. 57). Radical forms of political practice in the assembly were at once: (a) spatial practices with no predeter-mined strategies or designated leaders, and in which a diverse set of political activities co-existed without dominating each other; and (b) expressions of an amorphous political subject that offered an alternative form of existence against neoliberal urbanisation. As such, the activism practised in assemblies offered a powerful vision of an alternative society – one in which citizens were no longer imagined as consumers or entrepreneurs under the yoke of neoliberalism but were part of a collectivity connected through reciprocity and solidarity through creating new spaces of production and reproduction outside the realm of the state and capital (Sitrin, 2012, pp. 173–4).

Realising radical democracy in the assembly, by definition, involves deliberation – a lot of it (Polletta, 2002). As such, it helps people to escape from their isolation, offering refuge from atomisation and a way out of igno-rance about one another (Butler, 2014, p. xiii). Yet, assemblies also emerge 'to deliver a bodily demand for a more liveable set of economic, political condi-tions no longer afflicted by induced forms of precarity' (Butler, 2015, p. 11). They become an important part – if not the centre – of the critique and refu-tation of the neoliberal logic of promoting the 'individual responsibility', and prefigure a 'distinct ethical and social alternative' (Butler, 2015, p. 16). When bodies assemble in plurality, they define, produce and lay claim to the 'pub-lic' by seizing, reconfiguring and refunctioning the materiality of the space (Butler, 2015, p. 71). In Staal's words, 'the assembly is simultaneously a direct expression of the condition of precarity and a protest against it [. . .] when the precariat gathers its bodies in the form of an assembly, it also gains the potential to propose alternatives to the regimes that have forced it into this assembly in the first place' (Staal, 2017). Hence:

> a popular assembly is more substantive than just a meeting that is open to all
> residents. [It] is a political institution, where the whole point of the assembly

itself is to be the most important decision-making institution in the area where it is located [in order] to create a directly democratic polity that can challenge the prevailing powers. (Legard, 2011)

It was this spatial practice through which 'deliberation' in assembly movements was supplemented with 'direct action' that turned assembly into a 'political space in which citizens engage with each other to redress issues that states fail to address' (della Porta & Felicetti, 2018, p. 264). It also became an 'intentional' space where previously underrepresented groups could have their voices be heard and a truly plural grassroots activism could flourish (Juris, 2013). In the attempt to achieve these objectives, assembly politics did not succumb to universal principles or agreeable compromises in the liberal sense, but produced creative, innovative, experimental and experiential radical action, which gave the activism its prefigurative character (Breckman, 2020). Reciprocal recognition, improvised action, inclusive decision-making and consensus-building allowed the assembly to be able to establish relations of trust and cross-fertilisation among individuals, ideologies and activisms around common objectives and effectively address seemingly local or isolated issues as mutual problems (della Porta & Piazza, 2008, pp. 49–53). In a sense, the 'political', which was reduced to mere 'politics', 'policy-making' and 'policing' in the hands of professional politicians and experts, was brought back to the 'agora' for the benefit of each and every member of the political community (Argın, 2013, pp. 75–6).

Experimentation and constant innovation emerging from countless face-to-face interactions in horizontal, consensus-driven activism in open, inclusive public meetings became the engine of prefigurative politics in assemblies (della Porta & Mattoni, 2014). Specific rules, goal setting and task allocation and implementation allowed activists to experience a fundamentally new political organisation in a radically egalitarian way (Howarth & Roussos, 2022, pp. 10–11). Protocols and etiquette of communication (hand gestures, facilitation and other collectively agreed-upon conventions) paved the way for 'an alternative form of sociality and politics, in which equality was the core value and fundamental telos of social and political relations' (Breckman, 2020). In other words, by organising in – and as – assemblies, social movements of the 2010s rehearsed the kind of radical social change that they aspired to bring about (van de Sande, 2020, p. 398).

Forum

If the principle of assembly lay at the heart of radical democratic activism in contemporary social movements, one primary actualisation, materialisation and expression of assembly politics was the *forum*. Forums became, using Stavrides' words, 'new spaces of solidarity and communication [where] people [were] more able to demand social and economic justice [. . . and where] common space became a kind of performative representation of justice and equality' (Stavrides, 2013, p. 45). In forum meetings, the assembly became a critical element in turning activists into 'a people' when they asserted themselves through various actions (deliberating, silence, decision-making, task allocation, and so on) without reducing these to a single claim (Butler, 2015, pp. 156–7). In other words, a new 'we' was constantly negotiated and reconstituted through mundane daily (yet political) performances and enactments in the forum.

The seeds of first such forums were sown during the Global Justice Movement following the 1999 Seattle protests when various delegates from grassroots organisations as well as activist networks came together to exchange ideas and develop a road map to counter the harm inflicted by the neoliberal financial architecture. While World Social Forums (WSF) collectively worked out a vision for an alternative world (Sen & Waterman, 2007; Smith et al., 2012, 2014), the more inclusive and 'assembly-spirited' forums emerged following the 2008 financial crisis, convening in a broad range of places, from Puerta del Sol in Madrid to Syntagma square in Athens, from Rossio square in Lisbon to Tahrir in Cairo. In this renewed iteration, despite adopting a transnational discourse, forums were more context-specific and rooted in urban settings rather than floating around the planet like the WSF summits. Activists were less embedded in or affiliated to existing organisations and less connected through existing activist networks but instead found each other through individual interactions utilising communication technologies. Forum meetings could at times be long and tiresome, yet the horizontal, participatory, consensual and prefigurative activism went beyond an open market of ideas, or a carnival enjoyed collectively, but morphed into direct encounters between concerned citizens in inclusive and transparent public locations of the city where they formulated and executed concrete solutions to their immediate problems (della Porta, 2015, ch. 5) guided by 'counterhegemonic strains of thought' (Farmer, 2017), that is, a radical democratic vision for an alternative future.

Radical Democracy during the Gezi Episode

During the Gezi Episode, the first such radical political imaginaries began to appear in response to the immediate needs of the camp when activists settled in Gezi Park. Through familiar enactments of radical democracy, the political was reinvented, and the social reconstituted, under a dynamic 'collective reason' – rather than a pre-established 'directive reason' – which guided the activists' actions in the parks, neighbourhoods and other politicised sites of the city.

Radical Democracy as Assembly Politics in Gezi Park and Beyond

With the occupation of Gezi Park, activists and participants began to vocalise their frustration in different corners without reducing these plural voices to a single political language or succumbing to the prescriptions of tired political ideologies. The meetings – in committees formed in Gezi Park and later as a part of big park forums or in neighbourhood solidarities and squat houses – were always open to and inclusive of a variety of intersecting groups, including radical leftist groups, environmentalists, LGBTQIA+, women, Kemalists, anticapitalist Muslims, workers, college students, white-collar employees, and others. Almost a direct replica of her sisters, the park hosted a wide range of diverse ideas mostly from unaffiliated and non-aligned individuals with loose moderation and through special communication protocols. The occupation in Gezi Park became a performative activism lifestyle through the use of thematic workshops, a library, a free health clinic, free kitchens, 'revolution markets' and cafes where no monetary transactions were allowed, a make-shift mosque and yoga sessions and recreational activities for kids, among others. Turks embracing Kurds, soccer fans cursing the police rather than the rival teams, leftist cliques burying their war chests were all signs of a new modality of politics. More importantly, radical practices invented from the very first day of the occupation helped sever a dead part of 'revolutionary politics' that had weighed on most of these individuals who, now in the park, were no longer bothered by the nostalgia for the 'good old days' or by melancholia and pessimism that had consumed the Turkish left since the 1970s (Ersan, 2014, pp. 19–20; İplikçi, 2013, p. 144).

Once again, we find the 'assembly' as the organising principle and distinct expression of these core radical practices during the Gezi Episode. Here, too, various forms of assembly (from workshops and thematic groups to larger meetings) became the primary engine that propelled activism, gave it legitimacy and defined its method and characteristics regardless of the different forms these radical practices took in parks, solidarities or squat houses. Even during the days when a handful environmental activists started camping in Gezi Park to deter a sudden raid of the police and bulldozers to remove the trees, small gatherings had begun to take place to discuss defence strategies and other topics. These initial assemblies would lay the foundations for later forums during the occupation and afterwards. It was at these 'groundings' where people started to get to know each other and establish bonds of solidarity around a common purpose (Fırat, 2013, p. 37). Regardless of the spaces in which they were held, assemblies transformed the tired meanings of and associations with 'political meetings' and redefined even recreational activities, such as picnics or movie screenings, as political acts.

Forums of the Gezi Episode

Public park forums became places where the characteristics and principles of assembly politics were crystallised most notably, following the initial experimentation in Gezi Park. Although early forms of forum-style political activism in Turkey can be traced back to student mobilisations, especially to Resistance Committees (*Direniş Komiteleri*) of the Dev-Yol (Revolutionary Road, *Devrimci Yol*) movement within the radical left during the 1970s (Erdoğan, 2013; Gümrükçü, 2014, p. 224), it was the mobilisational and spatial dynamics of the Gezi Episode that fundamentally shaped the political character of the movement.

Forum meetings were already taking place during the two-week occupation of Gezi Park (Hürriyet Daily News, 2013). Yet more regular and increasingly larger forums would begin following the expulsion of the occupiers from the park (Gezgin, 2013). It was the Abbasağa Forum that first called its meetings 'park assemblies' and became an inspiration to channel the energy from the Gezi uprising into forums that were mushrooming around the country (Bakçay, 2013). Debates on how to organise, or whether becoming an organisation was necessary at all (seeing the inadequacy of existing organisations and the success of the unorganised masses) lasted for days. Social media, once again, became the main venue for communication between forums as well as among members of individual forums. However, attempts for establishing coordination between forums as well as different thematic sub-groups did not morph into a strictly centralised structure. Decisions were taken by consensus, and proposals – if accepted – were expected to be carried out by those who proposed them so that individuals could claim 'ownership' of the issues they brought up. Activists took responsibilities in ad hoc committees, which would dissolve when a task was completed or an issue was resolved (personal observation, Yoğurtçu Forum, 16 July 2014). Despite occasional hiccups, an exercise in direct democracy was in full force (Atılgan, 2013, pp. 14–15).

Staying vigilant and ready for street mobilisation around important local or national events (such as a permit issued by a local municipality to open a park for construction, or a murder at the hands of law enforcement) was an important aspect of forums' activism (personal observation, Yoğurtçu Forum, 16 July 2014). Yet, at a deeper level, it was the 'transformation of life along anti-capitalist principles' that has been the motivating and guiding principle in most of these forums. Activists wanted to revive what they called the 'solidarity economy', where they would engage in a host of creative activism, such as closing bank accounts, encourage shopping with local businesses and overall curbing consumption, organising 'do-it-yourself' style workshops (such as how to brew your own beer) to stop purchasing big brands, establishing exchange markets that would limit money transactions, and founding or supporting non-profit cooperatives, markets and restaurants (Atılgan, 2013, p. 16). Other assembly-oriented radical activism in forums included: inviting politicians, experts, journalists, artists, movie directors, and representatives of various organisations or groups for informative workshops, documentary screenings, establishing thematic groups and sub-committees to tackle local issues, solidarity kitchens and using guerrilla tactics to disrupt the ordinary flow of the economy (for initial reporting from various forums from around the country but mostly from Istanbul, see: Atılgan, 2013; Bakçay, 2013; Baysal, 2013; Çuhadar, 2013; Dinler, 2013; Gülün, 2013; Karakaş, 2013; Kibar & Tatari, 2013b; Özdemir, 2013; Yücel, 2013).

Overall, by rejecting the existing forms of political representation (especially the leadership and hierarchical structures of leftist groups) and by directly acting on ideas regarding alternative forms a democratic community, forums provided a ground for political mobilisation that cut across a variety of social movements and priorities. They 'revealed the possibility of establishing unexpected alliances across a variety of struggles for justice and recognition and, as such, showed the possibilities of transforming polarised debates into pluralised and decentralised public conversations' (Mendonça & Ercan, 2015, p. 279).

Below I focus on the Yoğurtçu Forum in order to trace different modalities of radical politics that emerged during the Gezi Episode. As one of the two forums that appeared in the immediate aftermath of the Gezi Park occupation, it assembled in Yoğurtçu Park in Kadıköy, a middle-class and relatively progressive district on the Anatolian side. Thanks to its long and unique career, the Yoğurtçu Forum could preserve, at least at the beginning, the most militant memories of clashes and first radical enactments of the Gezi movement. More importantly, the way the forum gave way to smaller forums, solidarities and squat houses and then took part in broader political movements, such as Birleşik Haziran, can illuminate the novelties of this radical democratic experience.

Yoğurtçu Forum

The Yoğurtçu Forum started spontaneously when a group of regular attendees of the Abbasağa Forum (which was gathering in Beşiktaş on the European side) decided to replicate the forum experience by gathering in Yoğurtçu Park (S. B., personal communication, 10 July 2015). In a truly improvised way, some of these individuals mobilised to gather the necessary apparatus (such as a sound system and chairs) to ensure a proper open-mic meeting similar to the ones in Abbasağa Forum could be held here, too (Y. O., personal communication, 30 June 30, 2015). The attendees mostly comprised 'learned' (*okumuş*) types (M. U., personal communication, 16 July 2014), a mix of residents in the immediate vicinity that would include those who were involved in leftist politics in various capacities in the past as well as younger white-collar professionals, most of whom had launched their 'political career' with the Gezi riots and the occupation of Gezi Park (Z. U., personal communication, 16 July 2015).

Similar to the forum experience in Gezi Park, Yoğurtçu Forum initially became a platform where people could share their thoughts and sentiments by utilising special communication protocols such as hand signs and gestures, rotating speakers, loose moderation and aiming for consensus rather than majority rule in decisions and so forth. There has been a great effort by those in charge of moderation to prevent the capture of the forum by representatives of political parties and more radical leftist groups with their propaganda using certain banners, slogans and flags (M. C. B., personal communication, 10 July 2015; Z. U., personal communication, 16 July 2015). Forum meetings, which initially took place almost every night, lasted for hours and involved both pragmatic matters (such as the type of action to be taken during certain events or protests) as well as broader political issues. Decisions were taken in the forum, rather than by an executive committee (M. C. B., personal communication, 10 July 2015), remaining true to the radical democratic character of assembly-style politics. Moreover, the forum sometimes hosted guests (politicians, academics, artists), which created a bridge between 'ordinary' people and the experts, further popularising and democratising the political debate.

From the very beginning, each task was undertaken on a voluntary basis. There was no set budget or agreed-upon hierarchy as would exist in a regular social movement organisation, and each activist would sign up for tasks and contribute funds from their own pocket (M. C. B., personal communication, 10 July 2015). The group would sometimes ask for resources (banners, sound equipment, and so forth) from other – and more formal – organisations (such as unions, political parties, or professional associations) to which some activists individually belonged (S. B., personal communication, 10 July 2015). As the forum grew larger, thematic sub-committees, workshops and study-groups on themes such as street art, photography, creative writing, children's art and entertainment were emerging. In its early days, there were about 100 such workshop ideas, some of which took hold whereas others were short-lived or did not even make it beyond mere proposals (such as 'Armenian language classes', Y. L., personal communication, 16 July 2014). Over time, groups representing different neighbourhoods began to create more localised initiatives and engaged in activities ranging from raising awareness to issues concerning their district to taking part in city-wide protests. Some of these initiatives would later evolve into 'neighbourhood forums' or 'solidarity groups' scattered in different parts of Kadıköy and beyond. Two of these solidarity groups (*Caferağa* and *Yeldeğirmeni*) would later take further steps to occupy two abandoned buildings and turn them into 'community centres' and 'neighbourhood houses' (Don Kişot Sosyal Merkezi and Caferağa Mahalle Evi).

In terms of the composition of its most regular attendees, it was possible to identify in Yoğurtçu Forum a number of 'elders', some of whom had prior political experience as members or sympathizers of the Dev-Yol tradition and would often allude to the Resistance Committee experience at the meetings.[1] Nevertheless, during the time I observed the forum, mostly young university students and white-collar professionals were at the forefront of mobilisation. Despite being respectful to the 'elders' in the group and acknowledging how instrumental the latter were for the political education of the group, they did not shy away from expressing their views or challenging what they saw as 'impediments' to their street activism: in that sense there was no obvious geriatric hierarchy or hegemony. Although elements of toxic masculine language could occasionally seep into meetings, a quota system and the principle of positive discrimination in favour of women was honoured. Traditional gender roles did not apply as men and women took equal responsibilities and occupied equal positions, something inherited from the Gezi Park occupation days (A. D., personal communication, 10 July 2015).

Throughout its time, some of the radical democratic activism that the Yoğurtçu Forum undertook included: mobilising against, and successfully interrupting, some of the projects by the Kadıköy municipal government (such as turning green areas into parking lots); raising awareness about stray animals; holding solidarity events to commemorate the 'martyrs of police violence'; recreational activities for children from low-income families; movie and documentary screenings; public meetings or educational workshops around themes such as 'what kind of a city do we want to live in' or 'what to do if got arrested'; organising protests against the conversion of public middle schools in the district to religious schools; protesting the demolition and rebuilding (as a billion-dollar multi-purpose centre) of a historical train station and the nearby seaport in Haydarpaşa to accommodate new high-speed train services; promoting and maintaining public vegetable gardens for sustainability; showing solidarity with local businesses and small restaurants against chain brands; and supporting refugees. While engaging in all these instances of activism, the group fought hard for – and took great pride in – maintaining the forum as 'identity-less' (*kimliksiz*) and 'non-belonging' (*aidiyetsiz*) and not falling prisoner to the agendas of more edgy leftist groups (Y. O., personal communication, 30 June 2015).

While Yoğurtçu Forum continued to have an appeal to different groups among the concerned public thanks to its size and power to call attention to more national events, different visions for its future began to surface. Some activists wanted to see it mutate into a political creature with an active political agenda and a broad roadmap whereas others found it hard to pursue in the forum a type of politics oriented towards local matters (M. C. B., personal communication, 10 July 2015). For the latter, Yoğurtçu Forum was too big and too distant to offer the spatial proximity and proper scale of political action to address the more urgent and local issues of neighbourhoods. When the anticipated coordination between Yoğurtçu and neighbourhood solidarity groups could not be established, the disagreements deepened and eventually separations from Yoğurtçu park forums accelerated (Z. U., personal communication, 16 July 2015). While these groups preferred to focus on the local, Yoğurtçu Forum tried to remain a political space in which 'higher level urban politics' could be debated and 'bigger actions' relevant to the whole city and country could be organised (U. U., personal communication, 13 July 2015).

While it retained prestigious presence on social media with thousands of followers and could mobilise many people for a protest or an event, the separations reduced Yoğurtçu Forum to a 'loyal cadre' of activists. Meetings became less frequent, and the attendance saw a significant decline. More importantly, the coming of the winter months brought an end to open park meetings and forced activists to retreat indoors to places such as the Barış Manço Centre. Neither May Day protests nor the first-year anniversary of the uprisings in 2014 could produce as strong a mobilisation as expected. By the summer of 2014, the Yoğurtçu moment had lost its appeal for most of the public who stopped attending in disappointment (O. S., personal communication, 11 August 2015). Despite that, according to its foremost activists, Yoğurtçu Forum played an important mission by educating many people from all walks of life and enlisting various ideological creeds into shared, collective mobilisation. In the words of one activist, 'when Gezi comes back again [these activists] know where to begin, whom to trust and what to do' (M. C. B., personal communication, 29 June 2016).

'Fluid Politics' during the Gezi Episode

In order to be able to understand the radical democratic dynamic in the Gezi Episode, I turn to various aspects of radical politics as they emerged from Yoğurtçu Forum and its offshoots. Rather than being confined to a particular temporal phase or a spatial unit, let alone being carried out only by particular political actor(s), these manifestations could precipitate in distinct configurations of 'space-time-political form'. Below I discuss two main modalities through which assembly-centred radical democratic practices gave way to what I call 'fluid politics' during the Gezi Episode.

Localised, Issue-based Politics

The first of these modalities can be summarised as localised, issue-based politics. As discussed earlier, the tendency to go smaller in scale and space (from big public parks to neighbourhoods to buildings, from large forum meetings to sub-committees, task forces and working groups) was already taking place in the course of the Episode. Some of these initiatives would later become the nuclei of various independent solidarity organisations with a focus on a single neighbourhood or district. This was a deviation from the experience during the two-week occupation in Gezi Park, and also from the early days of the bigger park forums where resentment, frustration, hopes and other thoughts and feelings about 'big politics' in the country would be the main motivation for attendance and driver of the meetings (for Ankara forums, see: Çelik & Ergenç, 2016, 2018).

The switch from broad topics in big politics to local issues was not abrupt. In various forums – especially in bigger ones – initial conversations continued for some time to be full of bigger political debates, such as how to build an effective umbrella movement to have impact in national politics or how to transform existing political parties to better respond to the concerns of the public. Slowly, the scale of politics and focus of agendas would shift to more pressing issues concerning the residents of the area in question, which began to shape the overall character and fragmented the trajectory of the movement. In Yoğurtçu Forum, as long, abstract and 'fruitless' discussions and political commentary began to cause weariness and exasperation by the end of 2013, the group adopted a parallel mission: debates on 'big politics' would continue during regular forum meetings alongside with more 'down-to-earth' activism (M. C. B., personal communication, 10 July 2015). Eventually, a more issue-based politics, often of concern to the Kadıköy district, began to take over the forum. Ad hoc committees and task forces would form and dissolve, allowing activists to easily switch from one task or committee to another. This accelerated the branching off of neighbourhood solidarities and squat houses and later paved the way for the establishment of Kadıköy Urban Solidarity (Kadıköy Kent Dayanışması) when several neighbourhood organisations came together to defend their 'right to the city' (Kadıköy Kent Dayanışması, n.d.).

One example of the impact of focusing on local issues in strengthening mobilisation was the rehabilitation of the Kurbağalıdere brook. When I started my fieldwork in Yoğurtçu Forum in the summer of 2014, this issue occupied an important place in the forum meetings. While observing the debates on the progress of their activism in terms of interacting with the municipality or reaching out to local residents as well as experts about possible solutions, I was impressed by the depth and breadth of knowledge the activists possessed (regardless of their age or occupation), even on very technical details, such as land ownership laws or other administrative regulations at the municipal level. As I learnt later, the group had in the past hosted educational seminars with experts to educate themselves and the public on the topic. Through their connections, they had sought help from outside organisations, such as the Union of Chambers of Turkish Engineers and Architects (TMMOB) or Turkish Medical Association (TTB). At the end of one of the meetings, the group decided to increase pressure on the Kadıköy municipality to resume the work for the rehabilitation of the brook, which had come to a halt. Some in the group proposed door-to-door canvassing and collecting signatures while others suggested reaching out to TBB as well as local organisations in Kadıköy and local and national media. More importantly, they decided to be ready for organising a street protest to make the issue even more visible (personal observation, Yoğurtçu Forum, 16 July 2014). This latter was yet another testimony that Yoğurtçu Forum in particular and forums in general never ceased to utilise the street as leverage for political action even when issues became more local.

Another example of successful issue-based mobilisation was undertaken by a smaller neighbourhood solidarity, Validebağ Defence (Validebağ Savunması), which was hailed as a model to be followed for 'it had no competing constituents (*bileşenler*)'. The organisation was established to defend a small grove, Validebağ Korusu, in the Üsküdar district where the local municipality developed plans to build a mosque and a parking lot for a nearby guesthouse for public school teachers and a nursing home (Akyıldız, 2015, pp. 35–41). While a neighbourhood watch (comprised mainly of retired residents of the nearby neighbourhoods) was already in place to protect the grove from destruction under various construction proposals since the 1990s, it was only when the incumbent local municipality controlled by the AKP began to decisively enforce a full-scale construction scheme in the early 2010s that the concerned residents connected with some of the younger activists who took part in Gezi protests (S. A., personal communication, 13 July 2015). Thanks to the 'heightened environmentalist sensitivities' in the immediate post-Gezi period, the call received great attention and an outpouring of support from lawyers, environmentalists, scholars, engineers, political groups and other forums around the district. In November 2014, the group officially took the name Validebağ Defence and created social media accounts to better coordinate and organise their activism. Barricades were built to keep guard, and any attempt by the municipality to build a construction site was immediately confronted by the group, which included getting involved in violent clashes with police and even getting arrested. In a sense, Validebağ Defence became a 'miniature Gezi', which conferred on it a high level of prestige.

Although many diverse individuals and groups got involved in Validebağ Defence when it was first formed, the core group decided to have the primary volunteers (*gönüllü*) – residents, the members of the former association formed by some of the retirees living in the area and others in the district – be at the forefront of activism while keeping those outside the inner circle simply as allies (S. A., personal communication, 13 July 2015). The primary volunteers agreed to take part in the defence with their 'resident' identity only, without bringing any other political affiliation into the group. This way the initiative could retain its 'neutrality' and autonomy from the influence of other groups who tried to impose their own political agendas to divert the defence from the main purpose of its activism (Y. S., personal communication, 13 July 2015).

Taking cues from this new mode of political activism around local issues, Yoğurtçu Forum began to reorient itself and function as a flexible 'movement organisation' mobilising around a specific issue each time, seeing its actions producing 'tangible results' while still maintaining its assembly character (M. C. B., personal communication, 10 July 2015). Activists realised that the local could become an important and useful venue, tool and strategy to organise dissent. As one of the activists put it: 'we came to the realisation that daily issues can guide the problems that citizens face on a regular basis, and from there a strong opposition and organisation can emerge. Solidarity can be established around smaller, local level issues, regardless of the victim or what their political position is' (Y. O., personal communication, 30 June 2015). For others, too, this type of mobilisation offered a political method where 'everybody can find a common ground in their own terms when upper-level politics (*üst siyaset*) cannot hear people's demands and the needs of life. Politics should be open to the demands coming from the bottom and be able to harmonise and organise these demands at a higher level' (A. D., personal communication, 10 July 2015). According to this view, existing political organisations or groups (*siyasetler*) could not wield the vision to fully understand and organise around local issues, and therefore it was 'a good thing that the people in a particular locality would take things in their own hands' (M. C. B., personal communication, 10 July 2015). For the Yoğurtçu Forum, the whole experience was also seen as a learning process, especially for the older generation in the group who used to reduce politics to tackling bigger issues. The move from abstract political targets to smaller-scale local issues and a pragmatic, issue-oriented political attitude became a valuable discovery (S. B., personal communication, 10 July 2015).

Nevertheless, this process of localisation and issue-based activism revealed an interesting duality in terms of the way that contentious politics was carried out during the Gezi Episode. On the one hand, bigger forums such as Yoğurtçu still carried – albeit in a declining way – the power to channel city-level or national political energy into a local issue or problem. For instance, the forum could inform and mobilise a city-wide and national audience to resist the government's attempts to convert a public school to a religious school in a neighbourhood in Kadıköy. This way, an ongoing bigger mobilisation around a deep political fault line (secular resistance against the AKP's Islamisation efforts) could be projected onto and replicated in a local case, helping the local gain visibility by – and garner support from – diverse groups who were not directly affected by this very issue. On the other hand, the same dynamic worked in the reverse direction, too. For instance, support for Kazova textile workers when they took over the factory and began to implement auto-management practices after the company went bankrupt could be reframed by park forums and neighbourhood solidarities as yet another instance of national and even global struggle against capitalism and hence could reproduce the support for this local issue in the context of a broader political movement. In other words, the forum structure could amplify the voice and impact of local struggles while connecting them to (and associating them with) larger ones. The sometimes-contradictory outcomes of this dual process (that is, descending from national or global to the local, and ascending from the local to the national or global almost simultaneously) will be addressed later in Chapter 6.

Political Hub

The second modality of assembly-centred radical democratic politics during the Gezi Episode is less about the content or scale of activism than the ways that activism could instigate a dynamic political hub by repurposing traditional political tools on certain occasions and inventing new ones in others. This found its expression in three ways.

Umbrella

As we have seen earlier, different individuals and groups from many walks of life (anti-capitalist Muslims, Alevis, Kurds, LGBTQIA+, women, youth and all others) joined the protests and supported each other against police brutality during the initial days of the Gezi uprising. This practice of solidarity continued during the occupation of Gezi Park, too, which was able to normalise – even if temporarily – relations between formerly adverse groups, such as leftist cliques, Kurds and Turks, seculars and the pious, and so forth.

In the aftermath of the occupation, emerging forums continued to bring individuals and groups together under an umbrella and provide a common ground for political mobilisation that cut across a variety of issues and priorities. Inheriting this experience from Gezi Park, Yoğurtçu Forum sought to become one such structure by amplifying the voices of many and making their issues a part of a larger political debate about democracy in Turkey. In its early days, Yoğurtçu Forum could bring together and facilitate the interaction and growing tolerance between ideologically opposed individuals and groups, which would have been unthinkable before Gezi considering the deep divides between these groups (Y. O., personal communication, 30 June 2015). Long and frequent forum meetings created an atmosphere where individuals got the opportunity to hear and interact with others (M. C. B., personal communication, 10 July 2015). More importantly, by connecting different individuals and groups (including experts as well as residents who were directly affected by an issue tackled by the forum) with each other helped establish stronger bonds among them and facilitated collaboration through developing common protocols that guided their concerted political action, such as deciding on the common slogans or banners to use during a joint rally and refraining from pushing individual agendas (S. B., personal communication, 10 July 2015; L. T. G., personal communication, 18 July 2014).

As these new relations were forming between activists and shaping the way radical democratic practices were being devised and undertaken in a horizontal, non-hierarchical manner, the possibility of a particular group claiming leadership and capturing the discourse faded. In many forums, certain hardline groups came to the realisation that they were not the leaders but students of this new political moment (Atılgan, 2013, pp. 14–15). In Yoğurtçu Forum, too, the fact that more 'edgy' political groups (especially the Turkish Communist Party, TKP) felt obligated to leave the park forum was testimony that the emerging politics was qualitatively different from what these groups were envisioning.

CATALYST

When the park forums such as Yoğurtçu began to invite guests (academics, architects, urban planners, civil engineers, but also artists and politicians) to discuss various topics in their meetings, they were turning the forum into a bridge between 'ordinary people' and 'experts' and as such 'socialising' knowledge and 'democratising' political debate. In other words, while bringing people, knowledge and resources together, the activism in forums, and later in neighbourhood solidarities and squat houses, also transformed these elements – through events and actions on matters that concerned the public – into 'catalysts' to raise political consciousness. As such, they were channelling and amplifying the political will among citizens to take matters in their own hands. In other words, by facilitating the information flow from narrow circles and high echelons of technical expertise to the collective public domain and encouraging the latter to take direct action or responsibility on political issues of all levels, forums were turning into a fertile ecosystem for the emergence of a new collective political attitude.

Another way that Yoğurtçu Forum acted as a political hub was through establishing connections with – and exerting pressure on – the local municipality of Kadıköy district. During the early days of the forum meetings, the Republican People's Party (Cumhuriyet Halk Partisi, CHP), the main opposition party of which the mayor of Kadıköy was a member, had provided resources such as sound systems, catering and other logistical assistance. The forum and municipality would keep the communication channels open later, too: some members of the forum had easy access to the mayor's office to pass on some of their demands and share their thoughts on such issues as the building of a shopping mall in Kadıköy, which eventually was withdrawn (Y. O., personal communication, 30 June 2015). In a sense, Yoğurtçu Forum could establish itself as an influential actor in institutional politics while transforming it.

The legacy of this political orientation would also emerge in different forms, especially when national politics accelerated during election periods. For instance, the 'After 10' (*10dan sonra*) initiative tried to convince progressive Turkish voters to vote for The Peoples' Democratic Party (Halkların Demokratik Partisi, HDP), a pro-Kurdish leftist party, during the June 2015 elections so that it could pass the 10% national threshold to have representation in the National Assembly. Some of the former Yoğurtçu Forum activists who took active part in the campaign put their forum experiences and vision into political organising, which included establishing local assemblies and connecting with voters directly in an assembly structure, rather than simply acting as a communication office or through canvassing. Some others who worked in the same campaign aimed to influence the HDP and make sure that its discourse embraced issues that left-leaning voters (Turks and Kurds together) cared about, such as establishing worker councils, ecological assemblies and other initiatives to effect lasting positive change through parliamentary action (Z. U., personal communication, 16 July 2015). The introduction of the forum principles into established politics helped, in a sense, move beyond forum politics as an abstract endeavour.

Calling Power

These two functions (being an umbrella and a political facilitator, enabler and catalyst) that made forums function as a political hub during the Episode were complemented by a third one in the specific case of Yoğurtçu Forum, which the activists proudly called the 'calling power' (*çağrı gücü*) and believed gave the forum its true dynamism and vigour. Even during times when its relevance was diminished, Yoğurtçu Forum could still call the crowds to mobilisation and would have a pivotal role in organising collective action. Some of the issues around which Yoğurtçu could mobilise crowds included protesting the military campaign on Rojava by Turkish armed forces, commemorating 'Gezi martyrs', the 17–25 December corruption scandal, protesting escalating violence perpetrated by the Israeli government on Gaza, problems of the Roma people or Syrian refugees in Istanbul, drawing attention to LGBTQIA+ issues, urban transformation and many others which belonged to the broader, higher-level political sphere and which could not be addressed by single-issue neighbourhood solidarities and forums (L. T. G., personal communication, 18 July 2014; U. U., personal communication, 13 July 2015).

The prestige and respect that Yoğurtçu Forum could garner from activists in other groups enhanced its *çağrı gücü* to mobilise otherwise separated or antagonist groups around bigger politics and keep street activism always an option. It was also this power that reinforced the forum's role as an enabler, amplifier and facilitator of political action by making issues more visible through its large presence on social media. In that sense, the forum was an elusive 'force' rather than an established organisation: it was at once a strategy, resource and motivation that could be brought into activism during rallies or events organised around local, national and even global issues.

'Fluid Politics'

All in all, the Gezi Episode witnessed the emergence of a new 'political creature' simultaneously appearing in a wide range of spaces, from streets and parks to neighbourhoods and squat houses. This was not a mere upgrade of institutional politics defined by representation, elections, political party affiliations or even simply protesting in the streets despite the mutual appeal to democracy these distinct forms of action shared. Rather, the assembly-centred forum model that encouraged participatory, consensus-oriented direct action without pre-decided principles in an inclusive, plural and non-hierarchical structure became the radical politics that could transform a particular space from which it emerged into a novel democratic experience under constant, globally connected mobilisation.

All this amounted to what I call 'fluid politics' – a modality of politics that emerged in tandem with 'fluid political identities' and 'fluid spaces' that I laid out in the previous two chapters. The Gezi Episode paved the way for activists to expand their political horizon through utilising flexible, multi-dimensional, poly-morphic modes of activism. Activists could easily float from one form of activism to another and sometimes occupied more than one political status simultaneously. Although there seemed to be a natural inclination towards local and issue-based politics, their fluid political identities and the fluid spaces they travelled enabled these activists to navigate between different scales of politics without feeling incoherent or inconsistent about it and to develop a more complex and nuanced political consciousness. They transgressed the assumed boundaries of political activism while prefiguring this new breed of radical politics.

In the case of the Yoğurtçu Forum, what emerged was not a new 'political subject' (*siyasi özne*), for its core activists reserved the term for more established political groups, organisations (such as political parties) or individuals as carriers of institutional politics (A. D., personal communication, 10 July 2015). For them, the forum was not an end in itself and never tried to become a political actor in the conventional understanding of the term (M. C. B., personal communication, 29 June 2016; A. D., personal communication, 4 August 2016). Instead, it embodied the act of organising and mobilisation. Yoğurtçu and others normalised politics as something undertaken by ordinary citizens on a daily basis and not necessarily by career politicians or insulated experts. They became sites for accumulation of political consciousness through which citizens' political subjectification was shaped beyond mere elections, political party affiliations or calendar-ised protests. In a sense, the politics emerging from the Gezi Episode became, borrowing from Ruth Wilson Gilmore, a 'rehearsal in life' (Gilmore, 2021), that is, a prefigurative act in organising in a novel and unprecedented way to capture the emerging impulse towards a new community. This is why many activists – not just in Gezi but globally – preferred to call themselves 'organisers' rather than 'activists' and certainly not 'partisans'. In this political movement, everyone was, borrowing from Denning (2021), a 'legislator' instead of being a passive cog in a rigid structure.

It is hard to miss the stark difference between this radical formulation of democracy and Erdoğan's emphasis on national will (*milli irade*) and the rule of the majority as the only source of democratic legitimacy. In the latter model, the marginalised could hope for class mobility only through their proximity to the party-state, which had no intention to address existing inequalities or forms of exclusion but would obscure these issues behind a rhetoric of the primacy of the 'ballot box' (S. Doğan, 2016, p. 263). As early as mid-June 2013, even before the occupation of Gezi Park was over, Erdoğan had begun a campaign of delegitimising and head-on attacking Gezi protests with his 'Respect for National Will' (*Milli İradeye Saygı*) rallies, first in Ankara, then in Istanbul after the occupation was dispersed. The divisive and exclusionary nature of his rhetoric became even more visible when he juxtaposed his version of political legitimacy through nation (*millet*) against what he called 'marauder, looter' (*çapulcu*) to describe and dismiss activists who later passionately re-appropriated the term as the basis of a new collective political identity (Harding, 2013). In a sense, the way radical democracy was experienced in Gezi Park and beyond normalised the idea of 'militant/resurgent citizen' – which found its most refined expression in *çapulcu* – against the passive 'voter' or 'docile rank-and-file' preferred by the establishment.

This also explains why the activists of Yoğurtçu Forum did not agonise or feel 'defeated' following the forum's demise. When I interviewed them for the last time in 2016, two of its most active members told me that the forum had reached its 'expiration date' and 'completed its mission' (M. C. B., personal communication, 29 June 2016; A. D., personal communication, 4 August 2016). For them, Yoğurtçu was different from a national political movement, such as Birleşik Haziran, Kadıköy Urban Defence or even a regular neighbourhood solidarity. Instead, it was a unique apparatus to facilitate politics and most importantly to reinforce the 'forum spirit' where individuals could gather and mobilise around local, less ideology-driven issues and become educated political subjects. In other words, it was important for Yoğurtçu Forum to remain as the heir of the Gezi uprising and preserve its autonomy without sacrificing its 'spirit' and 'mentality' (*zihniyet*) to 'politics as usual' while the principles and achievements of the forum experience could be transferred to larger political initiatives for real social impact.

Radical Praxis, Political Subjectivity and the Common in the Gezi Episode: Towards a New Political Community

In this final section, I highlight the ways through which radical democratic practices, especially those around the principles of assembly, shaped perceptions of collective subjectivity, belonging and solidarity during the Gezi Episode. That the activists became more knowledgeable, engaged and open and tolerant through constant mobilisation as a part of a global wave of social movements (as discussed in Chapter 3) and that their activism took various shapes as they strolled through many politicised sites in the city (as discussed in Chapter 4), conditioned the relationship between these prefigurative enactments of radical democracy and the imagination and solidification of a new political community. More importantly, I argue that it is from this relationship that the idea of the 'common' emerged as the guiding principle to reconstitute the social in the face of neoliberal destruction.

From Forums to the Common

During the square movements and occupations of the early 2000s, a subtle transition from 'public space' to the 'common' was taking place in tandem with the evolution of the forum structure from the congregation of organisations in World Social Forums towards assembly-driven local forums. The 'public realm' (the domain owned and controlled by the state) was being 'liberated' from state and market forces and replaced by radical ideas and practices in autonomous sites of direct or quasi-direct democracy (Hoskyns, 2014, p. 67). A multiplicity of radical political imaginaries and of emancipatory visions around the idea of the common were turning these sites into 'solidarity spaces' (Arampatzi, 2017). To better understand this transformation, we need to the trace the intricate relationship between commons, commoning and the common.

De Angelis and Harvie define commons as 'systems in which resources are shared by a community of users and producers, who also define the modes of use and production, distribution and circulation of these resources through democratic and horizontal forms of governance' (De Angelis & Harvie, 2013, p. 280). As such, 'ideas associated with the commons function as a productive supplement for the project of radical democracy by expanding its demands and strategico-theoretical orientation' (Howarth & Roussos, 2022, p. 2). Historically, commons were 'defence cushions' protecting the community 'from the excesses of capitalist processes, and at times even allow [members of the community] to avoid the discipline of capital' (Genç, 2018, p. 83). Their enclosure for private wealth accumulation therefore has always been destructive for urban as well as rural life. But it is the common-as-verb, that is, the act of 'commoning' that turns the commons as a resource collective into a praxis. It is, first and foremost, a movement against the enclosure and privatisation of shared urban spaces through gentrification and renewal projects: an act of self-defence against the neoliberal assault on the city and the social fabric it embraces. This includes all the 'discursive and material practices that not only counter forces of enclosure but also produce a sense of place and community' (B. Ö. Fırat, 2022, p. 1031).

Defending the commons became an important feature of the emancipatory struggles in the Global South, especially with Zapatistas in the mid-1990s as they focused mostly on the needs and survival of local communities through access and sustainable use of natural resources and collective production. Meanwhile various movements of the poor and the precariat, such as the rise of squat houses and other political practices, in urban centres in Europe or in the factory occupations of Argentina in the early 2000s were all becoming a part of the 'commoning' wave (B. Ö. Fırat, 2018, pp. 69–70). During the anti-austerity and pro-democracy movements in the 2010s, commoning became both a survival mechanism for the disadvantaged and marginalised, and a reaction by the urban middle class who experienced significant cultural and social impoverishment and loss of belonging due to the transformation of the city. In defiance of dispossession, initiatives such as collective kitchens, healthcare centres, day-care, non-commercial pharmacies, schools, producer cooperatives, exchange markets and vegetable gardens, in addition to assemblies in park encampments and occupations, emerged as solidarist, collaborative, egalitarian, self-ruling and radically democratic institutions of the collective will.

While 'commoning' relates to collectively producing, defending, reclaiming and reproducing the material needs of a community outside the realm of the market and state, it also embraces 'co-production of new systems of values, of producing what is of common value together' (De Angelis, 2010,

p. 958). Put differently, commoning is the act of reviving and redefining the community as a political statement and a means in the struggle for an alternative world. In contemporary social movements, the 'reversal in temporal order for radical social change' that this struggle needed was evident: instead of waiting for the transformation of institutions by force of a political revolution and pushing social change onto the community, mundane practices of everyday life, regardless of where they were undertaken (in the campsite of an occupied park or square, in a squat house, or even at a regular forum meeting) became the revolutionary force. The politics of commoning rejected state and market logic or power as the organising principle of the social and reclaimed what has been collectively produced and shared, not just in terms of food, shelter or any form of material resource but also of dreams and visions for a just future.

The transformative power of prefiguration in commoning is unmistakeable: actively building in the present time the values, habits, forms and social institutions of a collectively imagined future. Here, social change is immanent to the process in which the 'commons' (in plural) paves the way to the 'common' (in singular), the latter emphasising the 'constitutive' rather than 'reactive' or 'protective' quality of the radical politics they foster. As Federici argues, the common offers a deeper political critique with an alternative social organisation model in mind: a political project that attempts to restore a reworked form of solidarity sewn by a new social fabric – one that has been destroyed by neoliberalism when people lost their employment, residence, health, education and social bonds that held them together as a community. It encompasses attempts to reclaim control of everyday life, to re-appropriate the means of collective decision-making about issues concerning everyday life. Therefore, economic (pooling resources), political (collective decision-making) and social (community building) dimensions of the common are inseparable (Kontext TV, 2014).

The common and commoning during the social movements of the 2010s conferred on the latter a dual capacity: the radical democratic practices in these movements simultaneously became the politics of mobilising (to protect and reclaim common resources) and the politics of organising (to constitute a new community) against the neoliberal logic of social (dis)organisation. Moreover, the fact that the common involved the reappropriation of space (squares, parks, buildings) added an important dimension to these movements. As Stavrides puts it: 'Common spaces emerge as threshold spaces, spaces not demarcated by a defining perimeter. Whereas public space bears the mark of a prevailing authority that defines it, common space is opened space, space in a process of opening toward "newcomers"' (Stavrides, 2012, p. 589). It was in these spaces where:

> direct democracy can, perhaps, mean not only an equality of opinions but also a self-conscious synchronisation aimed at a commonly recognised cause [. . .] Inside the temporary space of the occupied square, people could develop new habits and new roles, new rhythms which characterised new forms of life in common. (Stavrides, 2013, pp. 46–7)

In the face of the urge for survival through solidarity in different corners of the city, the common served 'as both the form and the content of social relations that transcend the limitations and the market worshipping cynicism of contemporary capitalism' (Stavrides, 2020).

Finding the Common in the Gezi Episode

The Turkish word for the term commons (*müşterekler*) entered the lexicon of political activism in the late 1990s and early 2000s as an expression of resistance to the transfer of 'common resources' to private hands (B. Ö. Fırat, 2018, pp. 67–8). The commodification of natural resources and especially the construction of hydro-electrical power plants became notable instances when the idea of the commons was explicitly brought up in various protests (Adaman et al., 2016, p. 21). In the urban front, too, various neighbourhood associations emerged during the early years of the AKP rule in order to mobilise against renewal and transformation projects in their districts, creating platforms and alliances for education, information-sharing and consciousness-raising (Genç, 2018, pp. 85–6). These were often joined by other mobilisations to defend places of historical importance and public spaces in urban contexts, such as the Emek movie theatre in Istanbul (B. Ö. Fırat, 2022), which were also on the AKP's radar for commodification. Urban planners, lawyers, artists and scholars led campaigns against the enclosure of these common spaces and resources not just through legal battles, but especially through generating a counter-discourse emphasising accessibility, public interest and cultural heritage (Genç, 2018, p. 88).

The Gezi protests were a part of this lineage in defending the commons. As we saw earlier, they emerged as an act for protecting a collectively utilised resource, a public park, against the state-enforced enclosure disguised as urban renewal. Yet the uprising went beyond a mere act of defence and morphed into collective practices of producing and reproducing the common along the principles of solidarity, autonomy, justice and self-organisation. What Robin D. G. Kelley observes in the Black liberation movement in the US can be applied to the Gezi Episode: 'the challenges of solidarity and a deep understanding of the mechanisms of oppression generate the conditions and requirements for new modes of analysis, new ways of being together' (Kelley, 2022). Indeed, constant and globally connected mobilisation during the Gezi Episode evolved from protecting the commons to constituting the common, carrying with it new 'values and principles as freedom, equality, reciprocity, solidarity, trust, and self-governance' in different sites of the city (Genç, 2018, p. 92). The provision of food, shelter, healthcare, education, recreational activities and workshops, public gardens, and all other undertakings inherently prefigured a collective future beyond the AKP's neoliberal Islamist vision of Istanbul (Akbulut, 2016, pp. 291–2). These acts of commoning became a source of new subjectification that started to change the lives of those who took part in this collective effort (Yazıcı & Fırat, 2013). Therefore, the many politics of the Episode (from protests in the streets and Taksim square to the occupation of Gezi Park, from forums in the neighbourhood parks to squat houses) were in fact an alternative solidarity project rejecting the docile class of conservative, religious consumer-citizens that the AKP nurtured in favour of a bottom-up engagement that prioritised anti-capitalist, self-organised, non-hierarchical, non-representative and self-sufficient forms of political community.

Squat houses were the spaces where the politics of the common was most visible during the Gezi Episode. It was here where the fusion of space and politics nurtured a form of radical democracy that was not theoretical but directly relevant to shared resources and issues concerned with the house's immediate participants and the space within which it was located. Being a part of the squat house and building solidarity with locals as well as among themselves strengthened the relationships between activists from different backgrounds and political orientations (O. S., personal communication, 11 August 2015). More importantly, squat houses came to function as social centres where the 'lost feeling of community' was revived in a self-ruling, non-hierarchical social setting (Rittersberger-Tılıç, 2015, pp. 92–3).

Caferağa Solidarity, for instance, had initially begun as an attempt to reach out to the locals, yet became more active and gained a new character following the occupation of an abandoned building in the neighbourhood and turning it into a squat house. The occupation made it easier for the group to connect with the residents as well as with the participating individuals. Their calls for collaboration and solidarity were received warmly by feminists, vegans, refugees and other groups, who even held some of their meetings there. More established political groups, such as the HDP and CHP, with whom the group had no prior contacts or collaborations, also participated in the collective planning and organisation of some of the joint events (O. S., personal communication, 11 August 2015).

In Yeldeğirmeni Social Centre, too, house occupants as well as other groups that made up the broader forum decided to connect with the residents in the neighbourhood to collectively reclaim and reappropriate what was stolen from the public through commodification. Similar to the other squatting experiences around the world (Çoban, 2015), the neighbourhood was designated as the primary unit and the centre of the common in the broader effort to transform the city (*Yeldeğirmeni İşgal Evi'nde Yeni Bir Yaşam Kuruluyor*, 2013). Activists got actively involved in the matters of the neighbourhood, such as the provision of supplies for local schools or helping refugee children in the district. They also organised solidarity campaigns with the shopkeepers or created teams to help the elderly in need. In other words, squat houses both mobilised resources to improve the conditions of the city with a focus on local spaces and transformed the social relations within these spaces (Ülger et al., 2014).

Another important initiative that centred its politics on the pursuance of the common was the *Müştereklerimiz* ('Our Commons') group. Müştereklerimiz had its roots in the pre-Gezi period when it emerged as a collective to connect political struggles that shared a mutual concern for Istanbul, such as refugee solidarity groups, ecological collectives, feminists, trans individuals, anti-capitalists and other initiatives against urban transformation. As its name suggests, the group tried to establish itself as a platform where common issues could be addressed collectively rather than individually and separately because, as one of its members put it: 'the mechanisms of power and oppression surrounding us are the same' (B. A., personal communication, 12 July 2015). As the group declared in its manifesto: 'the urgent need of the present time is to create and multiply the spaces of opposition and solidarity to break off from this power-lessness and fragmentation [. . .] Starting with our commons, we reclaim what belongs to us!' (Müştereklerimiz, 2013).

Even before the Gezi Episode, Müştereklerimiz had established strong ties with environmental activists around the world, especially those based in differ-ent European cities. Their members were mostly university students or doing post-graduate studies and were well-connected to scholar-activist networks, closely following the world literature on ecological activism. They could also travel abroad and collaborate with some of the forums and squat movements in Europe to discuss and learn about occupations, cooperatives and other prac-tices of commoning from their counterparts (B. A., personal communication, 12 July 2015).

In the first days of the occupation, Müştereklerimiz attempted to coordi-nate many groups in Gezi Park, including taking part in organising the first forum (Çelik & Ergenç, 2018, p. 83). They tried to situate themselves as a liaison between these groups to amplify their impact as well as to help them develop the capacity to engage in new solidarity practices (Çelik & Ergenç, 2018, pp. 88–9). Their 'unstructured' structure allowed them organise fast and respond to the needs of the moment when other organisations, such as chambers, unions or political institutions were not able to operate as effectively (Fırat, 2013, p. 38). More importantly their efforts in commoning parallel social struggles would later become the basis of political agency and emerging political subjectivity in all forms of practices materialised in the parks, forums, neighbourhood solidarities and squat houses.

As the Gezi Episode unfolded, Müştereklerimiz offered a meso-level politi-cal strategy (in response to the localisation trend and to prevent forums from closing in on themselves) by establishing a 'middle field' (*orta alan*), a political space in which various local struggles could be synchronised and elevated to a broader political (and even electoral) agenda (B. A., personal communication, 12 July 2015). Yet, as the axis of political activism continued to shift to smaller forums and neighbourhood solidarities, Müştereklerimiz simply became one among many other groups rather than achieving a higher-level coordinator sta-tus to transform singular struggles into 'common' activism. According to one of its activists, Müştereklerimiz could not find 'anything different to say to' the forums and solidarities and eventually became weaker in their attempt to pull activism to a higher level (B. A., personal communication, 12 July 2015).

Praxis, Subjectivity, Citizenship and Political Community around the Common

What these particular examples of radical democratic activism around the concept of the common show us is that the social movements of the 2010s were expressions of a 'collective radical imagination that conjures and sustains visions of freedom even in the darkest times' (Kelley, 2022). The 'insurrectional' politics (Balibar, 2012) in these movements comprised egalitarian, horizontal, radical democratic forms and strategies that shaped the political vision of the activists with respect to solidarity, community and citizenship. These emancipatory struggles and accompanying practices were constitutive and 'proto-political' (Badiou, 2012) as they brought a heterogeneous body of individuals and groups together and turned them into 'a people' in the process: a new breed of 'insurgent citizens' for whom democracy was not limited to the formal mechanisms of liberal democracy but was envisioning a political community through a new ethics of living together while mobilising on the streets and other spaces in the city.

Once again, the idea and pursuance of the common was at the core of these 'community-oriented or community-inspired actions'. In other words, while individual instances of constant mobilisation operated in distinct rhythms, functions, routines, aesthetics and scope in different urban spaces, the square and occupation movements transformed these spaces of solidarity into 'common spaces' (Stavrides, 2012, p. 588) and spaces of the common. It was around this emerging common that ideas, visions and yearnings were assembled to constitute a reworked definition of the 'public' that prevented it from degenerating into a narrow, homogeneous form of community, embracing instead the complexity within which different communities tried to chart a common pathway (De Angelis & Stavrides, 2013).

During the Gezi Episode, one-dimensional identities that activists brought with themselves (as environmentalists, feminists, leftists, soccer fans and so forth) proved inadequate as the process of 'becoming' unfolded in response to the long-lost feeling of solidarity. Especially in the early days of the occupation of Gezi Park, numerous individuals bore testimony to the feeling of being transformed into something new that they had never experienced before (Eken, 2014, p. 434; also see: İplikçi, 2013; Uluğ & Acar, 2014). The new 'multitude' emerging from this process was not 'simply a mixture of the people and the sociological categories they represent[ed]' or simply recognition of other identities but rather an outcome of 'recomposition' through establishing new connections and 'reinventing themselves' (Karakayalı & Yaka, 2014, pp. 123–4).

Put differently, the Gezi Episode witnessed the emergence of an alternative solidarity project to that of the AKP's, building a new sense of identity against the docile class of citizens whose political capacity was 'reduced to the role of passive members of non-political society' (Lefebvre, 1969, p. 49). The rejection of the traditional, majoritarian, homogenising politics and a one-dimensional community built around a narrowly defined 'national will' in favour of an active, insurgent citizen gave the Gezi Episode a 'militant' character. This militancy found its ultimate expression in *çapulcu* as the foundation of a more inclusive and diverse urban citizenship with anti-capitalist tones. There is indeed a sense in the Turkish word *çapulcu* implying the act of prying on others' property, which fit nicely into what was actually unfolding during the Gezi Episode, that is, resisting commodification and reclaiming ownership of public spaces and resources 'stolen' from the people. The designation *çapulcu* proved useful as much for activists who appropriated it immediately in order to accentuate their defiance of private property and narrow political representation as for an authoritarian ruler posing as the 'guardian' of the rule of law and property of the nation. While this double-edged interpretation made the activists' political subjectivity precarious and always vulnerable to attacks from Erdoğan, the term still retained a romanticised modern-day iteration of heroic 'banditry' (*eşkiyalık*) to defend the commons of the people against the propertied class. The emerging militant and insurgent citizen, *çapulcu*, was in fact a 'common-er' floating from street clashes to the occupation of Gezi Park, from assemblies in neighbourhood forums to squatting in abandoned buildings, while prefiguring a new political community in which the common was at once the organising principle and the horizon.

* * *

All in all, globally connected activism in politicised spaces of the city was not simply about creating spaces for aggravated masses to interact with each other while expressing their thoughts and channelling their frustration. The interpenetration of the three dynamics of the Gezi Episode (mobilisational, spatial, radical democratic) drove these masses to embrace a new political subjectivity and nurtured a new idea of 'togetherness', a new expression of the 'demos'. In contrast to arguments regarding how radical politics that emerged from Gezi failed to contribute a 'genuine political alternative' (Akçalı, 2018), the process of building a new community with emphasis on the common was itself the political alternative. By radicalising the sphere of their everyday life (as experienced in squares, camps and then in park forums), the community became the source of political power. In other words, community and politics became inseparable as community became politics in, of and around the common. Borrowing from Caffentzis and Federici, 'a specific community [was] created in the production of the relations by which a specific common [was] brought into existence and sustained' (Caffentzis & Federici, 2014, p. 102). New political forms (such as 'assembly') and functions (such as 'calling power' and 'political hub') that accompanied the prefigurative practices of reclaiming, socialising and repurposing abandoned buildings, gardens and other unclaimed and stolen spaces and resources in the city, became 'rehearsals' in building a new political community.

Nevertheless, the claim that Gezi failed to offer a genuine alternative still merits a longer discussion, to which I turn in the next chapter.

Note

1. Documentaries on the implementation of 'neighbourhood committees' (modelled on Resistance Committees) in Fatsa (a small town on the coast of Black Sea) during the late 1970s would be shown in several forum meetings (Özkoray & Özkoray, 2013, p. 166). The nostalgia for the Fatsa experience would occasionally be revived in debates on Birleşik Haziran (see, for instance: Deli Gaffar, 2015, p. 38).

6

TROUBLE IN PARADISE?

Social movements are destined to fail if they can't create some sort of organisational structure [. . .] I attended numerous forums. I witnessed ordinary people calling for an organisation. Gezi was in fact a cry for organisation [. . .] We couldn't do it. Nobody could. This is why existing political groups (*siyasetler*) fell apart. (M. C. B., personal communication, 29 June 2016)

Yes, all these committees and branches emerged from forums, but they all fell apart later; they did not evolve into anything. Nothing is left from them. There was freedom in the forums to engage in identity politics and debate everything, but it was not connected to anything. (A. D., personal communication, 4 August 2016)

It did not occur to me until after the completion of my field work that these and other similar comments scattered through my interviews with Yoğurtçu Forum activists were in fact words of caution that the euphoric anticipation of a truly egalitarian society blinded many – including myself – to the dilemmas with which the whole process was marred. In this chapter, I interrogate the ambiguities and internal contradictions of the Gezi Episode. Questions such as 'how did even the most ardent supporters of prefigurative, radical democratic, assembly-style politics in forums, solidarities and squat houses end up prioritising conventional mechanisms of representative democracy that best functioned at the national level?' or 'why did its activists not regard Yoğurtçu

Forum and other radical democratic initiatives as a political end in itself, but rather a transition to what they saw as the "real politics" that could best be achieved through traditional forms of organisation, such as a political party?' Below I will demonstrate that these and other contradictions that arose from the three dynamics of the Gezi Episode deeply conditioned the efforts for the reconstitution of the social.

Explaining Gezi's Unravelling

Indeed, one common aspect of the global cycle of social movements in the 2010s was that they fizzled out of the political scene as rapidly as they emerged. Commentators who depict this as 'failure' often either express a genuine grief for a long-gone glimmer of hope for real social change or reveal their deep cynicism towards radical politics by claiming to have proved how 'nothing has changed'. More sober analyses aim to make sense of the aftermath of the movements in different parts of the world when most political conditions targeted by these movements remained intact or became worse, such as in Syria or Libya (Prashad, 2012). Yet, here too, the rise of authoritarian populism and increasing support for 'strongmen' in many parts of the world are linked to the alleged failures of the wave of anti-austerity and pro-democracy movements of the early twenty-first century (among many others, see: Cook, 2018, 2020; Ehrenberg, n.d.; Feldman, 2020; King, 2020; Kurzman et al., 2013; Mandour, 2019; TEDx Talks, 2017). Similar analyses appeared about the Gezi uprising to explain the inability of translating the energy and spirit from the Gezi experience into a more durable political structure (Balaban, 2022; Günay, n.d.; Özen, 2015). Among these explanations and observations, those which focus on the most immediate and visible factors that led to the eventual demise of forums and other radical democratic practices offer a useful entry point into this debate.

One theme that appears frequently is that political activism in forums in the aftermath of the Gezi uprisings was marred with 'too much talk' without achieving anything tangible and eventually pushing the public away in disappointment. Observers of the Gezi Episode as well as the activists often indicated that the masses who joined the Gezi protests in great numbers and diversity got 'tired of talks and nothing else' as countless ideas, committees or workshops failed to generate a coordinated political action (M. C. B., personal communication, 10 July 2015). In the early days of the park forums, meetings were often dominated by political commentary embellished with jargon and slogans reminiscent of the tired lexicon of the left, without 'actually touching people's lives' (A. D., personal communication, 10 July 2015). What made these meetings especially divisive was the ideological cleavages among different leftist groups going back to pre-Gezi times, leading to deep disagreements on how to transform the 'Gezi spirit' into a political movement. As discussed in Chapter 2, what had initially brought different individuals and political groups together was the anti-AKP sentiment defined mainly by defence of secularism, concerns about the city and its secular, Western urban fabric and protection of fundamental rights. This overarching defensive mode had allowed activists from a palette of ideological orientations to overcome their differences and unite around common goals, especially when these goals were increasingly centred around local and less controversial issues, such as the conversion of a public elementary school into a religious school, the destruction of a grove or the demolition of historic cultural sites. Yet when discussions switched to actively formulating broader political action, activists often failed in finding common ground. The way the debates were initially framed in large forum meetings, however, did not resonate, especially with the young activists who were politicised in unique circumstances, looking for and developing a different mode of politics since the early days of the uprisings. In the eyes of one Yoğurtçu activist, 'past tendencies of the leftist cliques could not be overcome' when they wanted to cling on to their 'micro powers' as 'generals without an army' (S. B., personal communication, 10 July 2015). Even after Yoğurtçu Forum broke up into smaller park forums, neighbourhood solidarities and squat houses, internal divisions within these very groups did not cease when – as some activists saw it – 'capriciousness, inflated egos and narrow identifications took politics hostage' (O. B., personal communication, 10 August 2015). These and similar disagreements and hostility between groups have often been interpreted as a factor that drained the forums' dynamism and prevented the activists from developing a broader, harmonious vision of politics.

Another theme that has often been brought up as an important factor for the demise of the Gezi movement was the proliferation of too many local and single-issue groups in the course of the Episode. As early as 2014, following the emergence of smaller park forums, neighbourhood solidarities and squat houses, core Yoğurtçu activists were complaining about these newly separated groups' lack of interest in collaboration with Yoğurtçu Forum. Each of these new solidarity groups, the activists later reported, were focusing on their narrow subjects and were not eager to engage in collective political mobilisation as they did during the active days of the Gezi protests (L. T. G., personal communication, 18 July 2014). On various occasions, such as 'Gezi's Remainder' (*Gezi'nin Bakiyesi*) meetings in 2014 – which had assembled various forums as well as individuals and activist groups to assess the overall state of political mobilisation since the beginning of the uprisings in May 2013 – there were some weak voices that suggested a framework in which smaller, neighbourhood-based solidarity groups would serve as contact points with local residents, directly addressing their problems and making the Gezi movement relevant to their lives, while bigger park forums such Yoğurtçu Forum could coordinate, synchronise and amplify these local initiatives under a broader common political agenda (Y. O., personal communication, 30 June 2015; also see some of the entries in the blog dedicated to these meetings: *Gezi'nin Bakiyesi*, n.d.). Yet, these expectations did not materialise, leading observers as well as the activists themselves to conclude that it was ultimately this fragmentation of activism during the Episode that prevented the emergence of concerted political mobilisation.

Heavy reliance on social media and other communication tools triggering rapid yet unstable and precarious activism is also often seen as a culprit for the ineffectiveness and eventual demise of the contemporary social movements around the world (Malchik, 2019). According to this line of argument, these movements did not spend as much time on organising on the ground or utilising existing organisations (such as unions, political parties and others) as their predecessors from the pre-digital era, which prevented the emergence and operationalisation of a political infrastructure for making collective decisions, negotiating with adversaries and challenging authority. More specifically, these movements could not produce 'network internalities' (Tufekci, 2017), the capacity to form durable networks and benefits emerging from these networks, because online mobilisation was too fast and unable to adapt to new paths. In the case of the Gezi uprisings, too, while the Yoğurtçu Forum and others often had a noticeable presence on social media, creating a portal for thousands of its followers for sharing news, raising consciousness and connecting and mobilising the participants when there was an event or protest to be organised, actual forum meetings became less and less attended, hosting only a handful of people who were already actively committed. For instance, during my field work, I joined some of the Yoğurtçu Park activists in a rally protesting the military operation launched by Israel in Gaza in July 2014. The rally was haphazardly organised on social media in the heat of the unfolding violence. I could witness the activists complaining about issues with communicating with other groups to coordinate the rally and disseminate the accurate logistical information. The miscommunication resulted in two different places being mistakenly announced as the place for the rally, which compromised the impact of the protest. Although younger, tech savvy activists had shouldered the burden in organising and publicising the event, the problems in communication and coordination could not be avoided, and thus the turnout was lower than expected.

Another argument often brought up to explain the short life span of the Gezi movement pertains to its 'organisational flaws', that is, its lack of a centralised structure with an effective leadership. The forceful refusal of a more traditional political structure in social movements dates back to the 1960s and 1970s when the 'new social movements' of the time – such as the feminist movement, gay and lesbian movement, student movement, anti-war movement and so on – were highly critical of the strict organisational structure of previous movements (see, for instance: Freeman, 1972). Yet the critique of this political position for a 'a purely horizontalist conception of radical democracy' (Mouffe, 2018) has recently become more pronounced because of its inability to bring about real radical transformation (see, for instance: Smith, 2016). It was not surprising to hear similar arguments tying the demise of the Gezi Episode to the lack of organisational structure, the absence of leadership and of a broader political agenda. The issue of organisational 'flaws' would sometimes be brought up with respect to the 'wrong choices' taken by activists due to their implicit or otherwise unwitting alleged narrow-mindedness, capriciousness and other 'middle-class tendencies' when they refused to follow the socialist lead, which would have provided the movement with much needed organisation and leadership (Balaban, 2022).

Along the same lines, the lack of an overarching body reminiscent of a general assembly (such as those that emerged in Greece and Spain or in some

Latin American countries in the earlier wave) that could have provided space for smaller forums, solidarities and squat houses to communicate and coordinate their activities was also brought up to explain the fizzling out of the Gezi spirit. Indeed, in the forums such as Yoğurtçu, the most visible and obvious impact of horizontalism and lack of institutionalisation was that all forms of activism could be achieved through 'volunteerism' in the absence of a solid bureaucratic body and of mechanisms for accountability. Moreover, the lack of centralised organisation was believed to cause decision-making processes to be long and arduous, especially at the beginning of the Episode when attendance in forums was high (Günay, n.d.).

While these factors may have contributed to the Gezi Episode's demise, I offer below an alternative set of explanations which, I argue, reveal deeper contradictions from within the three dynamics of the Episode (mobilisational, spatial, radical democratic) as they simultaneously shaped the whole movement. By highlighting these deeper issues to better capture the trajectory of this political experience, I argue that the very paradoxical features of the Episode activated several structural fault lines in the Turkish society, which ultimately led to the waning of the Gezi movement.

Contradictions in the Gezi Episode

Issues Pertaining to the Mobilisational Dynamic

One of the ways in which the mobilisational dynamic affected the Gezi Episode was the untenable speed of activism due to rapidly unfolding events – mostly in the national political scene – leading to fatigue and disorientation among activists. It was not only that many of these activists (especially the younger ones) were unable to make big life decisions in regard to their career or personal lives, nor was it solely that they saw dramatic reshuffling in their social circles because of over-commitment to activism (M. C. B., personal communication, 10 July 2015; A. D., personal communication, 10 July 2015). They were also ceaselessly responding to an almost daily changing political agenda comprising acts of violence, such as exploding bombs and military campaigns in the Kurdish-majority territories, national elections, social unrest following major workplace accidents (such as the Soma mining disaster, which claimed the lives of more than 300 people), among so many others. Activists, most of whom came to political maturation without prior experience, found themselves constantly mobilising without adequate time to organise, reflect on and digest what they had encountered. As some of the more seasoned activists observed, the overall mobilisation could not connect the nascent radical vision emerging from this politicisation process with the historical experiences and theoretical strength of the movements from the 1960s and 1970s. As a result, activism could easily be co-opted into 'lighter versions' of progressive politics with a narrow focus on local issues (S. B., personal communication, 10 July 2015). More importantly, the lack of institutionalisation due to fast pace intensified the disconnect between young, 'newly-minted' activists and the expectations of the masses. The latter, as some activists interpreted it, treated Gezi and Yoğurtçu as yet another official department that would accept petitions and take bureaucratic steps to accomplish things, while the former (Gezi activists) derided the 'ordinary folks' with this mindset for maintaining narrow-sighted, 'petit bourgeois' expectations and showed little patience to integrate them into the movement (O. B., personal communication, 10 August 2015; Y. O., personal communication, 30 June 2015). Consequently, the two sides could not find the time to develop mutual understanding and trust, nor could they develop a way to harness the political energy from the Gezi uprisings.

Another way the mobilisational dynamic had a negative impact on the Gezi Episode was the increasing rapidity and volatility of political activism in different urban sites, which made it impossible to sustain the shared identity that had nourished the 'Gezi spirit' in the early days of the Episode. As I discussed in Chapter 3, during early street protests and the occupation of Gezi Park, the anti-Erdoğan sentiment that embodied the collective resentment and frustration had helped create networks of trust among various groups. A discourse of liberation and dignity, often bolstered with humour on social media and graffiti on the walls, helped forge alliances. Differences could be deferred under immediate activism, such as erecting barricades, tending the wounded, occupying the square, surviving in the park and so forth. Yet, it proved difficult to sustain this momentum as the 'meaning of Gezi' became fragmented, with activists engaging in politics in multiple capacities and in different scales in park forums, neighbourhood solidarities and squat houses. Turning the anti-Erdoğan sentiment into a sustainable collective political identity became difficult, if not impossible, due to the 'fluidity' of subjectivities emerging in these multiple spaces. Despite the heavy use of social media, which gave the impression that networks of trust were robust and functioning towards achieving common (or at least well-coordinated) goals, in reality alliances could hardly go beyond sharing each other's social media posts without translating these ad-hoc alliances into a more concerted political action or enactments of citizenship. In other words, the pace of activism and its split nature paralysed the meaning of 'being committed' and sense of community.

Paradoxically, the spatiality of the movement was dragging it into a more localised space in which often the same people with similar concerns and priorities began the define the scope of mobilisation. Put differently, political subjectivities were beginning to 'calcify' as the sedentary phase of mobilisation was becoming the predominant mode in certain locales. It is the intensification of this contradictory situation (that is, hyper mobilisation and spatial calcification) to which I turn next.

Issues Pertaining to the Spatial Dynamic

As we saw in Chapter 4, the spatiality of the Gezi Episode created a segmented political cartography in Istanbul in which each site became home for a distinct type of politics thanks to its unique spatial characteristics. As the number of these sites increased, the range of their activism got trimmed further and political fragmentation of the Episode deepened: too many sites began to foster incompatible activism at different levels or scales that did not form a coherent and complementary political vision. While hyper-mobilisation prevented – as discussed above – the solidification of a common, overarching political identity during the Episode, the fluidity between different urban sites 'thickened' and activism within each site became even more insular and uncoordinated. For instance, in a neighbourhood solidarity, activists could come up with successful strategies for issues that concerned the neighbourhood, but that energy could not necessarily translate into a harmonised collective action with other groups in the city. The çapulcu identity that once fuelled activism slowly became faint as activism morphed into a routine set of activities coloured by the immediacy of daily problems or local manifestations of broader political fault lines. The tediousness of tasks in these local settings, such as regular meetings, planning, logistical decisions and other actions – all of which were necessary to maintain the ongoing efforts to continue for the movement to exist

(Glass, 2008, p. 13) – caused it to lose its dynamism and 'charisma', especially when the movement's global connections weakened and attempts to translate the lessons from other social movements in the world lost priority, eventually turning Gezi into a more parochial experience. This was especially true when bigger forums were split into smaller solidarities and squat houses, and the activists who could easily go in and out of different groups or sites became more suspicious of the politics (and the political vision) outside their immediate circle (Kuryel & Fırat, 2020).

One of the most visible consequences of such spatial (and eventually political) fragmentation of activism was 'loss of diversity' because only a fraction of the public joined the smaller solidarities after park forums lost their steam. In the Yoğurtçu Forum, for instance, only highly committed leftist activists (most of whom were independent and unaffiliated) remained and the whole forum experience became increasingly restricted to a leftist discourse. Feminists, LGBTQIA+ individuals, environmentalists, anarchists and other radical and moderate leftist groups seemed to have found their own platform for communication and networking, while the energy rising from multifaceted collective frustration could no longer be maintained.

Another consequence of spatial fragmentation was the mismatch between the characteristics of a politicised site in the city and the type of politics that activists advocated in that particular space. In various instances, attempts to carry out a certain (mostly national) political agenda in a particular site would backfire and further deepen existing cleavages. Yoğurtçu Forum, for instance, grew into a spatially awkward size for it was neither small enough to effectively reach out to the residents of smaller neighbourhoods in the district, nor big enough to be able produce powerful politics at the national level. Towards the end of its career, it became painfully clear that Yoğurtçu Forum did not comprise the most suitable and stable form to turn itself into a general assembly that would act as an overarching governing body where smaller groups could convene together and work on a common strategy for carrying out the type of politics required, imagined and prefigured following the protests and Gezi Park's occupation.

This 'space-politics mismatch' would become even more evident when smaller park forums, neighbourhood solidarities and squat houses – which had accumulated political power and shaped their political orientation around a local issue of immediate concern to them – found themselves debating how to take a political position in broader, national-level events, such as an upcoming presidential election or a national referendum. The sense of solidarity and community emerging from the political mobilisation around the local issue as the focus of a forum, solidarity or citizen initiative could easily be fractured in the face of such national questions (S. A., personal communication, 13 July 2015). Measures taken to prevent this would further deepen the inclination towards localisation, eventually turning these initiatives into small, insulated political islands where activists got stuck in narrow horizons and became increasingly less able (or willing) to 'flow' from one political style, scale or space to another, as was the case in the early days of the Gezi Episode. The broader political agenda that aimed to transform the political and reconstitute the social since the beginning of the Episode was thus compromised under this contradictory spatial dynamic at play.

The contrast between the experiences of Turkey and those of other countries during the rise and fall of their respective social movements can reveal the extent of the mismatch between the political vision and activism and the space in which it was imagined and enacted. For instance, in Argentina where the radical experiment lasted longer and had deeper implications with respect to the residents and activists involved, neighbourhood assemblies were closely linked to occupied and recuperated factories where the actual production process had come to a halt after their owners abandoned them (Sitrin, 2012; Also see: Vieta, 2016, p. 58; Mason-Deese, 2012). There were also assembly-based councils and communes in Venezuela where citizens organised themselves as agents of democratic self-government, which blurred the line between where one worked and lived (Ciccariello-Maher, 2016). In all these cases, a new set of practices, values and norms were formulated, debated and implemented in these locations in line with the demands of the new life once these production sites were resuscitated again by the very workers themselves. These workers organised autonomously and horizontally in these factories and established new ties to the neighbourhoods they were situated in, which resulted in the emergence of a unique vision for the future organisation of the society. The organic connection between, and mutual dependence of, the workplace and the neighbourhood shaped the emerging principles of citizenship and politics.

No similar connections that tied economic life to social life could be seen in the Gezi Episode, except for the creation of independent vegetable gardens and later small-scale food cooperatives that emerged in Kadıköy and a handful of other places (Işıl & Değirmenci, 2020; also see: Kadıköy Kooperatifi, 2017). Yoğurtçu and other forums were not backed by or did not directly contribute to any production-related occupation or a collective, with the exception of the Kazova textile factory – a short-lived collaboration and solidarity with the workers of a bankrupt firm whose workers confiscated the workshop and continued production (Taştan, 2013). Therefore, the way a territory was reclaimed in a neighbourhood had different implications in Argentina or Venezuela than in Turkey. In the former, the mobilisation was envisioning and actually built an alternative economic system in addition to rising up against an oppressive government, all in harmony with the needs and the expectations of the space where it was located (Sitrin, 2012, pp. 129–48, 179). The politics of the common in Turkey, however, could not connect this experiment with existing units of production in the localities where it emerged, which could have shaped the prefiguration and enactment of radical democracy.

All in all, the spatial fragmentation of urban revolt in Istanbul eventually forced Gezi activists to go even more local in their political activism and embrace a narrower iteration of the common. Spatially divided centres of political activism bolstered 'in-group, out-group' dynamics in these spaces, leading to a more isolationist, segregated co-existence of separate initiatives. The resulting insularity and loss of diversity led to the emergence of incompatible political visions at different levels or scales, which did not add up to a coherent, unified activism around a common goal.

Issues Pertaining to the Radical Democratic Dynamic

One of the contradictions that emerged during the Gezi Episode was the emphasis on – if not the fetish of – decentralised, non-hierarchical and leaderless organising as one of the main pillars of radical democratic activism. With their staunch refusal to create formal organisations and insistence on the 'logic of aggregation' (Juris, 2012) as the primary form of mobilisation, activists of the Gezi Episode, similar to others around the world, were coming to political maturation through a politics of what Jodi Dean (2016) calls a 'multitude of singularities', despite claiming to respond to neoliberalism's assault on the social. In other words, fetishising the performative assembly as a goal in and of itself – which offered no guarantees for a progressive let alone radical political imagination – ended up hurting the movement when these energies could not culminate in a solid, durable and transformative mobilisation, eventually leading to exhaustion, disillusionment and the ultimate capture by the authoritarian regime.

More importantly, such deep suspicion among activists towards pursuing radical politics in formal organisations was yet another symptom of the neoliberal *Zeitgeist* – now creeping into the very political activism that was fighting it – which aimed to replace the idea of an organised society with a narrow, conservative definition of community (also see: Brown, 2019). What emerged was similar to Lichterman's observation of 'public spirited commitment to politics' that 'emphasises individual voice without sacrificing the common good for private needs' (Lichterman, 1996, p. 4). While in Lichterman's eyes this type of activism creates collective identities and solidarity beyond narrower versions of traditional community, it can also be argued that the ever-increasing emphasis on the 'individualised' commitment to public good precludes the institutionalisation of activism and its achievements in the form of a new political community around 'the common'. Therefore, collective mobilisation in contemporary social movements seemed to have paradoxically fallen hostage to the very force it was against, that is, the individualisation and privatisation of everything under neoliberalism.[1] Accordingly, while the Gezi movement gravitated towards the common as the kernel of a new political community, the fact that radical assembly practices were undertaken as a multitude of autonomous individuals favouring a form of horizontalism that is suspicious of centrally organised power diminished the movement's transformative potential. As such, it could not go beyond 'connecting individualisms' to one another, falling short of reconstituting the social around the common.

A second contradiction that emerged from the common-oriented, radical democratic dynamic of the Gezi Episode relates to the scale and scope of radical imagination in activism. As we have seen earlier, in the effort to carry into the future the energy unleashed with the Gezi uprising, park forums and their offshoots progressively evolved from big political questions brought about by the immediacy of the political situation in the country (especially on getting organised and developing strategies against Erdoğan's Islamist conservative agenda in the city) towards an emphasis on more local issues, especially those concerning districts or neighbourhoods, to be able to 'engage in tangible activism' within the immediate spaces they occupied. 'Big politics', however, never fully disappeared in the political imagination. Despite prioritising the building of a new common through radical mobilisation in various urban sites, activists never fully abandoned the idea of engaging in 'old-style' leftist politics. Even the slogan 'everywhere is Taksim, resistance everywhere' served as an anchor to connect the symbolism of Gezi Park with broader political issues. Especially when forums began to lose their diversity, with mostly radical leftists remaining, the vocabulary of 'class struggle', 'revolution', 'strikes' and 'ideology' began to colour the discourse, vision and direction of these forums more manifestly. Whatever novelty in activism these forums and their offspring introduced, the expectation was still that these initiatives ultimately would tie into a familiar political struggle and especially to class struggle because, as one of the Yoğurtçu activists rhetorically asked during an interview: 'why forum if it won't touch anything?' ('*bir şeye dokunmayacaksa niye forum?*') (O. B., personal communication, 10 August 2015). The inability to achieve this was often seen as a reason behind the unravelling of the movement, with the optimistic caveat that this was a lesson well-learned and 'when Gezi comes back again, the revolutionary left will be ready and prepared' (Y. O., personal communication, 30 June 2015).

The problem with such ambition was that while activists wanted to transform the whole society into a more democratic and inclusive political community as a part of a broader political fight, the tools they could find in their arsenal were still appropriate primarily for local activism. The assembly structure in forums, solidarities and squat houses – which claimed to offer 'concrete' steps in solving 'real problems' concerning the very locale they were situated in – did not provide the most suitable and stable spatial setting for 'big politics' that permeated the Gezi Episode. Yet, the way politics unfolded in Turkey (elections, increasing authoritarianism of the AKP, the end of the peace process with the Kurds, and so on) was forcing the activists to commit themselves to broader, traditional politics, stealing the primacy of the novel radical democratic practices.

For example, in Don Kişot squat house, where the most prominent politics was of local nature, one could observe an uneasy co-existence of local and national visions of political activism. Deep cleavages had begun to emerge within the squat community as early as 2014 regarding how to continue their activism and into what form the squat experience had to be transformed. There was a more anarchist, libertarian group, which defended the idea of establishing a 'real' squat house in which occupants should live without rules, pre-determined protocols or big decisions regarding politics: they were interested in a type of politics defined by building a life along the principles of anarchism in the house and in the neighbourhood. On the other side, there were those who aspired to have an impact on 'real politics' or at least were looking to take a position on national matters (such as the parliamentary elections) as the Gezi Episode was unfolding. These divisions became so deep that they eventually led to the final breaking up of the solidarity into two distinct entities (O. B., personal communication, 10 August 2015; Z. U., personal communication, 16 July 2015).

In other words, despite the gravitation towards local activism, the power of the broader political activism was too strong to be ignored in the local space where prefigurative politics was cultivated. It was as if a 'fictitious national space' always found its way into the minds of activists, even though they were experimenting with novel radical democratic practices that required the local physical space as the locus and scope of activism. Activists sought to elevate their political mobilisation beyond the confines of localism into this national space, which they believed would be more suitable for 'effective' political outcomes, even if it meant being open and vulnerable to political manipulation.[2] Consequently, this oscillation between 'small' (which could produce policy solutions, gather expertise from different stakeholders and increase the level of knowledge as well as internal harmony at the expense of the sphere of impact and range of interest) and 'big' (more abstract discussions on politics and activism, fuelling passion in political debates, energising crowds for mobilisation yet causing deeper divisions and preventing the implementation of more feasible, reasonable ideas) visions of politics in the Gezi Episode turned park forums, neighbourhood solidarities and squat houses into contradictory political spaces torn between opposite directions.

Yoğurtçu Forum's Dilemma

Yoğurtçu Forum's trajectory best demonstrates this tension between the local and national scopes of radical activism. As discussed in Chapter 5, Yoğurtçu

Forum felt obligated to follow course in going more local as the centre of gravity for political activism had been moving within the city's inner veins – from parks to neighbourhoods to buildings. When the forum was mobilising around local issues (such as the rehabilitation of the Kurbağalıdere brook that cut across the district), the emerging politics would become more concrete (supported by sound information and policy recommendations), consensus would be easier to reach and the outcome would be more effective and tangible. This type of local activism, however, circumscribed the forum's reach, dynamism and impact, which it had inherited from the early Gezi days. According to its activists, it could not provide a 'political ground (*siyasi zemin*)' to evolve into a nation-wide struggle because 'we are stuck in Kadıköy' (M. C. B., personal communication, 10 July 2015). Accordingly, the overall mobilisation experience would be dull, repetitive, mundane and tiresome, leading to decline in interest and hope in its transformative, 'utopian' potential.

This stood in sharp contrast to 'big politics', which was always prominent among the forum activists even when they were deeply occupied with local issues. High attendance in forum meetings or during collective mobilisation would only be possible when there was an important event such as a commemoration or a protest over broader issues, such as the state violence in the Kurdish areas of the country or in support of Palestine. In such instances, when 'big politics' was at the centre of activism, however, tensions would surface quickly, exposing ideological divisions, generating unending and unproductive debates for hours in a vague and incoherent (if not conspiracy-laden) language that would cause the clarity and harmony of politics be lost.

Under these two opposite forces, Yoğurtçu Forum found it increasingly difficult to become an 'overarching political body', a coordinating power broker for local initiatives in Istanbul around a broader agenda or strategy, which further weakened its mobilisation and drained its radical vision. While, as we saw earlier, other local initiatives, solidarities and forums blossomed separately from Yoğurtçu, the loyal forum activists I interviewed – for whom local activism was never enough as a form of true political engagement – began to gravitate towards big, national, electoral politics but with one new ingredient they felt they were bringing with them: the 'forum spirit'. They believed this spirit – which was itself a product of radical experience emerging from the forum structure inherited from the early days of the Gezi Park occupation – had to be infused into existing traditional, national-level politics because ultimately it was this latter type of politics that mattered the most. For one of its foremost activists, Yoğurtçu Forum was too weak to respond to the demands of the times and had completed its mission: the spirit was important yet insufficient for it could not be translated into 'real politics' outside the forum (A. D., personal communication, 4 August 2016). Another activist believed that while there had always been a yearning for 'real politics' among the people, Yoğurtçu and other smaller forums were never able to fully translate this yearning into constructive institutional politics except for smaller, local triumphs (M. C. B., personal communication, 29 June 2016). For other activists, too, there was an urgent need to carry out the local and national struggles simultaneously by a broader organisation because otherwise the movement would remain fragmented (S. B., personal communication, 10 July 2015).

As Yoğurtçu Forum wavered under this oscillation between the tendency to go local in its activism and the will to have a voice at the national level, the forum experience eventually imploded and gave way to two separate structures of political mobilisation: the Birleşik Haziran movement and Kadıköy Urban Defense (Kadıköy Kent Savunması). While the Kadıköy Urban Defence emerged – and survived to date – as a citizens' initiative for local and environmental issues particularly in the Kadıköy district, it is the now defunct Birleşik Haziran that best illustrates the contradictions in the Yoğurtçu experience.

Birleşik Haziran

Birleşik Haziran began its political career in 2014 as an initiative by a number of scholars and representatives from political parties, revolutionary leftist organisations, unions and non-governmental organisations in order to form a broad 'anti-capitalist, anti-imperialist, anti-fascist' front against the AKP regime. By the end of the year, special forums began to take place in various districts in Istanbul, Ankara, Izmir and other cities to discuss the establishment of a 'United Opposition' (*Birleşik Muhalefet*), which would later become the Birleşik Haziran movement ('*Birleşik Haziran Hareketi' Yola Çıktı*, 2014). The movement declared its mission as organising the public in various spaces (neighbourhoods, workplaces, villages) all over the country for the establishment of an 'anti-imperialist, pro-labour, anti-fascist, secular, solidaristic, democratic and independent republic' (Güvenç, 2015). As such, it strived to be the emblem of the long-waited transformation among the revolutionary left, a renewed hope for otherwise ineffective, dispersed leftist political organisations that could not predict, steer or shape the Gezi uprising (Deli Gaffar, 2015, p. 37). It claimed to be rooted in the 'street' and the 'assembly' thanks to the forum legacy it inherited and preserved, which needed to be scaled up to the national level with political targets, such as a new constitution, new presidential system, defence of secular education, ecology, women's equality and others. It also tasked itself to make sure that the 'resistance' and 'revolt' dynamics were multiplied through 'commoning' the struggles beyond mere cooperation between existing organisations and structures and by novel mechanisms that connected millions who rose up to demand full control of their fate during the Gezi uprisings (İşleyen, 2014, pp. 41–3). What was needed in this endeavour was a revolutionary movement untarnished by 'ethnic nationalism' or liberalism but one that pursued a left-leaning patriotism (*yurtseverlik*) in a pro-social, secular and pro-enlightenment opposition (Yanardağ, 2014, pp. 32–5).

The fact that by 2016 almost all activists who were still active in Yoğurtçu Forum joined the Birleşik Haziran movement was testament to their attraction to national-level, electoral political mobilisation because for them the forum experience in Yoğurtçu 'did not correspond to real politics' ('*gerçek siyasette karşılığı yoktu*'). True, Yoğurtçu Forum could prepare banners and organise rallies against an issue such as 'corruption' but simply undertaking these actions – as the argument followed – did not make the forum a transformative political actor, subject or agent to address any issue at its core. Birleşik Haziran, on the other hand, had the potential to be more powerful and 'actually do something about it' (M. C. B., personal communication, 29 June 2016). Despite its diverse, inclusive and flexible structure, Yoğurtçu Forum would not necessarily produce politics that could effect 'real social change' while Birleşik Haziran had 'bigger dreams of creating a new country, a new world'. For Yoğurtçu activists, who were now also Birleşik Haziran delegates, doing politics in the latter was different with respect to its impact and audience: one would feel accountable to the whole nation rather than just fellow activists in a forum or the residents in that locality (A. D., personal communication, 4 August 2016). By moving beyond the 'identity politics' that was pervasive in many forums and activist groups, Birleşik Haziran was 'trying to establish itself as a political subject' ('*siyasi özne olmaya çalışıyor*'), focusing on such issues as labour, class struggle, secularism, state violence, imperialism and so forth. That was how it 'defined the diameter of politics' ('*siyasetin çapını ona göre belirliyor*') (A. D., personal communication, 4 August 2016).

Here the very conceptualisation of political power and 'real social change' was what made activists gravitate towards a more established, traditional political style over forum and assembly politics. Yet, the nature of the politics pursued by Birleşik Haziran – defined by tackling large-scale national issues through institutionalising horizontal activism along vertical political organisation – intensified disagreements within the movement. Some Yoğurtçu activists in the movement could observe that although it was a less diverse group (especially in terms of the political orientation of its constituents) than the Yoğurtçu Forum during its earlier days, it was still more difficult to find a common ground in Birleşik Haziran because the type of discussions, topics to address and actions to take differed widely in scale and content. The assembly nature of politics in Yoğurtçu and other forums made it easier to mediate differences of opinion, whereas issues that would not even be a matter of argument in the forum became highly contentious in Birleşik Haziran's party assembly (A. D., personal communication, 4 August 2016).

This oscillation between the forces of local and national politics demonstrates the limit of the activists' radical political imagination as it conditioned the characteristics of the emerging political community. The political experience in Birleşik Haziran stood in contrast to the radical political orientation towards the creation of a new common in the assembly, which worked best at the intersection of constant radical mobilisation at the local scale while being connected to its global counterparts. As the political horizon of the Gezi Episode could not fully shake off its national ambitions, activists often found themselves drawn into traditional politics whose language was not suitable to express the essence of the common-oriented radical politics they were pursuing. With national political agendas becoming more pressing, and as Birleşik Haziran found itself deeply involved in electoral politics, the vision of radical democracy risked being watered down and even falling from view.

Reconstituting the Social in Difficult Times

The above-mentioned contradictions emerging from the three dynamics (mobilisational, spatial and radical democratic) that were prevalent during the

Gezi Episode prevented the movement from adequately tackling at least two political questions.

Declining Primacy of Radical Activism in the Face of State Violence

As we saw in Chapter 2, the Gezi protests were as much the culmination of urban discontent as they were a result of the AKP's failure in maintaining its hegemonic position through 'mechanisms of consent'. The 17–25 December 2013 revelations of government corruption that involved some of the cabinet members and Erdoğan's own son had in particular compelled the party and its leader to heavily fall back on 'mechanisms of coercion' to silence dissent. Following the Gezi uprisings, an unofficial 'state of exception' became the modus operandi of the government through recoding statutory laws that regulated non-governmental organisations (such as the association of architects and engineers, trade unions) or other legal bodies (such as the council of judges and prosecutors) (Öztürk, 2021, ch. 5). The new authoritarianism of the state would be cemented, especially with the escalation of armed conflict in Kurdish-majority regions, the failed coup attempt in 2016 and numerous instances of terrorism, all of which helped Erdoğan shore up support from his followers and consolidate his declining legitimacy, and it served as a prelude to fundamental changes in the political regime.

In such a precarious political environment, being a political objector in streets, forums or squat houses was becoming increasingly dangerous. Intensifying repression against citizens, especially in the form of curtailing basic rights (such as right to assembly, speech and so on) and criminalising dissent discouraged the general public from openly involving in activism. The declining participation in activism brought with it a paradox. In order to make up for the loss of interest and attendance, Yoğurtçu and other forums offered a safe space where activists knew each other, and the issues they tackled did not often trigger immediate retaliation from the police. The spatial dynamic of the Gezi Episode was in full force towards localisation of politics, yet the fragmentation of the political space, once again, came at the expense of the scope of the prefigurative political experiment being compromised: with streets becoming less available for expression of dissent, parks or neighbourhoods could not effectively produce the type of radical activism that would generate a stronger force to address the bigger questions of transforming politics but instead were conducive to focusing solely on less controversial local issues. The type of political vision emerging from these politicised urban sites was no match for the violence perpetrated by the state.

Consequently, the constant state of emergency in national politics stole the primacy of the radical democratic vision promised by assembly and forum practices. Priorities had to shift from prefigurative experimentations of radical democracy to more urgent events as they unfolded almost daily. As one of the Yoğurtçu Forum activists told me in an interview we had just a day after the bombing in Atatürk Airport in June 2016, which claimed the lives of more than 40 people:

> Today [with escalating terror, increasing authoritarianism, war on Kurds, and so on] such [prefigurative, radical, forum style] politics is impossible – we are in the middle of a war. Nobody would be taken seriously if they came to the forum with a political agenda about this or that issue and said 'let's talk about these alternative thoughts and proposals'. People would say 'now is not the right time or place to deal with this issue'. (M. C. B., personal communication, 29 June 2016)[3]

These factors explain why activists in Yoğurtçu and others gravitated towards a higher-level, national political organisation such as Birleşik Haziran. Activists who came of political age through constant mobilisation in various sites of the city around the idea of the common found themselves compelled to take positions in a political matrix whose rules were increasingly defined by the grammar of traditional politics. This is why an activist who experienced direct, horizontal, prefigurative political activism in a squat house would find no contradiction in also hustling for the success of the candidate of a political party during the presidential election. More importantly, the same activist would find herself adopt the language, vision, strategies and overall politics of the same political party, which would require her take a position in the existing social and political cleavages without having the power to redefine or transform these cleavages. Consequently, the imagination of a democratic political community built through radical prefigurative political experiences became impossible to sustain.

The Impact of the Kurdish Question on Radical Activism

While the Gezi Episode marked one of the rare periods in Turkish politics during which time an opportunity arose for ethnic Turks to engage with the 'Kurdish question' beyond the state's framing and propaganda, it also witnessed the implications of this issue, activating deep fault lines in radical left politics. As early as the first days of Gezi park's occupation, there were instances when the Kurdish group in the park was harassed by hard-line nationalist left groups, especially the young sympathisers of the national socialist Workers' Party (İşçi Partisi) and Turkish Youth Union (Türk Gençlik Birliği) when the former brought in posters of Abdullah Öcalan, the captive leader of the Kurdish freedom movement. The initial scuffles were defused by other groups to allow the Kurdish activists stay in the park without being subjected to any more harassment. Afterwards, reports of positive interactions between the Kurds and the rest of the park occupants became commonplace. The forum experience following the dispersion of the Gezi occupation also helped Turkish and Kurdish activists connect with each other, creating channels for uneasy dialogues and mutual understanding. Collective activism occurred, with protests such as that in Kadıköy for the murder of Medeni Yıldırım in Lice being one such example of these comradely interactions. Some activists believed that the diverse composition of the forums as well as the open space that allowed for different ideas and topics to be discussed bravely, helped the Peoples' Democratic Party (Halkların Demokratik Partisi, HDP) pass the 10% threshold and enter the national assembly in the June 2015 elections (Y. O., personal communication, 30 June 2015).

These interactions with the Kurds and genuine soul-searching helped the Turkish left gain prestige, especially among younger citizens who had been developing deep suspicions towards the statist discourse. Over time, however, mistrust began to build up, especially among the Turkish activists who became increasingly disillusioned when their Kurdish counterparts did not automatically follow their lead in activism, as they were expecting them to do. This resentment dated back to the early days of the Gezi riots when the foremost leaders and spokespeople of the Kurdish movement were reluctant to give their full support (Hamsici, 2013). Some members of Yoğurtçu Forum even blamed the Kurds for pursuing a selfish political agenda and for prioritising a politics of ethnic identity rather than a mutual agenda for a collective struggle (M. C. B., personal communication, 10 July 2015; A. D., personal communication, 10 July 2015). They were dismayed by what they saw as 'disinterest' by the Kurdish groups in having a shared and coordinated activism and would complain that the Kurds did not 'honour their part of the agreement' (that is, not using certain slogans or banners during co-organised events or protests) but would instead 'steal the agenda' during protests or commemorations (M. C. B., personal communication, 29 June 2016).

Birleşik Haziran, too, would subtly blame the HDP for having more social democratic (as opposed to socialist) tendencies, and even for rubbing shoulders with the 'conservative, religious' sectors of the Kurdish community. Claims about Kurds' alleged support for Erdoğan's bid for presidency and accusations that they were not leftist, socialist or pro-labour enough to embrace the whole country became widespread (Kozanoğlu, 2015; Yurtsever, 2014). So much so that Birleşik Haziran presented itself as a non-Kurdish left alternative for many Gezi activists to engage in big politics while embodying a more progressive patriotic stance in leftism ('*yurtseverlik*') in a blend of anti-imperialist, worker-oriented and pro-secular jargon. As such, it strived to become a refuge for both the mainstream and radical Turkish left, which was increasingly wary of – and resentful towards – the organised Kurdish opposition, which it saw as carrying too much 'ethnic' tones in their politics.

It is important to remember that the roots of this tension between the Turkish and Kurdish left dates back to the 1960s and 1970s when the latter became increasingly estranged from political analyses and agendas adopted by the former regarding the 'Kurdish Question' (Yeğen, 2014). Disagreements deepened and divisions became unavoidable when the Kurdish left – especially with the force of armed struggle led by PKK from the 1980s onwards – began to develop its own theses and strategies of liberation, triggering an internal crisis among the Turkish left, which has long considered itself to be the 'older brother' – a guardian and mentor to Kurds in the revolutionary struggle (Ünlü, 2018, pp. 273–4; 288–95). It was not surprising, therefore, that nationalist undertones during the Gezi Episode – foiled in a rhetoric of universalism as opposed to particularism, such as the defence of secularism or a socialist revolution for all rather than pursuing narrow ethnic rights – could be heard among the leftist voices when it came to the Kurdish issue. While the latter could be discussed more sympathetically in the open format of forum meetings, tensions could still arise.

At a Yoğurtçu Forum meeting, for instance, the appearance of then head of the HDP, Selahattin Demirtaş, as a guest speaker in one of the earlier forums generated an unusually tense discussion among the participants of the meeting (personal observation, Yoğurtçu Park, 12 August 2014). Over time, many regular attendees lost interest and left Yoğurtçu and other forums, accusing them of becoming too radical or too lenient towards what they saw as 'separatist terrorism'. Similar tensions rose more frequently in other political spaces, such as Caferağa and Yeldeğirmeni squat houses, where activists had to navigate internal divisions stemming from disagreements about their political stance during the parliamentary election in 2015 (O. B., personal communication, 10 August 2015; O. S., personal communication, 11 August 2015; Z. U., personal communication, 16 July 2015). As divisions grew wider, 'Kurdish elements' in these political spaces, as well those sympathetic to the Kurdish position, preferred to prioritise working for the HDP's campaign in the election. This upset the autonomous, multiple-faceted, diverse character of the squat houses as well as other forums and solidarities, while the centre of gravity of political activism and organisation, once again, shifted to the national level. These spaces lost their primacy and effectiveness because the issues often discussed in forums once again faded in such a political urgency of the election, harming the prospects for an alternative political community that had emerged at the beginning of the Gezi Episode.

As could be expected, sympathisers of the Kurdish movement within the Turkish left kept their distance to Birleşik Haziran, deepening the latter's fragmented and fragile composition. Eventually the Kurdish question prevented the formation of true solidarity, paved the way for splits and led to the disappearance of many groups from the political scene. The glimmer of camaraderie and collaboration between the Turkish left and the Kurdish movement that fostered synergy and hope in the early days of the Gezi Episode was lost to mistrust and resentment. The escalation of violence following the June 2015 election and the collapse of the 'peace process' changed the whole calculus of politics once again. All this tragedy played into Erdoğan's hands and helped him maintain his increasingly authoritarian politics.

Once again, the immediacy of national politics that demonstrated itself through escalating state violence and the inability to settle disagreements on the Kurdish question prevented a full-fledged development towards a new conception of political citizenship around the idea of the common. It forced activists to oscillate between national and local perspectives on politics during which the primary focus on building the common and transforming society towards a new political community beyond nation-state was lost.

Notes

1. I am grateful to Derya Özkaya for drawing my attention to this connection.
2. Çelik and Ergenç (2018) talk about the negative impact of the national and local elections on the forums in Ankara, where established political organisations and political party affiliates tried hard to steer forums into their own political agendas.
3. Breines describes a similar development in student movements in the US in the 1960s when the movement had to recalibrate its activism from more prefigurative, radical political experimentation to more urgent, daily politics as the Vietnam war began to dominate the national political agenda (Breines, 1989, p. 64).

7

CONCLUSION

As I type these final words, there is still rubble on the ground from the two powerful earthquakes that hit south-eastern Turkey in February 2023, claiming more than 50,000 lives and leaving millions without an inhabitable home. This catastrophe of biblical proportions came at the tail end of a global pandemic, which brought the world to a halt for almost three years and made millions perish. Yet even before all this, an ever-intensifying suspicion, if not pessimism, had already been settling in among those who were dreaming of and fighting for a better Turkey and world, after having mobilised for an inclusive and democratic political community in Taksim Square, Gezi Park and numerous neighbourhoods and other places. When bombs began to explode, when the armed conflict with Kurdish guerillas began to escalate and when the failed coup attempt provided the pretext for a constitutional change that turned the country's political system into a neo-sultanate, the word 'Gezi' became synonymous with crime and terrorism in official mouths. Prominent civil society leaders such as Osman Kavala, Mücella Yapıcı, Can Atalay and others were convicted with unsubstantiated charges and grave disregard for even the most basic principles of justice. Could it really be that we were all too naïve when we thought we saw the dawn of a new Turkey in Gezi Park in June 2013?

Feminist, LGBTQIA+, environmentalist, anti-racist movements and others have been hailed – and rightly so – for their achievements (no matter how small, slow or incomplete these may have been) in expanding the scope of democracy through inclusion, recognition and representation. The pro-democracy and anti-austerity movements of the early twenty-first century, however, are often remembered for their 'failure' and how their 'spring' turned into 'winter'. They face criticism for failing to make even a tiny dent in the existing order, let alone overthrow it.

Yet, despite appearing to be defeated, this new generation of movements has, at the very least, shown that those who have suffered its most severe consequences are no longer convinced that the system can be fixed. Gezi and her sisters, as I demonstrated in this book, did not conceptualise or experiment with new democratic norms and practices simply to innovate in political participation and deliberation, or repair failing political institutions or bring social injustices and inequalities to a bearable level. In a constant state of mobilisation, activists with fluid political identities organised in various corners of the city and pursued a radical politics around the idea of the common. That is, by blurring the line between community-making and rebellion, the movements of the twenty-first century became 'rehearsals' in prefiguring and gradually building a new world.

The 'rehearsal' metaphor is not arbitrary but a nod of gratitude to the late Immanuel Wallerstein who preferred this expression to point out that the movements that erupted during the late 1960s, to which he referred as 1968, were a 'revolution of and in the world-system' (Wallerstein, 1989, p. 431; also see: Arrighi et al., 1989).[1] For Wallerstein, 1968 was a rehearsal in shaking to the core (and ultimately replacing) the capitalist world-system which, for him, had arrived to its metastatic crisis. The neoliberal turn from the 1980s onwards – which provides the political and economic backdrop for this book's arguments – was a partially successful yet ultimately futile effort to avert this crisis by intensifying the conservative attack on the post–Second World War redistributive pact (i.e., the welfare state) abandoning developmental policies and commodifying all aspects of life.

To this day, there is no sign that capitalism is able to find a cure to rescue itself from demise. Continuous and contagious economic crises resulting from a cascade of speculative bubbles wreaked havoc in societies from Latin America to East Asia during the 1990s and early 2000s. The last of these was the 2008–9 housing market crash whose impact was so vast that questioning the

CONCLUSION | 159

survival of capitalism became commonplace even in the mainstream media. Meanwhile, financial manipulations, not to mention corporate and state corruption, allowed mind-blowing profits being made in fictitious commodities, such as social media frenzies or cryptocurrencies – all unpredictable, volatile and wildly swinging, and yet flawlessly facilitating the transfer of enormous wealth to what eventually became the 'one percent'. Increasing wealth polarisation, accompanied and exacerbated by rising unemployment at the world level and proletarisation of white-collar professionals whose dreams of a comfortable middle-class life were constantly crushed, went hand-in-hand with the atomisation of individuals, distrust in organisations and other symptoms of decay in social fabric. As Wallerstein observed, when institutions 'on which people rely to guarantee their immediate security seem to be faltering seriously [. . .] both antisocial crime and so-called terrorism have come to seem to most people more widespread than in the past they think they remember' (Wallerstein, 2022, p. 32). The ensuing confusion, resentment and fear were compounded by tectonic developments, such as the Covid-19 pandemic or the invasion of Ukraine by Russia, furthering uncertainty and fluctuations in 'the markets, the geopolitical alliances, the stability of state boundaries, employment, debts, taxes, and the groups we blame for the crisis' (Wallerstein, 2015, p. 167). All this was unfolding on the backdrop of the decline of American hegemony with the US losing wars it started or finding itself unable to convince the world to follow its lead. Despite the rise of various regional powers, either as individual states (such as China) or as groups and pacts (such as BRICS, an intergovernmental organisation comprising Brazil, Russia, India, China and South Africa), no viable candidate could emerge for a new world leadership in charge of the interstate system that harboured and nurtured capitalism for 500 years. On top of all this, and echoing what the 'new social movements' of the late 1960s criticised, neither social democratic or leftist parties that came to power nor radical leftist movements could deliver their promises. The pale glimmer of 'hope' that came with the 'pink tide' that carried leftist politics to power in Latin America in the late 1990s and early 2000s was countered by the rise of authoritarian 'strongmen' and proto-fascisms all over the world, further evincing the extent of volatility, unpredictability and disequilibrium in the system.

It is in this broader context that we witnessed the resurgence of labour and other social movements in many parts of the world by the end of the twentieth century. The Zapatistas in the mid-1990s and the Global Justice Movement in the early 2000s, later to be joined by Occupy Wall Street and Arab Spring along with their global offspring in the early 2010s, became landmarks in this global collective action by bringing together embattled labour movements: environmentalist, social justice and identity-based movements, and many discontented yet less organised groups and individuals in the Global South and Global North. According to Wallerstein, these movements 'managed to change world discourse, moving it away from the ideological mantras of neo-liberalism to themes like inequality, injustice, and decolonisation' (Wallerstein, 2012). Nothing, not even the pandemic and mandatory isolation could deter this mobilisation. On the contrary, the growing direness of their situation empowered people to resist and protest even more, sometimes in the form of wildcat strikes, work stoppages and all possible ways of refusal to show up for work, and at other times as rallies for racial justice and abolition. As of this writing, in the belly of the beast that is the US, where labour militancy has been historically weak, one cannot but notice an impressive uptick in strikes, unionising efforts and development of fresh and innovative forms of organ-ising under more diverse, inclusive and democratic leadership in a variety of public and private sector professions, including teachers, graduate assistants, Hollywood screen writers and actors and service sector workers in multina-tional giants such as UPS, Amazon and Starbucks, among others. All in all, the growing strength and frequency of these and other movements all over the world stands as testament that no matter how hard it tries to avoid it, the capitalist world-system continues to create its own 'grave diggers'.

More importantly, these movements did not just protest but gathered around 'a common objective – struggle against the social ills consequent on neoliberalism – and a common respect for each other's immediate priorities' (Wallerstein, 2002, p. 37). Occupy Wall Street protests and their future incar-nations provided the opportunity to 'think about the realities of the struc-tural crisis of capitalism and the major geopolitical transformations that are occurring' (Wallerstein, 2011). Even when they were suppressed or co-opted later, social eruptions dubbed the Arab Spring were 'heir to 1968' with their anti-imperialist, anti-exploitation and profoundly egalitarian spirit (Waller-stein, 2013a). And the most recent wave of this movement cycle, to which Gezi belongs, nurtured the spirit of Porto Alegre and the World Social Forum with their openness, inclusivity (especially of the Global South), horizontalism, internal democracy, but most important of all, with their dare to assert that 'another world is possible' (Wallerstein, 2022, p. 25). All of them 'rehearsed' strategies against multiple forms of inequality, oppression and exploitation in their unique ways but within a common, collective and connected framework rather than as separate realms.

There is no doubt that by the second half of 2010s, 'the global political struggles that seemed so relatively favorable to the Global Left a decade ago [. . .] have been reversed' (Wallerstein, 2016), which led to more pessimistic analyses about this latest wave of social movements. Still, 'fading of the overt protests [. . .] does not indicate failure of the protests', as Wallerstein (2013b) noted. They leave a legacy for the future, by putting major issues on the public agenda and increasing scepticism about governments' ability to tackle these issues. If 1968 was indeed a rehearsal for exposing the irresolvable contradictions of the system, including the inept alternatives offered as the only path to the promised new world, the movements of the twenty-first century can be seen as – borrowing from Moghadam (2017) – the final 'dress rehearsal' for they went beyond simply being an expression of resentment, rage or disappointment. They emboldened the masses not only to dream about the possibility of a different world but actually build it through world-making practices, ranging from occupations, assemblies, cooperatives, mutual aid and care networks, among many others. Similar to what Breines (1989) observed with the US student movement in the 1960s, the movements of the twenty-first century, too, harboured and acted on utopian dreams for a more profound, radical change in the organisation of the society through practical, everyday activism. Maybe as we approach 'the end of the world as we know it' (Wallerstein, 2001), we find that life, community and politics are becoming – by necessity – even more inseparable.

A sober assessment of Gezi's legacy, then, requires us to move beyond fetishising political forms (such as a political party or a centralised organisation) or tangible political outcomes (being successful in national elections or carrying out a full-fledged revolution) because as one observer of the Gezi Park protests noted, 'Gezi fundamentally changed the foundations and the language of politics. This is new because Gezi doesn't suggest any power practices. Quite the contrary – Gezi is a certain outlook on life, it's the practice of judging power'

(Letsch, 2014). Considering the rich political reflection and experience that emerged from this attempt at reconstituting the social, an indispensable condition for a healthy and robust democratic life, the word 'defeat' – or even 'victory' – cannot gauge the real change Gezi effected in society. Radical democratic organising from streets to park forums, from neighbourhood solidarities to squat houses and cooperatives redefines the horizon of the emancipatory struggles beyond resisting market or state coercion, and prefigures a new political community.

Yet the dilemmas I laid out in Chapter 6 still wait to be addressed: is the triple modality of activism in the movements of the twenty-first century 'flawed by design'? How can the 'real democracy' that these movements promise be realised and formalised beyond an elusive dream when the three dynamics they engender begin to work against each other? How can they strike a balance between organisational stability, institutional durability and mobilisational dynamism in an erratic global political context? Most important of all: how can they defend the political community that they are building against attacks that aim for its destruction?

It is true that collective struggles for a just, inclusive and democratic society promise no guarantees, especially when we expect the arc of radical politics to bend towards reconstituting the social in the midst of neoliberal destruction. Yet, what the past three decades have shown is that even when they become dysfunctional, inefficient, disorganised and vulnerable in the face of internal contradictions and external threats, even when they are silenced, criminalised and eventually crushed, social movements can still reincarnate to activate the collective will. In times of urgency, they can produce 'new ways of living where people get to create systems of care and generosity that address harm and foster well-being' (Spade, 2020, p. 2). As both the source and carriers of 'radical hope' for a more democratic political community, Gezi and her sisters could resurface in different forms when that very hope they preserved was direly needed. When mutual aid networks were activated during the pandemic and chains of care and assistance were formed beyond national borders as a part of the earthquake relief efforts in Turkey, it became clear that social movements such as Gezi do not merely organise, harmonise, amplify voices of dissent and then simply disappear. Rather, they are incubators for future political action to mobilise people for surviving hardship and tackling the underlying causes of their situation. This is why no matter how inconsistent and imperfect it was in that relatively short episode, Gezi made people realise their power to build a new, democratic political community. There is every reason to believe that 'when Gezi comes back again' it will continue its venture right from where it left off.

North Attleboro
April 2023

Note

1. I am grateful to Barış Ünlü for drawing my attention to this connection.

BIBLIOGRAPHY

31 mayıs 2013 taksim gezi parkı polis saldırısı. (2013, May 31). ekşi sözlük. https://eksisozluk.com/31-mayis-2013-taksim-gezi-parki-polis-saldirisi--3853414?p=62

Adaman, F., Akbulut, B., & Kocagöz, U. (2016). Giriş. In F. Adaman, B. Akbulut, & U. Kocagöz (Eds), *Herkesin, Herkes İçin: Müşterekler Üzerine Bir Antoloji*. Metis Yayınları.

Ağartan, K. (2018). Türkiye'de Özelleştirme Karşıtı Hareketlerin Seyri. In O. Savaşkan & M. Ertan (Eds), *Türkiye'nin Büyük Dönüşümü: Ayşe Buğra'ya Armağan* (1st ed.). İletişim Yayınları.

Ahunbay, Z., Dinçer, İ., & Şahin, Ç. (Eds) (2016). *Neoliberal Kent Politikaları ve Fener-Balat-Ayvansaray* (1st ed.). Türkiye İş Bankası Kültür Yayınları.

Akay, H. (2015). *Türkiye'de İnsani Güven(siz)lik—2014-2015* (978-605-84715-1-1). Helsinki Yurttaşlar Derneği. https://hyd.org.tr/attachments/article/175/TR%27de%20insani%20guvensizlik.pdf

Akbulut, B. (2016). Sonuç. In F. Adaman, B. Akbulut, & U. Kocagöz (Eds), *Herkesin, Herkes İçin: Müşterekler Üzerine Bir Antoloji*. Metis Yayınları.

Akçalı, E. (2018). Do Popular Assemblies Contribute to Genuine Political Change? Lessons from the Park Forums in Istanbul. *South European Society and Politics, 23*(3), 323–40.

Akçaoğlu, A. (2018). *Zarif ve Dinen Makbul: Muhafazakar Üst-Orta Sınıf Habitusu* (1st ed.). İletişim Yayınları.

Aksoy, E., & Güzey Kocataş, Ö. (2017). Gecekondu Alanlarında Uygulanan Kentsel Dönüşüm Projelerinin Meşruiyet Zemini Olarak Yoksulluk ve Suç. *Karadeniz*

Teknik Üniversitesi Sosyal Bilimler Enstitüsü Sosyal Bilimler Dergisi, 7(14), 275–95.

Akyıldız, S. (2015). *Yeni Toplumsal Hareketler: Validebağ Direnişi Üzerinden Çevre Hareketleri* [Masters Thesis, Maltepe University]. https://openaccess. maltepe.edu.tr/xmlui/bitstream/handle/20.500.12415/775/10063199. pdf?sequence=1&isAllowed=y

Altınay, A. G. (2014). Direnenlerin Pedagojisi. In K. İnal (Ed.), *Gezi, İsyan, Özgürlük*. Ayrıntı Yayınları.

Altunok, Ö. (2013). Beni de Sayın Demek İçin Oradaydım. *Mesele Dergisi, 79*, 36–7.

Ancelovici, M., Dufour, P., & Nez, H. (Eds) (2016). *Street Politics in the Age of Austerity: From the Indignados to Occupy*. Amsterdam University Press.

Araman, S. (2013). Şekeriniz Bittiyse Don Kişot'un Kapısını Çalın. *Evrensel*. https:// www.evrensel.net/haber/72408/sekeriniz-bittiyse-don-kisotun-kapisini-calin

Arampatzi, A. (2017). The Spatiality of Counter-Austerity Politics in Athens, Greece: Emergent 'Urban Solidarity Spaces'. *Urban Studies, 54*(9), 2155–71.

Argın, Ş. (2013). *Gezi'nin Ufkundan: Liberal Demokrasinin Krizi, Kamusallık ve Sol*. Agora Kitaplığı.

Arrighi, G., Hopkins, T. K., & Wallerstein, I. (1989). *Antisystemic Movements*. Verso.

Arslanalp, M. (2014). Yerinde Duramamak. *Birikim, 302*, 52–4.

Atalay, C. (2013, July). Hukuksuzluğa Karşı Yurttaş Hareketi. *Express, 136*, 30.

Atayurt, U. (2013, July). Demokratik Cumhuriyetin İlk 15 Günü. *Express, 136*, 26–9.

Atılgan, Y. (2013, August). Yeniden Öğrenirken. *Bir+Bir, 24*, 14–16.

Avcı, Ö. (2012). *İki Dünya Arasında: İstanbul'da Dindar Üniversite Gençliği* (1st ed.). İletişim Yayınları.

Avtur, S. (2014). 21. Yüzyılda Değişen Toplumsal Hareketler. *Praksis, 34*.

Aydın, S. (2012). İstanbul'da 'Orta Sınıf' ve Kapalı Siteler. *İdeal Kent, 6*, 96–123.

Badiou, A. (2012). *The Rebirth of History: Times of Riots and Uprisings* (G. Elliott, Trans.; 1st ed.). Verso.

Bailey, M. (2020). The Neoliberal City as Utopia of Exclusion. *Globalizations, 17*(1), 31–44. https://doi.org/10.1080/14747731.2019.1603799

Baiocchi, G. (2005). *Militants and Citizens: The Politics of Participatory Democracy in Porto Alegre*. Stanford University Press.

Bakçay, E. (2013, August). Doğrudan Demokrasi. *Bir+Bir, 24*, 12–13.

Bakioğlu, A. (2022). *Büyük Madenci Yürüyüşü: Zonguldak'ın Büyük Grevi (1990-1991)* (1st ed.). İletişim Yayınları.

Balaban, U. (2022, July 3). Gezi Neydi? *İnsan Hakları Okulu*. https://blog. insanhaklariokulu.org/gezi-neydi/

Bali, R. (2020). *Tarz-ı Hayattan Life Style'a* (13th ed.). İletişim Yayınları.

Balibar, E. (2012). The 'Impossible' Community of the Citizens: Past and Present Problems. *Environment and Planning D: Society and Space, 30*(3), 437–49.

Balkan, E., & Öncü, A. (2018). Convergence and Competition Among the New Turkish Middle Classes. *Current History, 117*(803), 350–4.

Barnett, C. (2014). What Do Cities Have to Do with Democracy? *International Journal of Urban and Regional Research, 38*(5), 1625–43.

Başer, B. (2015). Gezi Spirit in the Diaspora: Diffusion of Turkish Politics to Europe. In I. David & K. Toktamış (Eds), *Everywhere Taksim: Sowing the Seeds for a New Turkey at Gezi* (1st ed., pp. 251–66). Amsterdam University Press.

Batuman, B. (2013a). Political Encampment and the Architecture of Public Space: TEKEL Resistance in Ankara. *International Journal of Islamic Architecture, 2*(1), 77–100.

Batuman, B. (2013b, June 12). Meydan, Sokak, Park: Direnişle Yeniden Üretilen Kamusal Mekân. *TMMOB Mimarlar Odası Ankara Şubesi Bülten, June-July 2013*(107), 5–8.

Batuman, B. (2018). *New Islamist Architecture and Urbanism: Negotiating Nation and Islam through Built Environment in Turkey* (1st ed.). Routledge.

Baysal, E. (2013, August). Kıyımın Daniskası. *Bir+Bir, 24*, 23.

Belbağ, A. G., Üner, M. M., Cavusgil, E., & Cavusgil, S. T. (2019). The New Middle Class in Emerging Markets: How Values and Demographics Influence Discretionary Consumption. *Thunderbird International Business Review, 61*(2), 325–37.

Benhabib, S. (2013, September 9). *The Gezi Park Protests and the Future of Turkish Politics.* Dissent Magazine. https://www.dissentmagazine.org/online_articles/the-gezi-park-protests-and-the-future-of-turkish-politics-an-interview-with-seyla-benhabib

Benlisoy, F. (2012). *21. Yüzyılın İlk Devrimci Dalgası: Fransa ve Yunanistan'dan Arap İsyanı, The Occupy Hareketleri ve Kürt Baharına.* Agora Kitaplığı.

Benski, T., Langman, L., Perugorría, I., & Tejerina, B. (2013). From the Streets and Squares to Social Movement Studies. *Current Sociology, 61*(4), 541–61.

'Birleşik Haziran Hareketi' Yola Çıktı. (2014, October 20). https://haber.sol.org.tr/soldakiler/birlesik-haziran-hareketi-yola-cikti-haberi-98879

Bizim İçin Gezi, Çocuklarımıza Anlatacağımız Sivil Bir Devrim. (2013, July). *Mesele Dergisi, 79*, 33–5.

Blee, K. M. (2014). *Democracy in the Making: How Activist Groups Form* (1st ed.). Oxford University Press.

Blokland, T. (2012). *Community as Urban Practice*. Polity Press.

Bookchin, M. (2021). *From Urbanization to Cities: The Politics of Democratic Municipalism*. AK Press.

Bora, T. (2014). Gezi ve Orta Sınıf. *Birikim*, *302*, 23–33.

Bora, T. (Ed.). (2021). *İnşaat Ya Resulullah* (4th ed.). İletişim Yayınları.

Bora, T., Bora, A., Erdoğan, N., & Üstün, İ. (2011). *'Boşuna mı Okuduk?' Türkiye'de Beyaz Yakalı İşsizliği* (1st ed.). İletişim Yayınları.

Boratav, K. (2013). Olgunlaşmış Bir Sınıfsal Başkaldırı: Gezi Direnişi. In Ö. Göztepe (Ed.), *Gezi Direnişi Üzerine Düşünceler* (pp. 15–20). NotaBene Yayınları.

Boratav, K. (2016). *1980'li Yıllarda Türkiye'de Sosyal Sınıflar ve Bölüşüm* (3rd ed.). İmge Kitabevi Yayınları.

Breckman, W. (2020, November 23). Can the Crowd Speak? *Public Books*.

Breines, W. (1989). *Community and Organization in the New Left, 1962–1968: The Great Refusal* (2nd ed.). Rutgers University Press.

Brenner, N., Marcuse, P., & Mayer, M. (Eds) (2011). *Cities for People, Not for Profit: Critical Urban Theory and the Right to the City* (1st ed.). Routledge.

Brown, W. (2015). *Undoing the Demos: Neoliberalism's Stealth Revolution*. Zone Books.

Brown, W. (2019). *In the Ruins of Neoliberalism: The Rise of Antidemocratic Politics in the West*. Columbia University Press.

Brownlee, B. J., & Ghiabi, M. (2016). Passive, Silent and Revolutionary: The 'Arab Spring' Revisited. *Middle East Critique*, *25*(3), 299–316.

Buck-Morss, S. (2013a). A Commonist Ethics. In S. Zizek (Ed.), *The Idea of Communism* (1st ed., Vol. 2, pp. 57–76). Verso.

Buck-Morss, S. (2013b, October 31). *On Translocal Commons and the Global Crowd* [Colloquim]. Bogazici Chronicles, Bogazici University, Istanbul.

Buğra, A. (2008). *Kapitalizm, Yoksulluk ve Türkiye'de Sosyal Politika* (1st ed.). İletişim Yayınları.

Buğra, A., & Keyder, Ç. (2006). The Turkish Welfare Regime in Transformation. *Journal of European Social Policy*, *16*(3), 211–28.

Bulut, G. (Ed.). (2010). *Tekel Direnişi Işığında Gelenekselden Yeniye İşçi Sınıfı Hareketi* (1st ed.). NotaBene Yayınları.

'Bunu Yaşayan Aynı Kalamaz'. (2013, July). *Express*, *136*, 51.

Burawoy, M. (2018). A New Sociology for Social Justice Movements. In M. Abraham (Ed.), *Sociology and Social Justice* (1st ed., pp. 20–33). SAGE Publications.

Bürkev, Y. (2013). Sınıf, Toplumsal Muhalefet ve Siyasal Rejim Açısından Gezi Direnişi. In Ö. Göztepe (Ed.), *Gezi Direnişi Üzerine Düşünceler* (pp. 29–44). NotaBene Yayınları.

Butler, J. (2014). Foreword. In U. Özkırımlı (Ed.), *The Making of a Protest Movement in Turkey*. Palgrave Macmillan.

Butler, J. (2015). *Notes Toward a Performative Theory of Assembly*. Harvard University Press.

Caffentzis, G., & Federici, S. (2014). Commons Against and Beyond Capitalism. *Community Development Journal, 49*(supplement 1), 92–105.

Candan, A. B., & Kolluoğlu, B. (2008). Emerging Spaces of Neoliberalism: A Gated Town and a Public Housing Project in Istanbul. *New Perspectives on Turkey, 39*, 5–46.

Carvin, A. (2013, June 6). In Turkey, Protesters Proudly Call Themselves 'Looters'. *NPR*. https://www.npr.org/sections/parallels/2013/06/05/188935332/in-turkey-protesters-proudly-call-themselves-looters.

Casalucci, M., & Anghelinas, E. (2010, July 4). *European Sociale Forum, Istanbul 1-4th of July 2010: Final Assembly and Thematic Declarations*. Europe Solidaire Sans Frontièrs. http://www.europe-solidaire.org/spip.php?article17966.

Cassano, J. (2013, June 1). The Right to the City Movement and the Turkish Summer. *Jadaliyya*. https://www.jadaliyya.com/Details/28710.

Castel, R. (2003). *From Manual Workers to Wage Laborers: Transformation of the Social Question*. Transaction Publishers.

Castells, M. (2015). *Networks of Outrage and Hope: Social Movements in the Internet Age* (2nd ed.). Polity Press.

Çavdar, A. (2010, December). Müslüman Gettoda Çakma Modernite. *Express, 115*, 44–8.

Çavdar, A. (2016a). AKP's Housing Policy: TOKI as the Loyalty Generator. *Journal Für Entwicklungspolitik (JEP), 32*(1/2), 42–63.

Çavdar, A. (2016b, September 14). *Re-placing Ottomans: How to Understand AKP's Istanbul*. Turkologentag Second European Convention on Turkic, Ottoman and Turkish Studies, Hamburg.

Çavdar, A. (2019). As if They Will Never Die: Islamism's Dream of Capital Accumulation. *South Atlantic Quarterly, 118*(1), 23–40.

Çavdar, A. (2020). Kutsal Hırsın Beton Gölgesi: Çamlıca Camii Neyin Anıtı? In Ş. Geniş (Ed.), *Otoriter Neoliberalizmin Gölgesinde: Kent, Mekân, İnsan* (1st ed., pp. 243–96). Nika Yayınları.

Çavdar, A. (2021). Görünür Fanteziler: Büyüklük Kimde Kalsın? İn T. Bora (Ed.), *İnşaat Ya Resulullah* (4th ed., pp. 113–30). İletişim Yayınları.

Çelik, Ö., & Ergenç, C. (2016). Ankara'nın Kent Mücadelesi ile İmtihanı. *Saha Dergisi, 3*, 11–16.

Çelik, Ö., & Ergenç, C. (2018). Gezi Sonrası Mahalleye Çekilmek: Ankara'da Mahalle Forumları Pratiği. *Iktisat Dergisi*, *539*, 81–95.

Celikates, R. (2021). Radical Democratic Disobedience. In W. E. Scheuerman (Ed.), *The Cambridge Companion to Civil Disobedience* (pp. 128–52). Cambridge University Press.

Çetin, M. (2016). Spatial Anarchy in Gezi Park Protests. In R. J. White, S. Springer, & M. L. de Souza (Eds), *The Practice of Freedom: Anarchism, Geography, and the Spirit of Revolt*. Rowman & Littlefield Publishers.

Çetinkaya, Y. D. (2020). Toplumsal Hareketler, Devrim ve Siyaset (1999-2020). *Katkı*, *10*, 37–48.

Ciccariello-Maher, G. (2016). *Building the Commune: Radical Democracy in Venezuela*. Verso.

Çoban, F. (2015). *Sokak Siyaseti: Siyasalın Gündelik Kuruluşu Bağlamında Bir İnceleme*. Metis Yayınları.

Cook, S. A. (2018, July 5). Strongmen Die, but Authoritarianism Is Forever. *Foreign Policy*.

Cook, S. A. (2020, September 5). The End of Hope in the Middle East. *Foreign Policy*.

Coşar, S., & Yücesan-Özdemir, G. (Eds) (2012). *Silent Violence: Neoliberalism, Islamist Politics and the Akp Years in Turkey*. Red Quill Books.

Coward, M. (2012). Between Us in the City: Materiality, Subjectivity, and Community in the Era of Global Urbanization. *Environment and Planning D: Society and Space*, *30*(3), 468–81.

Çuhadar, B. (2013, August). Kilimlerimizle, Fikirlerimizle. *Bir+Bir*, *24*, 24–5.

Dahlberg, L. (2013, February 26). Radical Democracy in Contemporary Times. *E-International Relations*.

De Angelis, M. (2010). The Production of Commons and the 'Explosion' of the Middle Class. *Antipode*, *42*(4), 954–77.

De Angelis, M., & Harvie, D. (2013). The Commons. In M. Parker, G. Cheney, V. Fournier, & C. Land (Eds), *The Routledge Companion to Alternative Organization*. Routledge.

De Angelis, M., & Stavrides, S. (2013, December). Başka Bir Dünyanın Peşinde: Massimo De Angelis ve Stavrides ile Müşterekler. *Express*, *139*, 30–2.

Dean, J. (2016). *Crowds and Party*. Verso.

Deli Gaffar. (2015, April). Fatsa'dan Haziran'a: Zafer Bize Göz Kırpıyor. *Redaksiyon*, *12*, 37–8.

della Porta, D. (Ed.). (2009). *Democracy in Social Movements*. Palgrave Macmillan.

della Porta, D. (2014a). Learning Democracy: Cross-Time Adaptation in Organisational Repertoires. In D. della Porta & A. Mattoni (Eds), *Spreading Protest: Social Movements in Times of Crisis*. ECPR Press.

della Porta, D. (2014b). *Mobilizing for Democracy*. Oxford University Press.

della Porta, D. (2015). *Social Movements in Times of Austerity: Bringing Capitalism Back into Protest Analysis*. Polity Press.

della Porta, D. (Ed.). (2017). *Global Diffusion of Protest: Riding the Protest Wave in the Neoliberal Crisis*. Amsterdam University Press.

della Porta, D. (2020). *How Social Movements Can Save Democracy*. Polity Press.

della Porta, D., & Diani, M. (2006). *Social movements: An Introduction* (2nd ed.). Blackwell Publishing.

della Porta, D., & Felicetti, A. (2018). Democratic Deliberation, Social Movements and the Quest for Democratic Politics. *Partecipazione & Conflitto*, *11*(1), Article 1.

della Porta, D., & Mattoni, A. (2014). Patterns of Diffusion and the Transnational Dimension of Protest in the Movements of the Crisis: An Introduction. In D. della Porta & A. Mattoni (Eds), *Spreading Protest: Social Movements in Times of Crisis*. ECPR Press.

della Porta, D., & Piazza, G. (2008). *Voices of the Valley, Voices of the Straits: How Protest Creates Communities* (1st ed.). Berghahn Books.

della Porta, D., & Rucht, D. (Eds) (2015). *Meeting Democracy: Power and Deliberation in Global Justice Movements*. Cambridge University Press.

Demiral, S. (2018). Sosyal Tabakalar ve Kentsel Katmanlar: İstanbul'da Mekansal Ayrışma Biçimleri. In Sunar, Lütfi (Ed.), *Türkiye'de Toplumsal Tabakalaşma ve Eşitsizlik* (2nd ed., Vol. 2, pp. 71–99). Nobel.

Demirok, İ., Tepeli, A. D., & Yalçınöz, B. (2013). 'Bağzı' Psikoloji Söylemlerine Gezi'den Bir Bakış. *Teorik Bakış*, *2*, 125–37.

Demirtaş-Milz, N. (2020). Neoliberal Kentsel Politikalar ve Sosyal Ayrışma. In Ş. Geniş (Ed.), *Otoriter Neoliberalizmin Gölgesinde: Kent, Mekân, İnsan* (1st ed., pp. 85–122). Nika Yayınları.

Denning, M. (2021). Everyone a Legislator. *New Left Review*, *129*, 29–44.

Dikeç, M. (2018). *Urban Rage: The Revolt of the Excluded* (1st ed.). Yale University Press.

Dikeç, M., & Swyngedouw, E. (2017). Theorizing the Politicizing City: Theorizing The Politicizing City. *International Journal of Urban and Regional Research*, *41*(1), 1–18.

Diken. (2016, December 12). *Bir Buçuk Yılda 33 Bombalı Saldırıda 461 Kişi Hayatını Kaybetti—363'ü Sivil*. Diken. https://www.diken.com.tr/bir-bucuk-yilda-33-bombali-saldirida-461-kisi-hayatini-kaybetti-363u-sivil/.

Dinler, D. (2013, August). Bir Halaya Gider Gibi. *Bir+Bir*, *24*, 22.

Doğan, A. E. (2013). Hegemonya Krizine Dönülürken Tarihsel Momentin Gerekleri. *Praksis, Special Issue*, 95–104.

Doğan, S. (2016). *Mahalledeki AKP Parti İşleyişi, Taban Mobilizasyonu ve Siyasal Yabancılaşma* (1st ed.). İletişim Yayınları.

Doğru, H. E. (2021). *Çılgın Projelerin Ötesinde: TOKİ, Devlet ve Sermaye* (1st ed.). İletişim Yayınları.

Douzinas, C. (2014). Notes Towards an Analytics of Resistance. *New Formations, 83*, 79–98.

Eckardt, F. (2015). City and Crisis: Learning from Urban Theory. In F. Eckardt & J. R. Sánchez (Eds), *City of Crisis: The Multiple Contestation of Southern European Cities* (pp. 11–29). Transcript Publishing.

Edwards, G. (2014). *Social Movements and Protest* (1st ed.). Cambridge University Press.

Ehrenberg, J. (n.d.). What Can We Learn From Occupy's Failure? *Palgrave Communications, 3*(1), Article 1.

Eken, B. (2014). The Politics of the Gezi Park Resistance: Against Memory and Identity. *South Atlantic Quarterly, 113*(2), 427–36.

Elicin, Y. (2014). Neoliberal Transformation of the Turkish City Through the Urban Transformation Act. *Habitat International, 41*, 150–5.

Elicin, Y. (2017). Defending the City: Taksim Solidarity. *Journal of Balkan and Near Eastern Studies, 19*(2), 105–20.

Eraydın, A. (2008). The Impact of Globalisation on Different Social Groups: Competitiveness, Social Cohesion and Spatial Segregation in Istanbul. *Urban Studies, 45*(8), 1663–91.

Ercan-Bilgiç, E., & Kafkaslı, Z. (2013). *Gencim, Özgürlükçüyüm, Ne İstiyorum? ##direngeziparkı Anketi Sonuç Raporu*. Istanbul: Bilgi University.

Erder, S. (2002). *Kentsel Gerilim* (2nd ed.). Uğur Mumcu Vakfı Yayınları.

Erdik, A. (2017, November 13). Yeni Muhafazakârlar Orta Sınıfı Keşfederse. *Eleştirel Kültür Dergisi*. https://www.ekdergi.com/yeni-muhafazakarlar-orta-sinifi-kesfederse/

Erdi-Lelandais, G. (2014). Space and Identity in Resistance against Neoliberal Urban Planning in Turkey: Resistance against neoliberal urban planning in Turkey. *International Journal of Urban and Regional Research, 38*(5), 1785–1806.

Erdi-Lelandais, G. (2016). Gezi Protests and Beyond: Urban Resistance Under Neoliberal Urbanism in Turkey. In M. Mayer, C. Thörn, & H. Thörn (Eds), *Urban Uprisings: Challenging Neoliberal Urbanism in Europe* (1st ed. 2016 edition). Palgrave Macmillan.

Erdoğan, F. E. (2013). *Faşizme Karşı Demokratik Halk İktidarı Yolunda Direniş Komiteleri*. Pratika.

Erkilet, A. (2014, April 1). Dönüşen Şehir. *Al Jazeera Türk Dergi, Special Issue*. http:// dergi.aljazeera.com.tr/2014/04/01/donusen-sehir/

Erman, T. (2016a). Kentsel Dönüşümün Eleştirel Analizi. In İ. Kaya (Ed.), *Yeni Türkiye'nin Toplumsal Yapısı*. İmge Kitabevi Yayınları.

Erman, T. (2016b). *'Mış Gibi Site' Ankara'da Bir TOKİ-Gecekondu Dönüşüm Sitesi* (1st ed.). İletişim Yayınları.

Ersan, V. (2014, July). Başkaldırı, Sosyalistlerin 'Hedef Saptırıcı' Gördüğü Alanda Patladı. *Mesele Dergisi, 91*, 18–20.

Evcimen, G. (2019). *The Politics of Middle Class Professionals and The Global South's Recent Protest Wave: The Political Agency of Professionals in the Gezi Protests and Beyond* [Ph.D]. Binghamton University.

Farmer, A. D. (2017). Epilogue. In A. D. Farmer (Ed.), *Remaking Black Power: How Black Women Transformed an Era*. University of North Carolina Press.

Farro, A. L., & Demirhisar, D. G. (2014). The Gezi Park Movement: A Turkish Experience of the Twenty-first-century Collective Movements. *International Review of Sociology, 24*(1), 176–89.

Feldman, N. (2020). *The Arab Winter*. Princeton University Press.

Felicetti, A. (2018). *Deliberative Democracy and Social Movements*. Rowman & Littlefield Publishers.

Fırat, B. Ö. (2018). Global Movement Cycles and Commoning Movements. In E. Erdoğan, N. Yüce, & Ö. Özbay (Eds), *The Politics of the Commons: From Theory to Struggle*. Sivil ve Ekolojik Haklar Derneği (SEHAK).

Fırat, B. Ö. (2022). A Double Movement of Enclosure and Commons: Commoning Emek Movie Theatre in Three Acts. *City, 26*(5–6), 1029–44.

Fırat, K., Kocabıçak, E., Özbakır, M., Bulut, V., Günay, Ö. S., & Bulut, N. (2021, August). Düşleri, Ümitleri Açığa Çıkaran Mekanlar. *Express, 176*, 17–21.

Fırat, Z. (2013, July). Sonuç Ne Olursa Olsun Biz Kazandık. *Express, 136*, 36–8.

Fominaya, C. F. (2014). *Social Movements and Globalization: How Protests, Occupations and Uprisings are Changing the World* (2014th ed.). Red Globe Press.

Fominaya, C. F. (2020). *Democracy Reloaded: Inside Spain's Political Laboratory from 15-M to Podemos: Inside Spain's Political Laboratory from 15-M to Podemos*. Oxford University Press.

Freeman, J. (1972). The Tyranny of Stuctureless. *The Second Wave, 2*(1), 20–33.

Fresko, L. (2013, June 2). Diren Gezi, Day 6. *Mashallah News*. https://www. mashallahnews.com/diren-gezi-6th-day/.

Gambetti, Z. (2009). Conflict, 'Commun-ication' and the Role of Collective Action in the Formation of Public Spheres. In S. Shami (Ed.), *Publics, Politics and Participation: Locating the Public Sphere in the Middle East and North Africa* (p. 312). Social Science Research Council.

Gambetti, Z. (2014). Occupy Gezi as the Politics of the Body. In U. Özkırımlı (Ed.), *The Making of a Protest Movement in Turkey*. Palgrave Macmillan.

Gedikli, A. Ö. (2021, June 15). İstenmeyen Kentliler: Dışlanan kent yoksulunun ana akım medyada temsili, Çinçin örneği. *Textum Dergi*. https://textumdergi. net/istenmeyen-kentliler-dislanan-kent-yoksulunun-ana-akim-medyada-temsili-cincin-ornegi/.

GENAR'ın yaptığı Gezi Parkı anketi. (2013, June 12). *Yeni Şafak*. https://www. yenisafak.com/foto-galeri/gundem/genarin-yaptigi-gezi-parki-anketi-5684.

Genç, F. (2018). Urban Social Movements and the Politics of the Commons in Istanbul. In E. Erdoğan, N. Yüce, & Ö. Özbay (Eds), *The Politics of the Commons: From Theory to Struggle*. Sivil ve Ekolojik Haklar Derneği (SEHAK).

Geniş, Ş. (2007). Producing Elite Localities: The Rise of Gated Communities in Istanbul. *Urban Studies, 44*(4), 771–98.

Geniş, Ş. (Ed.). (2020). *Otoriter Neoliberalizmin Gölgesinde: Kent, Mekân, İnsan* (1st ed.). Nika Yayınları.

Gezen, A. (2014, May). Bir 'Ağaç'tan 'Ortaklığa' İşgal Evleri. *Redaksiyon, 8*, 54–6.

Gezer, Ö., Popp, M., & Trenkamp, O. (2013, June 3). Revolt in Turkey: Erdogan Losing Grip on Power. *Der Spiegel*.

Gezgin, U. B. (2013, June 22). *Kadıköy Forumu Notları: Kimliğini Kaybedip, Bulmak*. Bianet.

Gezi Parkı Eylemleri Yepyeni Bir Fiil Yarattı: Çapullamak. (2013, June 5). *Hürriyet Kelebek*, https://www.hurriyet.com.tr/kelebek/gezi-parki-eylemleri-yepyeni-bir-fiil-yaratti-capullamak-23440261.

Gezi'nin Bakiyesi. (n.d.). Gezi'nin Bakiyesi Blog. Retrieved January 30, 2023, from http://gezininbakiyesi.blogspot.com/.

Gilmore, R. W. (2021). Foreword. In R. Maynard & L. B. Simpson, *Rehearsals for Living*. Haymarket Books.

Glass, P. G. (2008). *La Vida Junta: An Ethnography of Participatory Democracy, Everyday Activity, Collective Action Frames and the Reproduction of the Zapatista Social Movement in Los Angeles*. University of California, Los Angeles.

Graeber, D. (2002). The New Anarchists. *New Left Review, 13*, 61–73.

Gülün, S. (2013, August). İnsanca Yaşama Talebi. *Bir+Bir, 24*, 17.

Gümrükçü, S. B. (2010). The Rise of a Social Movement: The Emergence of Anti-Globalization Movements in Turkey. *Turkish Studies, 11*(2), 163–80.

Gümrükçü, S. B. (2014). *Reconstructing a Cycle of Protest: Protest and Politics in Turkey, 1971-1985.* University of Zurich.

Gümüş, P., & Yılmaz, V. (2015). Where Did Gezi Come From? Exploring the Links Between Youth Political Activism Before and During the Gezi Protests. In I. David & K. Toktamış (Eds), *Everywhere Taksim: Sowing the Seeds for a New Turkey at Gezi* (1st ed., pp. 231–48). Amsterdam University Press.

Günay, Ö. (n.d.). *Haziran İsyanı ve Örgütlenme.* Emek Atölyesi. Retrieved January 30, 2023, from https://emekatolyesi.org/Guncel/haziran-isyani-ve-orgutlenme#.Y9g6_XbMJnK

Gürcan, E. C., & Peker, E. (2015). *Challenging Neoliberalism at Turkey's Gezi Park: From Private Discontent to Collective Class Action* (1st ed.). Palgrave Macmillan.

Güven, E. (2013, July). Hayat Barikatta O'lum. *Tempo, 54,* 76–81.

Güvenç, S. (2015, April). Seçimleri Aşan Bir Mücadele. *Redaksiyon, 12,* 49.

Hamsici, M. (2013, August 29). *Cemil Bayık: 'Gezi'de yanlışlar yaptık'.* BBC News Türkçe, https://www.bbc.com/turkce/haberler/2013/08/130828_cemil_bayik_3_gezi_cemaat.

Harding, L. (2013, June 10). Turkish Protesters Embrace Erdoğan Insult and Start 'capuling' Craze. *The Guardian.*

Hardt, M., & Negri, A. (2004). *Multitude: War and Democracy in the Age of Empire* (1st ed.). Penguin Books.

Harmanşah, Ö. (2014). Urban Utopias and How They Fell Apart: The Political Ecology of Gezi Park. In U. Özkırımlı (Ed.), *The Making of a Protest Movement in Turkey* (pp. 121–33). Palgrave Macmillan.

Harvey, D. (2013). *Rebel Cities: From the Right to the City to the Urban Revolution* (1st ed.). Verso.

Haug, C., & Rucht, D. (2015). Structurelessness: An Evil or an Asset? A Case Study. In D. della Porta & D. Rucht (Eds), *Meeting Democracy: Power and Deliberation in Global Justice Movements* (pp. 179–213). Cambridge University Press.

Henden-Şolt, H. B. (2019). Kentsel Dönüşüme Eleştirel Bakış. *Balkan ve Yakın Doğu Sosyal Bilimler Dergisi, 5*(2), 78–89.

Hoffman, L. M. (2014). The Urban, Politics and Subject Formation. *International Journal of Urban and Regional Research, 38*(5), 1576–88.

Holston, J. (2009). *Insurgent Citizenship: Disjunctions of Democracy and Modernity in Brazil* (1st ed.). Princeton University Press.

Hoskyns, T. (2014). *The Empty Place: Democracy and Public Space.* Routledge.

Howarth, D., & Roussos, K. (2022). Radical Democracy, the Commons and Everyday Struggles during the Greek Crisis. *The British Journal of Politics and International Relations*, *25*(2).

Hürriyet Daily News. (2013, June 15). *Gezi Park Protesters Hold Forums to Discuss Next Move*. Hürriyet Daily News, https://www.hurriyetdailynews.com/gezi-park-protesters-hold-forums-to-discuss-next-move--48857.

Id, D. (2011, November 12). *Occupy Oakland Egypt Solidarity March, 11/12/11*. Indybay.

IMECE. (2011, March). Foruma Doğru: IMECE 4. Yıl Forumu Öncesi Yapılan Toplantıların Özeti. *İMECE || Toplumun Şehircilik Hareketi Forumu*.

İnsel, A. (2014, June). Başbakan Merhametsiz Muktedir. *Tempo Arşiv*.

İplikçi, M. (2013). *Biz Orada Mutluyduk* (1st ed.). Doğan Kitap.

İşeri, G. (2015). *Ateşin ve Sürgünün Gölgesinde—Kentsel Dönüşüm* (2nd ed.). NotaBene Yayınları.

Işık, O., & Pınarcıoğlu, M. M. (2021). *Nöbetleşe Yoksulluk: Sultanbeyli Örneği* (13th ed.). İletişim Yayınları.

Işıl, Ö. S., & Değirmenci, S. (Eds) (2020). *Yaşamı Örgütleyen Deneyimler: Kadınlar Dayanışma Ekonomilerini ve Kooperatifleri Tartışıyor*. NotaBene Yayınları.

Isin, E. F. (2009). Citizenship in flux: The figure of the activist citizen. *Subjectivity*, *29* (1), 367–88.

İşleyen, Ö. (2014, May). Haziran'ın Birleşik Muhalefeti. *Redaksiyon*, *8*, 41–3.

Juris, J. (2004). Networked Social Movements: Global Movements for Global Justice. In M. Castells (Ed.), *The Network Society: A Cross-Cultural Perspective* (pp. 341–62). Edward Elgar.

Juris, J. (2012). Reflections on #Occupy Everywhere: Social media, Public Space, and Emerging Logics of Aggregation. *American Ethnologist*, *39*(2), 259–79.

Juris, J. (2013). Spaces of Intentionality. In J. Juris & A. Khasnabish (Eds), *Insurgent Encounters*. Duke University Press.

Kadıköy Kent Dayanışması. (n.d.). *Details about Kadıköy Kent Dayanışması*. Facebook. Retrieved February 26, 2023, from https://www.facebook.com/KadikoyKentDayanismasi/about_details.

Kadıköy Kooperatifi (Director). (2017, November 9). *Kadıköy Kooperatifi 1 Yaşında!* https://www.youtube.com/watch?v=I-4VgXa21Lo.

Kapsali, M., & Tsavdaroglou, C. (2016). The Battle for the Common Space, from the Neo-liberal Creative City to Rebel City and Vice Versa. In R. J. White, S. Springer, & M. L. de Souza (Eds), *The Practice of Freedom: Anarchism, Geography, and the Spirit of Revolt* (pp. 153–84). Rowman & Littlefield Publishers.

Karakaş, B. (2013, August). İsyan Hareketinin Nitelikli 20'si. *Bir+Bir*, *24*, 20–1.

Karakaş, Ö. (2018). Gezi Assemblages: Embodied Encounters in the Making of an Alternative Space. *Studies in Social Justice, 12*(1), 38–55.

Karakatsanis, L. (2019). International Solidarity Perplexed: From the Certainties of Gezi Park to Post-coup Complexities. In N. Christofis (Ed.), *Erdoğan's 'New' Turkey* (1st ed.). Routledge.

Karakayalı, S., & Yaka, Ö. (2014). The Spirit of Gezi: The Recomposition of Political Subjectivities in Turkey. *New Formations, 83*(1), 117–38.

Karaman, O. (2013). Urban Neoliberalism with Islamic Characteristics. *Urban Studies, 50*(16), 3412–27.

Karataşlı, Ş. S. (2020). Kapitalizm, Emek ve Artık Nüfus: 21. Yüzyılda İşçi Hareketlerini Nasıl Anlamalı? *Katkı, December*(10), 13–36.

Kardeşoğlu, S. (2022, June 13). Kentler En Zengin ve En Yoksullara Kalacak. *Birgün*.

Kaya-Erdoğan, E. (2020). Maltepe Karyesinden Maltepe'ye: İnşaatın, Sermayenin ve Kentsel Hareketlerin Odağı. In Ş. Geniş (Ed.), *Otoriter Neoliberalizmin Gölgesinde: Kent, Mekân, İnsan* (1st ed., pp. 39–85). Nika Yayınları.

Keith, M., & Pile, S. (Eds) (1993). *Place and the Politics of Identity*. Routledge.

Kelley, R. D. G. (2022, August 1). *Twenty Years of Freedom Dreams*. Boston Review.

Keyder, Ç. (Ed.). (1999). *Istanbul: Between the Global and the Local*. Rowman & Littlefield Publishers.

Keyder, Ç. (2005). Globalization and Social Exclusion in Istanbul. *International Journal of Urban and Regional Research, 29*(1), 124–34.

Keyder, Ç. (2010). Istanbul into the Twenty-First Century. In D. Göktürk, L. Soysal, & I. Tureli (Eds), *Orienting Istanbul: Cultural Capital of Europe?* (1st ed., pp. 25–34). Routledge.

Keyder, Ç. (2013a, June 19). Law of the Father. *LRB Blog*. https://www.lrb.co.uk/blog/2013/june/law-of-the-father.

Keyder, Ç. (2013b, August 1). Yeni Orta Sınıf. *Bilim Akademisi*. https://bilimakademisi.org/wp-content/uploads/2013/09/Yeni-Orta-Sinif.pdf.

Keyder, Ç. (2013c, September 5). Gezi Parkı Protestoları Bağlamında Yeni Orta Sınıflar, Neoliberal Dönüşüm ve Yoksulluk. *Konuşa Konuşa*.

Keyder, Ç. (2014a, January 20). Gezi Muhalefeti – Nedenler, Beklentiler. *Al Jazeera Türk Dergi*, http://everywheretaksim.net/tr/al-jazeera-turk-dergi-gezi-muhalefeti-nedenler-beklentiler-caglar-keyder/.

Keyder, Ç. (2014b, July 3). Yeni Orta Sınıfa Dikkat. *Taraf*. https://acikradyo.com.tr/arsiv-icerigi/yeni-orta-sinifa-dikkat.

Keyman, E. F., & Koyuncu Lorasdağı, B. (2010). *Kentler: Anadolu'nun Dönüşümü, Türkiye'nin Geleceği*. Doğan Kitap.

Kibar, S., & Tatari, B. (2013a, July). Birkaç Ağaç, Her Türlü İnsan. *Tempo, 54*, 62–71.

Kibar, S., & Tatari, B. (2013b, August). Forumlarda Neler Oluyor? *Tempo, 55,* 64.

Kilkenny, A. (2013, June 3). Occupy Gezi: International Solidarity for Turkey's Uprising. *The Nation.*

King, S. J. (2020). *The Arab Winter: Democratic Consolidation, Civil War, and Radical Islamists.* Cambridge University Press.

Kioupkiolis, A., & Katsambekis, G. (2014). Radical Democracy and Collective Movements Today: Responding to the Challenges of Kairos. In A. Kioupkiolis & G. Katsambekis (Eds), *Radical Democracy and Collective Movements Today: The Biopolitics of the Multitude versus the Hegemony of the People* (pp. 1–15). Routledge.

Koç, G. (2015). A Radical-Democratic Reading of the Gezi Resistance and the Occupy Gezi Movement. In G. Koç & H. Aksu (Eds), *Another Brick in the Barricade: The Gezi Resistance and Its Aftermath* (pp. 164–88). Wiener Verlag für Sozialforschung.

Koca, A., Çalışkan, Ç. O., Kaya, E., & Akgün, G. (Eds) (2013). *Kentleri Savunmak: Mekan, Toplum ve Siyaset Üzerine.* NotaBene Yayınları.

Koçak, H. (2011). İstanbul Emeksizleştirilirken. *İstanbul Üniversitesi Siyasal Bilgiler Fakültesi Dergisi, 44,* 41–8.

Kolluoğlu, P. (2020). A 21st Century 'Repertoire': Affective and Urban Mobilization Dynamics of the Gezi Commune. *Interface, 12*(1), 437–63.

Koloğlu, D., Gençtürk, D., Kazaz, G., Mavituna, H. İ., & Şen, S. (Eds) (2015). *Polis Destan Yazdı: Gezi'den Şiddet Tanıklıkları* (1st ed.). İletişim Yayınları.

Kömürcü, D. (2014). Gezi Parkı Direnişi ve Siyasal Olanın Geri Dönüşü. In E. Abat, E. Bulduruç, & F. Korkmaz (Eds), *Bizim Bir Haziranımız: Haziran Ayaklanması Üzerine Notlar.* Patika Kitap.

Kömürcüoğlu, H. (2015). *Y Kuşağını Anlamak Bir Gezi Parkı Araştırması.* Doğu Kitabevi.

Konda. (2013). *Gezi Parkı Araştırması.* Konda Araştırma ve Danışmanlık. https://konda.com.tr/duyuru/5/gezi-parki-arastirmasi.

Konda. (2014). *Gezi Raporu.* Konda Araştırma ve Danışmanlık. https://konda.com.tr/rapor/67/gezi-raporu.

Kontext TV (Director). (2014, October 23). *Silvia Federici: The Struggle for the Commons.* https://www.youtube.com/watch?v=oJwFT3a3J_4&ab_channel=KontextTV

Kozanoğlu, H. (2015, August). Direnişin Coğrafyası ve Politikası. *Redaksiyon, 13.*

Kural, B. (2013, October 22). *Don Kişot Yeldeğirmeni'ni İşgal Etti.* Bianet. https://www.bianet.org/bianet/toplum/150716-don-kisot-yeldegirmeni-ni-isgal-etti

Kurtuluş, H. (2003). Mekânda Billurlaşan Kentsel Kimlikler: İstanbul'da Yeni Sınıfsal Kimlikler ve Mekânsal Ayrışmanın Bazı Boyutları. *Doğu Batı Dergisi, 6*(23), 75–96.

Kurtuluş, H. (2011). Gated Communities as a Representation of New Upper and Middle Classes in Istanbul. *İstanbul Üniversitesi Siyasal Bilgiler Fakültesi Dergisi*, 44, 49–65.

Kurtuluş, H. (2012, April). Orta Sınıfın Sosyo-Mekânsal Yeniden İnşası. *Express*, 127.

Kurtuluş, H. (Ed.). (2016). *İstanbul'da Kentsel Ayrışma* (2nd ed.). Bağlam Yayınları.

Kuryel, A., & Fırat, B. Ö. (2020, April 30). Şimdi Neredeyiz? Burdayız. . . . *Bir+Bir*. https://birartibir.org/simdi-neredeyiz-burdayiz/

Kurzman, C., Fahmy, D. F., Gengler, J., Calder, R., & Whitson, S. L. (2013, May 20). Arab Winter—Viewpoints. *Contexts*.

Kuyucu, T. (2020). Türkiye'de Sosyal Konut Politikasının Paradoksu. In Ş. Geniş (Ed.), *Otoriter Neoliberalizmin Gölgesinde: Kent, Mekân, İnsan* (1st ed., pp. 123–54). Nika Yayınları.

Laclau, E., & Mouffe, C. (2001). *Hegemony and Socialist Strategy: Towards a Radical Democratic Politics* (2nd ed.). Verso.

Lee, Y. (2022). *Between the Streets and the Assembly: Social Movements, Political Parties, and Democracy in Korea*. University of Hawaii Press.

Lefebvre, H. (1969). *The Explosion: Marxism and The French Upheaval*. Monthly Review Press.

Lefebvre, H. (1991). *The Production of Space* (D. Nicholson-Smith, Trans.). Wiley-Blackwell.

Lefebvre, H. (2003). *The Urban Revolution*. University of Minnesota Press.

Lefebvre, H. (2013). *Rhythmanalysis: Space, Time and Everyday Life*. Bloomsbury Academic.

Legard, S. (2011, July 8). *Popular Assemblies in Revolts and Revolutions*. New Compass. http://new-compass.net/articles/popular-assemblies-revolts-and-revolutions

Letsch, C. (2013, June 3). Turkey Protests Unite a Colourful Coalition of Anger Against Erdogan. *The Guardian*. https://www.theguardian.com/world/2013/jun/03/turkey-protests-coalition-anger-erdogan

Letsch, C. (2014, May 29). A Year After the Protests, Gezi Park Nurtures the Seeds of a New Turkey. *The Guardian*. https://www.theguardian.com/world/2014/may/29/gezi-park-year-after-protests-seeds-new-turkey

Lichterman, P. (1996). *The Search for Political Community: American Activists Reinventing Commitment*. Cambridge University Press.

Linklater, A. (1998). *Transformation of Political Community: Ethical Foundations of the Post-Westphalian Era*. Polity Press.

Lorey, I. (2015). *State of Insecurity: Government of the Precarious*. Verso.

Magnusson, W. (2014). The Symbiosis of the Urban and the Political. *International Journal of Urban and Regional Research*, *38*(5), 1561–75.

Malchik, A. (2019, May 6). Why In-Person Protests Are Stronger Than Online Activism—The Atlantic. *The Atlantic*, https://www.theatlantic.com/technology/archive/2019/05/in-person-protests-stronger-online-activism-a-walking-life/578905/.

Mandour, M. (2019, December 5). *The Poverty of Protest. openDemocracy*, https://www.opendemocracy.net/en/north-africa-west-asia/poverty-protest/.

Mashallah Team. (2013, June 9). Gezi Park Occupation (liveblog). *Mashallah News*, https://www.mashallahnews.com/gezi-park-occupation-liveblog/.

Mason, P. (2013). *Why It's Still Kicking Off Everywhere: The New Global Revolutions* (Revised and updated edition). Verso.

Mason-Deese, L. (2012, September 10). The Neighborhood is the New Factory. *Viewpoint Magazine*, https://viewpointmag.com/2012/09/10/the-neighborhood-is-the-new-factory/.

Massey, D. (1995). Thinking Radical Democracy Spatially. *Environment and Planning D: Society and Space*, *13*(3), 283–8.

Mayer, M. (2011). The 'Right to the City' in Urban Social Movements. In N. Brenner, P. Marcuse, & M. Mayer (Eds), *Cities for People, Not for Profit: Critical Urban Theory and the Right to the City* (1st edition, pp. 63–85). Routledge.

Mayer, M. (2016). Neoliberal Urbanism and Uprisings Across Europe. In M. Mayer, C. Thörn, & H. Thörn (Eds), *Urban Uprisings: Challenging Neoliberal Urbanism in Europe* (1st ed. 2016 edition). Palgrave Macmillan.

McCurdy, P., Feigenbaum, A., & Frenzel, F. (2016). Protest Camps and Repertoires of Contention. *Social Movement Studies*, *15*(1), 97–104.

McDonald, K. (2002). From Solidarity to Fluidarity: Social Movements Beyond 'Collective Identity'. *Social Movement Studies*, *1*(2), 109–28.

Mendonça, R. F., & Ercan, S. A. (2015). Deliberation and Protest: Strange Bedfellows? Revealing the Deliberative Potential of 2013 Protests in Turkey and Brazil. *Policy Studies*, *36*(3), 267–82.

Menser, M. (2018). *We Decide! Theories and Cases in Participatory Democracy*. Temple University Press.

Miessen, M., & Mouffe, C. (2012). *The Space of Agonism: Markus Miessen in Conversation with Chantal Mouffe* (N. Hirsch & M. Miessen, Eds). Sternberg Press.

Miller, B. (2000). *Geography and Social Movements: Comparing Antinuclear Activism in the Boston Area*. University of Minnesota Press.

Moghadam, V. M. (2017). The Semi-Periphery, World Revolution, and the Arab Spring: Reflections on Tunisia. *Journal of World-Systems Research*, *23*(2), 620–36.

Mostafavi, M. (Ed.). (2017). *Ethics of the Urban: The City and the Spaces of the Political.* Lars Muller.

Mouffe, C. (2018). *For a Left Populism.* Verso.

Müştereklerimiz. (2013, June 8). Our Commons—Who, why? *Müşterekler*, http:// mustereklerimiz.org/ourcommonswhowhy/.

Naumov, V. (2015). *The Belarusian Maidan in 2006: A New Social Movement Approach to the Tent Camp Protest in Minsk* (1st ed.). Peter Lang GmbH.

Nez, H. (2016). 'We Must Register a Victory to Continue Fighting': Locating the Action of the Indignados in Madrid. In M. Ancelovici, P. Dufour, & H. Nez (Eds), *Street Politics in the Age of Austerity: From the Indignados to Occupy.* Amsterdam University Press.

Ofer, I., & Groves, T. (Eds) (2017). *Performing Citizenship: Social Movements across the Globe.* Routledge.

Oikonomakis, L., & Ross, J. E. (2016). A Global Movement for Real Democracy? The Resonance of Anti-Austerity Protest from Spain and Greece to Occupy Wall Street. In M. Ancelovici, P. Dufour, & H. Nez (Eds), *Street Politics in the Age of Austerity: From the Indignados to Occupy.* Amsterdam University Press.

Öktem, B. (2011). İstanbul'da Neoliberal Kentleşme Modelinin Sosyo-Mekansal İzdüşümleri. *İstanbul Üniversitesi Siyasal Bilgiler Fakültesi Dergisi*, *44*, 23–40.

Öktem Ünsal, B. (2015). State-led Urban Regeneration in Istanbul: Power Struggles between Interest Groups and Poor Communities. *Housing Studies*, *30* (8), 1299–1316.

Olivier, B. (2014). Signs of Radical Democracy? Deleuze, Badiou, Rancière and Tahrir Square, 2011. *Theoria*, *61*(139), 1–21.

Özcimbit, A. (2013, June 2). Gezi Parkı Eyleminin Analizi. Kimler katılmakta? Hükümet Huzur İçin Acil Ne Yapmalı? *Milliyet Blog*, http://blog.milliyet.com. tr/gezi-parki-eyleminin-analizi-kimler-katilmakta--hukumet-huzur-icin-acil-ne-yapmali-/Blog/?BlogNo=417406.

Özdemir, N. (2013, August). Yepyeni Bir Dil. *Bir+Bir*, *24*, 18–19.

Özden, B. A., & Bekmen, A. (2015). Rebelling against Neoliberal Populist Regimes. In I. David & K. Toktamış (Eds), *Everywhere Taksim* (pp. 89–104). Amsterdam University Press.

Özen, H. (2015). An Unfinished Grassroots Populism: The Gezi Park Protests in Turkey and Their Aftermath. *South European Society and Politics*, *20*(4), 533–52.

Özer, S. (2014). *Gezi'nin Yeryüzü Kardeşleri: Direnişin Arzu Coğrafyaları* (1st ed.). Otonom Yayıncılık.

Özet, İ. (2019). *Fatih-Başakşehir: Muhafazakâr Mahallede İktidar ve Dönüşen Habitus* (1st ed.). İletişim Yayınları.

Özgür, D. (2013, July). Gerçek Katarsis. *Express, 136*, 31–4.

Özkaya, D. (2024). '(Re)creating a New Gezi': The Affective Politics of Saying No to the Presidential System in the Aftermath of Popular Uprisings. In B. Ayata & C. Harders (Eds), *The Affective Dynamics of Mass Protests: Midan Moments and Political Transformation in Egypt and Turkey*. Routledge.

Özkaya Günaydın, B. (2021, March 14). 'Çığlıkta Ahenk Aranmaz', Tarlabaşı Dayanışması İnsanlık Dersi Veriyor. *Yeni Bir Mecra*, https://yeni1mecra.com/tarlabasi-dayanismasi/.

Özkırımlı, U. (2014). Introduction. In U. Özkırımlı (Ed.), *The Making of a Protest Movement in Turkey*. Palgrave Macmillan.

Özkoray, E., & Özkoray, N. (2013). *Bireyselleşme ve Demokrasi: Gezi Fenomeni*. İdea Politika Yayınları.

Öztürk, A. E. (2021). *Religion, Identity and Power: Turkey and the Balkans in the Twenty-first Century*. Edinburgh University Press.

Parkinson, J. R. (2012). *Democracy and Public Space: The Physical Sites of Democratic Performance*. Oxford University Press.

Penpecioğlu, M., & Taşan-Kok, T. (2020). Yabancılaşma, Hayal Kırıklığı ve Mücadelenin Umudu: Kentleşme Koşullarında Plancının Habitus'u Nasıl Değişiyor? In Ş. Geniş (Ed.), *Otoriter Neoliberalizmin Gölgesinde: Kent, Mekân, İnsan* (1st ed., pp. 325–58). Nika Yayınları.

Polletta, F. (2002). *Freedom Is an Endless Meeting: Democracy in American Social Movements*. University of Chicago Press.

Prashad, V. (2012). *Arab Spring, Libyan Winter*. AK Press.

Prentoulis, M., & Thomassen, L. (2013). Political Theory in the Square: Protest, Representation and Subjectification. *Contemporary Political Theory, 12*(3), 166–84.

Press, E. (2013, January 14). When Democracy Is In the Streets: An Appraisal of the Occupy Movement. *Public Books*.

Ramazanoğulları, H. (2022). After the Protest: Istanbul Park Forums and People's Engagement in Political Action. *Social Movement Studies, 21*(4), 420–35.

Resneck, J. (2014, December 24). *Squats of Istanbul: After Gezi, The Fight Continues Over Public Space. Occupy.com*, https://www.occupy.com/article/squats-istanbul-after-gezi-fight-continues-over-public-space#sthash.EwxTVH35.hXE3LcXa.dpbs.

Rittersberger-Tılıç, H. (2015). Squatting (in Turkey): A Practice of Transforming Public Spaces into Commons? In N. Konak & R. Ö. Dönmez (Eds), *Waves of Social Movement Mobilizations in the Twenty-First Century: Challenges to the Neo-Liberal World Order and Democracy*. Lexington Books.

Rivas-Alonso, C. (2015). Gezi Park: A Revindication of Public Space. In I. David & K. Toktamış (Eds), *Everywhere Taksim: Sowing the Seeds for a New Turkey at Gezi* (1st ed., pp. 231–48). Amsterdam University Press.

Rolnik, R. (2019). *Urban Warfare: Housing Under the Empire of Finance*. Verso.

Romão, J. (2009, July 8). *European Social Forum on Its Way to Istanbul*. Transform! Europe, https://www.transform-network.net/fr/blog/article/european-social-forum-on-its-way-to-istanbul/.

Roos, J. (2013, June 19). Assemblies Emerging in Turkey: A Lesson in Democracy. *ROAR Magazine*, https://roarmag.org/essays/assemblies-emerging-in-turkey-a-lesson-in-democracy/.

Rossi, U. (2017). *Cities in Global Capitalism* (1st ed.). Polity Press.

Ruccio, D. F. (2013, June 3). Heterotopia in Istanbul. *Occasional Links & Commentary*, https://anticap.wordpress.com/2013/06/03/heterotopia-in-istanbul/.

Rutland, T. (2013). Activists in the Making: Urban Movements, Political Processes and the Creation of Political Subjects: Activist subjects in the making. *International Journal of Urban and Regional Research, 37*(3), 989–1011.

Rutz, H., & Balkan, E. M. (2010). *Reproducing Class: Education, Neoliberalism, and the Rise of the New Middle Class in Istanbul* (1st ed.). Berghahn Books.

Said, A., & Moore, P. (2021). Dialectics of Hope and Despair in the Arab Uprisings. *MERIP Report: Revolutionary Afterlives, Winter*(301).

Samaddar, R. (2012). The Politics of a Political Society. In A. Ghudavarty (Ed.), *Reframing Democracy and Agency in India* (1st ed., pp. 125–52). Anthem Press.

Sandıkçı, E., & Yılmaz, S. (2014, July). Bize Ait Bir Kent. *Bir+Bir, 50*, 50–1.

Saraçoğlu, C. (2015). Haziran 2013 Sonrası Türkiye'de İdeolojiler Alanının Dönüşümü: Gezi Direnişi'ni Anlamanın Yöntemleri Üzerine Bir Tartışma. *Praksis, 37*.

Şardan, T. (2013, June 23). 2.5 Milyon Insan 79 İlde Sokağa İndi. *Milliyet*, https://www.milliyet.com.tr/gundem/2-5-milyon-insan-79-ilde-sokaga-indi-1726600.

Schmid, C. (2011). Henri Lefebvre, the Right to the City, and the New Metropolitan Mainstream. In N. Brenner, P. Marcuse, & M. Mayer (Eds), *Cities for People, Not for Profit: Critical Urban Theory and the Right to the City* (1st ed., pp. 42–62). Routledge.

Şen, B. (2011). Kentsel Mekânda Üçlü İttifak: Sanayisizleştirme, Soylulaştırma, Yeni Orta Sınıf. *İstanbul Üniversitesi Siyasal Bilgiler Fakültesi Dergisi, 44*, 1–21.

Sen, J., & Waterman, P. (Eds) (2007). *World Social Forum: Challenging Empires* (2nd ed.). Black Rose Books.

Şengül, T. (2015). Gezi Başkaldırı Ertesinde Kent Mekânı ve Siyasal Alanın Yeni Dinamikleri. *METU Journal of the Faculty of Architecture*, *32*(01), 1–20.

Seni, N. (2013). Polarization in a Culturally Changing Society. *Hérodote*, *148*(1), 122–37.

Şentürk, B. (2015). *Bu Çamuru Beraber Çiğnedik: Bir Gecekondu Mahallesi Hikayesi* (1st ed.). İletişim Yayınları.

Sewell, W. H. (2001). Space in Contentious Politics. In R. R. Aminzade, J. A. Goldstone, D. McAdam, E. J. Perry, S. Tarrow, C. Tilly, & W. H. Sewell. *Silence and Voice in the Study of Contentious Politics*. Cambridge University Press.

Sewell, W. H. (2005). Three Temporalities. In W. H. Sewell (Ed.), *Logics of History*. The University of Chicago Press.

Sewell, W. H., & McAdam, D. (2001). It's About Time: Temporalities in Social Movements and Revolutions. In R. R. Aminzade, J. A. Goldstone, D. McAdam, E. J. Perry, S. Tarrow, C. Tilly, & W. H. Sewell, *Silence and Voice in the Study of Contentious Politics*. Cambridge University Press.

Sitrin, M. (2012). *Everyday Revolutions: Horizontalism and Autonomy in Argentina* (Illustrated edition). Zed Books.

Sitrin, M., & Azzellini, D. (2014). *They Can't Represent Us! Reinventing Democracy From Greece To Occupy* (1st ed.). Verso.

Smith, J. (2016). Social Movements and Political Moments: Reflections on the Intersections of Global Justice Movements & Occupy Wall Street. In M. Ancelovici, P. Dufour, & H. Nez (Eds), *Street Politics in the Age of Austerity: From the Indignados to Occupy*. Amsterdam University Press.

Smith, J., Byrd, S., Reese, E., & Smythe, E. (Eds) (2012). *Handbook on World Social Forum Activism* (1st ed.). Routledge.

Smith, J., Karides, M., Becker, M., Brunelle, D., Chase-Dunn, C., & Porta, D. D. (2014). *Global Democracy and the World Social Forums* (2nd ed.). Routledge.

Soğukdere, Ö. (2014, June). Gezi Parkı'nda Aç Kapa Dönemi. *Tempo Arşiv*, 4–9.

Soja, E. W. (2000). *Postmetropolis: Critical Studies of Cities and Regions*. Wiley-Blackwell.

Sosyal Demokrasi Vakfı. (2020). *Türkiye'nin Gençliği Araştırması Raporu*. Sosyal Demokrasi Vakfı, http://sodev.org.tr/wp-content/uploads/2020/05/detayli_rapor.pdf.

Spade, D. (2020). *Mutual Aid: Building Solidarity During This Crisis (and the Next)*. Verso.

Staal, J. (2017). Assemblism. *E-Flux, 80*, https://www.e-flux.com/journal/80/100465/assemblism/.

Standing, G. (2016). *The Precariat: The New Dangerous Class* (Reprint edition). Bloomsbury Academic.

Stanek, L. (2011). *Henri Lefebvre on Space: Architecture, Urban Research, and the Production of Theory*. University of Minnesota Press.

Stavrides, S. (2012). Squares in Movement. *South Atlantic Quarterly, 111*(3), 585–96.

Stavrides, S. (2013). Contested Urban Rhythms: From the Industrial City to the Post-Industrial Urban Archipelago. *The Sociological Review, 61*(1_suppl), 34–50.

Stavrides, S. (2020, May 8). Life as Commons. *Undisciplined Environments*, https://undisciplinedenvironments.org/2020/05/08/life-as-commons/.

Sunar, L. (2018). Giriş: Türkiye'de Tabakalaşma ve Eşitsizliği Tartışmak. In Sunar, Lütfi (Ed.), *Türkiye'de Toplumsal Tabakalaşma ve Eşitsizlik* (2nd ed., Vol. 1, pp. 1–32). Nobel.

Szolucha, A. (2016). *Real Democracy Occupy: No Stable Ground*. Routledge.

Tanülkü, B. (2012). Güvenlikli Siteler Arası Rekabet: 'Ahlâklı Kapitalizm' in Kimlik Üzerindeki Etkisi. *İdeal Kent, 6*, 124–53.

Tarrow, S. (2005). *The New Transnational Activism* (1st ed.). Cambridge University Press.

Taştan, D. (2013, October 18). *Hedefimiz Patronsuz Bir Hayat*. soL, https://haber.sol.org.tr/sonuncu-kavga/hedefimiz-patronsuz-bir-hayat-haberi-81203.

TEDx Talks (Director). (2017, February 24). *Amr Hamzawy: The Failed Struggle for Democracy in the Arab World, and What's Next*, https://www.youtube.com/watch?v=DKdpnzVMWR4.

Thörn, H., Mayer, M., & Thörn, C. (2016). Re-Thinking Urban Social Movements, 'Riots' and Uprisings: An Introduction. In M. Mayer, C. Thörn, & H. Thörn (Eds), *Urban Uprisings: Challenging Neoliberal Urbanism in Europe*. Palgrave Macmillan.

Tilly, C. (2000). Spaces of Contention. *Mobilization, 5*(2), 135–59.

Tilly, C. (2003). Contention over Space and Place. *Mobilization, 8*(2), 221–5.

Tilly, C. (2008). *Contentious Performances*. Cambridge University Press.

Tokdoğan, N. (2018). *Yeni Osmanlıcılık: Hınç, Nostalji, Narsisizm*. İletişim Yayınları.

Tol, G., & Alemdaroğlu, A. (2020, July 15). Turkey's Generation Z Turns Against Erdogan. *Foreign Policy*, https://foreignpolicy.com/2020/07/15/turkey-youth-education-erdogan/.

Tonak, E. A. (2013). İsyanın Sınıfları. In Ö. Göztepe (Ed.), *Gezi Direnişi Üzerine Düşünceler* (pp. 21–8). NotaBene Yayınları.

Toplumun Şehircilik Hareketi. (2014). The Urban Roots of Gezi, Istanbul. In C. Mathivet (Ed.), *Take Back the Land! The Social Function of Land and Housing, Resistance and Alternatives* (pp. 78–83). Ritimo.

Tufekci, Z. (2017). *Twitter and Tear Gas: The Power and Fragility of Networked Protest*. Yale University Press.

Tuğal, C. (2016). *The Fall of the Turkish Model: How the Arab Uprisings Brought Down Islamic Liberalism*. Verso.

Tuğal, C. (2021). Urban Symbolic Violence Re-Made: Religion, Politics and Spatial Struggles in Istanbul. *International Journal of Urban and Regional Research*, 45(1), 154–63.

Turam, B. (2013). The Primacy of Space in Politics: Bargaining Rights, Freedom and Power in an İstanbul Neighborhood. *International Journal of Urban and Regional Research*, 37(2), 409–29.

Turam, B. (2015). *Gaining Freedoms: Claiming Space in Istanbul and Berlin*. Stanford University Press.

Turam, B. (2017). Split City versus Divided State in Turkey: Contrasting Patterns of Political Opposition to AKP's Authoritarianism. *Contemporary Islam*, 11(2), 185–99.

Türkmen, N. (2012). *Eylemden Öğrenmek: Tekel Direnişi ve Sınıf Bilinci*. İletişim Yayınları.

Türküsev, S. (2015). *Muhafazakar Burjuva: Sınıf Atlamış Dindarların Yaşam Tarzları* (1st ed.). Akis Kitap.

Uca, O. (2016). *Türkiye'de Orta Sınıfın Fotoğrafı: Akışlar ve İlişkiler Maddi Olmayan Emeğe Sahanın Eleştirisi*. NotaBene Yayınları.

Ülger, Z., Sandıkçı, E., Yoldaş, B., & Akın, Ş. (2014, May). Kadıköy'de Bir Hayalet Dolaşıyor: Yeldeğirmeni Dayanışması. *Redaksiyon*, 8, 36–7.

Uluğ, Ö. M., & Acar, Y. G. (2014). *Bir Olmadan Biz Olmak* (1st ed.). Dipnot Yayınları.

Uluğ, Ö. M., & Acar, Y. G. (2019). 'Names will never hurt us': A qualitative exploration of çapulcu identity through the eyes of Gezi Park protesters. *British Journal of Social Psychology*, 58(3), 714–29.

Ünal Çınar, R. (2012). *Ecdadın İcadı: AKP İktidarında Bellek Mücadelesi* (1st ed.). İletişim Yayınları.

Üner, M. M., & Güngördü, A. (2016). The New Middle Class in Turkey: A Qualitative Study in a Dynamic Economy. *International Business Review*, 25(3), 668–78.

Ünlü, B. (2018). *Türklük Sözleşmesi: Oluşumu, İşleyişi ve Krizi*. Dipnot Yayınları.

Ünsal, Ö. (2013). *Inner City Regeneration and the Politics of Resistance in Istanbul: A Comparative Analysis of Sulukule and Tarlabası* (Ph.D, University College London), http://openaccess.city.ac.uk/13026/.

Ünsal, Ö. (2014). Neoliberal Kent Politikaları ve Direnişin Siyaseti: İstanbul'da Yeni Kentsel Muhalefet. İn C. Özbay & A. B. Candan (Eds), *Yeni İstanbul Çalışmaları: Sınırlar, Mücadeleler, Açılımlar* (1st ed., pp. 109–23). Metis Yayınları.

Ünsal, Ö., & Kuyucu, T. (2010). Challenging the Neoliberal Urban Regime: Regeneration and Resistance in Başıbüyük and Tarlabaşı. In D. Göktürk,

L. Soysal, & I. Tureli (Eds), *Orienting Istanbul: Cultural Capital of Europe?* (1st ed.). Routledge.

Uşaklıgil, E. (2014). *Bir Şehri Yok Etmek* (1st ed.). Can Yayınları.

Üstündağ, E. (2004, April 16). European Social Forum Prepares in Istanbul. *Bianet English*, https://m.bianet.org/english/politics/32814-european-social-forum-prepares-in-istanbul.

Uzunçarşılı-Baysal, C. (2015a). Kötücül Siluet. İn K. İnal, N. Sancar, & U. B. Gezgin (Eds), *Marka Takva Tuğra: AKP Döneminde Kültür ve Politika* (1st ed., pp. 125–38). Evrensel Basım Yayın.

Uzunçarşılı-Baysal, C. (2015b, August 15). *Kentsel Dönüşümde Suçlulaştırma Bahanesine Geri Dönüş*. Bianet, https://www.bianet.org/biamag/toplum/166826-kentsel-donusumde-suclulastirma-bahanesine-geri-donus.

van de Sande, M. (2020). They Don't Represent Us? Synecdochal Representation and the Politics of Occupy Movements. *Constellations, 27*(3), 397–411.

Vardar, N. (2013, February 4). Başbakan'ın Topçu Kışlası Israrı. *Bianet*, https://www.bianet.org/bianet/kent/144084-basbakan-in-topcu-kislasi-israri.

Vasudevan, A. (2023). *The Autonomous City: A History of Urban Squatting* (2nd ed.). Verso.

Vatansever, A. (2018). Proletarya ile Orta Sınıf Arasında: Siyasi Aktör Olarak Prekarya. In Sunar, Lütfi (Ed.), *Türkiye'de Toplumsal Tabakalaşma ve Eşitsizlik* (2nd ed., Vol. 1, pp. 181–218). Nobel.

Vatansever, A., & Gezici Yalçın, M. (2015). *'Ne Ders Olsa Veririz'—Akademisyenin Vasıfsız İşçiye Dönüşümü* (1st ed.). İletişim Yayınları.

Vieta, M. (2016). Autogestion: Prefiguring a 'New Cooperativism' and the 'Labour Commons'. In C. DuRand (Ed.), *Moving Beyond Capitalism*. Routledge.

Volk, C. (2021). On a Radical Democratic Theory of Political Protest. *Critical Review of International Social and Political Philosophy, 24*(4), 437–59.

Voulvouli, A. (2007). *Arnavutköy District Initiative: From Environmentalism to Transenvironmentalism: Practicing Democracy in a Neighbourhood of Istanbul* (Ph.D, University College London), https://www.academia.edu/562947/Arnavutk%C3%B6y_District_Initiative_From_Environmentalism_to_Transenvironmentalism_Practicing_Democracy_in_a_Neighbourhood_of_Istanbul.

Voulvouli, A. (2011). Grassroots Mobilisation in Turkey: The Transnational Character of Local Environmental Protests. *International Journal of Academic Research, 3*(1).

Wacquant, L. (2007). *Urban Outcasts: A Comparative Sociology of Advanced Marginality* (1st ed.). Polity.

Wallerstein, I. (1989). 1968, Revolution in the World-System: Theses and Queries. *Theory and Society, 18*(4), 431–49.

Wallerstein, I. (2001). *The End of the World As We Know It: Social Science for the Twenty-First Century*. University of Minnesota Press.

Wallerstein, I. (2002). New Revolts Against the System. *New Left Review, 18*, 29–39.

Wallerstein, I. (2011, October 15). The Fantastic Success of Occupy Wall Street. *Commentaries*, https://iwallerstein.com/fantastic-success-occupy-wall-street/.

Wallerstein, I. (2012, January 1). The World Left After 2011. *Commentaries*, https://iwallerstein.com/world-left-2011/.

Wallerstein, I. (2013a, February 14). Turmoil in Tunisia and Egypt: Beginning or End of the Revolutions? *Commentaries*, https://iwallerstein.com/turmoil-tunisia-egypt-beginning-revolutions/.

Wallerstein, I. (2013b, July 1). Uprisings Here, There, and Everywhere. *Commentaries*, https://iwallerstein.com/uprisings/.

Wallerstein, I. (Ed.). (2015). *The World is Out of Joint: World-Historical Interpretations of Continuing Polarizations*. Paradigm Publishers.

Wallerstein, I. (2016, November 1). The World Social Forum Still Matters. *Commentaries*, https://iwallerstein.com/the-world-social-forum-still-matters/.

Wallerstein, I. (2022). *The Global Left: Yesterday, Today, Tomorrow*. Routledge.

Warner, M. (2005). *Publics and Counterpublics*. Zone Books.

Wisniewska, A. (2017, July 13). From Civil Society to Political Society. *openDemocracy*, https://www.opendemocracy.net/en/can-europe-make-it/from-civil-society-to-political-society/.

Wood, P. B. (2017). *Citizenship, Activism and the City: The Invisible and the Impossible* (1st ed.). Routledge.

Yalçıntaş, A. (Ed.). (2015). *Creativity and Humour in Occupy Movements: Intellectual Disobedience in Turkey and Beyond* (1st ed.). Palgrave Pivot.

Yanardağ, M. (2014, May). Tarihin Çağrısı ve Cezası. *Redaksiyon, 8*, 32–5.

Yazıcı, G., & Fırat, B. Ö. (2013, December). Hepimiz İştirakçiyiz. *Express, 139*, 34–6.

Yeğen, M. (2014). Türkiye Solu ve Kürt Sorunu. In M. Gültekingil (Ed.), *Modern Türkiye'de Siyasal Düşünce—Sol* (Vol. 8). İletişim Yayınları.

Yeldeğirmeni İşgal Evi'nde Yeni bir Yaşam Kuruluyor. (2013, December 6). *Muhalefet*, https://muhalefet.org/haber-yeldegirmeni-isgal-evinde-yeni-bir-yasam-kuruluyor-51-8827.aspx.

Yıkılmaz, G., & Kumlu, S. (Eds) (2011). *Tekel Eylemine Kenar Notları*. Phoenix Yayınevi.

Yıldırım, C. (2018). Neoliberal Dönemde Türkiye'de Sınıflar ve Değişen Orta Sınıf. In Sunar, Lütfi (Ed.), *Türkiye'de Toplumsal Tabakalaşma ve Eşitsizlik* (2nd ed., Vol. 1, pp. 101–28). Nobel.

Yıldırım, Y., & Gümrükçü, S. B. (2017). TEKEL-HES ve Gezi Parkı Protestoları Ekseninde Türkiye'de Eylem Dalgalarının Sürekliliği ve Değişimi. *Pamukkale Üniversitesi Sosyal Bilimler Enstitüsü Dergisi, 26*, 388–405.

Yılmaz, A., Toydemir, B., Keskin, C., Yıldırım, C., Kocabıçak, E., Elhan, E., Seymen, F., Kalyoncu, G., Kılıç, H., Fırat, K., Özbakır, M., Mıhçı, M., Ülker, N., Bulut, N., Elhan, N., Günay, Ö. S., Yıldırım, T., Uludağ, Ü., Bulut, V., . . . Karşı Lig. (2020). *Yeniden İnşa Et: Caferağa ve Yeldeğirmeni Dayanışmaları Yatay Örgütlenme Deneyimi*. NotaBene Yayınları.

Yılmaz Şener, M. (2018). 'Kendinizin CEO'su Olun!' Kendi Kendini Yöneten Bilgi İşçileri. In Sunar, Lütfi (Ed.), *Türkiye'de Toplumsal Tabakalaşma ve Eşitsizlik* (2nd ed., Vol. 1, pp. 245–74). Nobel.

Yörük, E., & Yüksel, M. (2014). Class and Politics in Turkey's Gezi Protests. *New Left Review, 89*.

Yücel, V. (2013). Park Cemiyetleri. *Teorik Bakış, 2*, 77–86.

Yücesan-Özdemir, G. (2014). *İnatçı Köstebek: Çağrı Merkezlerinde Gençlik, Sınıf ve Direniş*. Yordam.

Yurtsever, H. (2014, May). Zamanı Gelmiş Bir Düşüncenin Gücü. *Redaksiyon, 8*, 24–8.

Zerubavel, E. (2021). Toward A Concept-Driven Sociology: Sensitizing Concepts and the Prepared Mind. In W. H. Brekhus, T. DeGloma, & W. R. Force (Eds), *The Oxford Handbook of Symbolic Interactionism*. Oxford University Press.

Personal Communications

A. D. (2015, July 10).

A. D. (2016, August 4).

B. A. (2015, July 12).

L. T. G. (2014, July 18).

M. C. B. (2015, July 10).

M. C. B. (2016, June 29).

M. U. (2014, July 16).

O. B. (2015, August 10).

O. S. (2015, August 11).

S. A. (2015, July 13).

S. B. (2015, July 10).

U. U. (2015, July 13).

Y. L. (2014, July 16).

Y. O. (2015, June 30).

Y. S. (2015, July 13).

Z. U. (2015, July 16).

INDEX

EU representative:
Easy Access System Europe
Mustamäe tee 50, 10621 Tallinn, Estonia
Gpsr.requests@easproject.com

www.ingramcontent.com/pod-product-compliance
Lightning Source LLC
Chambersburg PA
CBHW050650270326
41927CB00012B/2967

9 781399 525916